If These **WALLS** *Could* **TALK:**
CHICAGO CUBS

Stories from the
Chicago Cubs Dugout,
Locker Room, and Press Box

Jon Greenberg

30 YEARS®
TRIUMPH
BOOKS

Library of Congress Cataloging-in-Publication Data

Names: Greenberg, Jonathan author.
Title: If these walls could talk : Chicago Cubs : stories from the Chicago
    Cubs dugout, locker room, and press box / Jon Greenberg.
Description: Chicago, Illinois : Triumph Books LLC, [2019]
Identifiers: LCCN 2019013069 | ISBN 9781629376547
Subjects: LCSH: Chicago Cubs (Baseball team)—Anecdotes. | Chicago Cubs
    (Baseball team)—History.
Classification: LCC GV875.C6 G75 2019 | DDC 796.357/640977311—
dc23 LC record available at https://lccn.loc.gov/2019013069

This book is available in quantity at special discounts for your group or organization. For further information, contact:
    Triumph Books LLC
    814 North Franklin Street
    Chicago, Illinois 60610
    (312) 337–0747
    www.triumphbooks.com

Printed in U.S.A.
ISBN: 978-1-62937-654-7
Design by Amy Carter
Page production by Patricia Frey

To my mom, Stephanie, for always believing in me
And to Jen, Gabe, and Sloane for putting up with me

CONTENTS

INTRODUCTION

On October 4, 2015, Cubs president Theo Epstein stood on the 100-level concourse of Miller Park talking to a reporter about the present and the future. For the first time since taking the Sisyphean task of rebuilding the Cubs nearly four years earlier, the present was worth talking about.

As we talked, the Cubs were in the process of winning their 97th game of the season, 3–1 over the Milwaukee Brewers. There wasn't much to watch. The Cubs were already in the playoffs, though there was a faint chance they could host the Pittsburgh Pirates in the Wild Card Game if the Pirates lost that day. But even though that would mean a little more money and home-field advantage, the Cubs preferred to go on the road. Wrigley Field was a house of horrors for previous playoff teams.

We watched the Pirates win their 98th game on Joe Maddon's TV in the visiting manager's office after the game and no one complained.

As Theo and I talked for a half-hour, Cubs fans, and even some Brewers fans, kept coming up to Epstein to take pictures. This wasn't uncommon. From the moment a fan spotted Epstein in a North Side Starbucks in the fall of 2011, he was the face of the franchise. With a hat (usually representing Pearl Jam) pulled low, Epstein could walk the streets of Lakeview relatively unbothered. At a Cubs game, wearing a navy sports coat and a plaid shirt, it was a little more difficult.

What was keeping Epstein up at night as he mentally prepared for this important milepost in the Cubs rebuild?

"Unfulfilled hopes," he told me for an ESPN story. "In October, you have a special team, and you want to see a special run. There's such an arbitrary nature to it sometimes. A ball bouncing a certain way or a bleeder down the line or something. You want to see teams get what they deserve. I think our guys deserve a lot."

That magical season wasn't quite unexpected—the Cubs did fire Rick Renteria to hire Joe Maddon and signed Jon Lester—but it still felt a little like free money.

And the eventual trip to the National League Championship Series turned into real money as well, as the Cubs' coffers increased, if only incrementally, enough to help pay for major lineup additions that winter.

Epstein is wrongly referred to as a "genius," in the same way that calling a surefire Hall of Famer "the greatest of all time" is misleading. But his mind does work in advance, and at the time, he was thinking that a playoff series loss, perhaps to the Cardinals, might be worth as much in future capital as a series win because it would spur his boss, Cubs chairman Tom Ricketts, into spending more money in the off-season. That's what happened in Boston when the Red Sox kept losing to the Yankees, culminating in that heartbreaking playoff exit in 2003. Epstein wasn't building for a divisional series win, but he got one anyway.

After that NDLS win over hated St. Louis came the NLCS, where a four-game sweep by the Mets had the psychological effect he was looking for. After all, the Cubs and Mets had their own history, and the manner in which the Mets pitchers silenced the Cubs' bats in that series resonated with everyone.

At the time of our discussion, Epstein couldn't be certain what was ahead for the Cubs that month or that winter—too many variables—but he had a pretty good guess they would win the Wild Card Game, thanks to Jake Arrieta, and that they would have some money to spend in the off-season. But he told me he had no guarantee that Ricketts would open the vault. Ricketts did, in a way, signing Jason Heyward (eight years, $184 million), Ben Zobrist (four years, $56 million), and John Lackey (two years, $32 million).

During our conversation, I brought up how I was there when the Cubs lost their 100th game of a 101-loss season in 2012—a game that featured Jason Berken as the starting pitcher and Dave Sappelt as the leadoff hitter. Even for the Cubs, a 100-loss season was rare. But Epstein, perhaps feeling vindicated, wanted to talk about the following October, when he met with the media for his end-of-season press conference, right after he fired manager Dale Sveum, a sharp-edged hitting teacher who was not the right man for that particular phase of the rebuild.

"I remember the questions in that press conference were so negative, so negative," he said. "And meanwhile, we felt great about what was going on because we knew how talented the young players were and how much the organization had turned around, as far as infrastructure and talent. But it hadn't manifested at the big leagues. I remember stopping at one point and saying, 'Look guys, you might look at this as a failure right now, but I can tell you outside this organization, outside this city, people are saying the Cubs are going to be really fucking good pretty soon.' And we are."

Flash forward a few years to 2018—a World Series bookended by two NLCS appearances—and I'm talking to Epstein again as the Brewers are chasing down the Cubs in the NL Central in late September and he's not so hopeful and he's not so happy. He could see what was coming.

The Cubs' run of three straight NLCS appearances ended unceremoniously at Wrigley Field on October 2, 2018, in the Wild Card Game. The Cubs were only playing in that game because the Brewers got red hot in late September, winning their last eight games of the regular season, including a divisional tiebreaker game at Wrigley Field on October 1.

Epstein was wary of his team going down the stretch. While the 2015 Cubs sprinted into the Wild Card Game, cocksure and confident, the 2018 Cubs were self-aware. They knew the magic wasn't there. The Cubs won 95 games and the prevailing storyline following that 13-inning loss to Colorado was: Will Joe Maddon get fired?

Before 2015, the idea of the Cubs winning 95 games and being disappointed enough for a change at manager was hard to believe. But because of the run that started that season, nothing less than a serious chance to make and win the World Series would be considered a success.

The 2018 Cubs were the worst (and only) 95-win team in the franchise's history. Though to put it more optimistically, they were also the ninth Cubs team to ever win more than 90 games and the fourth in the last four years.

What does it say about the Cubs that fans could name every team that's won 90 games off the top of their head?

Try it, I'll give you a second.

So aside from 2015–18, the Cubs won 90-plus games in 1969, 1984, 1989, 1998, and 2008. No, they didn't do it in 2003. They won 88 games that year and 89 in 2004.

The Cubs' 2018 season was odd, discomfiting, a slog at times. It wasn't very joyful. While the players got along fine with each other, relationships with some coaches were strained. The front office was consistently concerned with what they were seeing and what they weren't.

That led to an epic end-of-the-season press conference where Epstein, without calling anyone out, laid bare the team's flaws and what needed to change.

Joe Maddon would stay, but not get a contract extension. Epstein made that public at the GM meetings soon after the World Series.

The Cubs fired hitting coach Chili Davis, who had joined the organization the previous winter when he was billed as the best in the business. The Cubs couldn't score at the end of the season and Davis' all-fields approach, which was supposedly what the team lacked under previous hitting coach John Mallee, didn't mesh with the actual talent—he lost Kris Bryant and Anthony Rizzo early, a bad sign. The young Cubs hitters regressed (aside from Javy Báez) and the Cubs wound up rehiring a former organizational hitting instructor in Anthony Iapoce.

Pitching coach Jim Hickey resigned weeks later. Hickey had been rumored to be on his way out and he left for "personal reasons" that weren't disclosed.

That big free agent–spending spree fans were looking for in the 2018 off-season? That was off the table because of budgetary concerns. A blockbuster trade would help. But who were the Cubs going to deal? Any of their position players they would want to trade were at low points in their value.

With the same team as 2018, the Cubs were immediate playoff contenders, and if things shook out with Yu Darvish, in the running for the pennant as well. But in a sport where you're getting better or getting worse, where were the Cubs after four years and a World Series?

And what does it say about the job Epstein and company had done that one World Series and four straight postseason appearances weren't enough?

Some fans were eager to believe the Cubs had a trick up their sleeve, that unnamed sources and Epstein's own quotes about the team's budgetary limits were just a cover for a late pouncing on Bryce Harper. The latter part would've made sense. The free agent market for Harper was limited because of his price tag (believed to be upward of $300 million) and because of league-wide concerns about the competitive balance tax and the idea that blockbuster free agents weren't worth the money. The CBT was serving as a de facto salary cap and luxury tax payments were seen as wasteful.

But there were no tricks. The Cubs simply didn't have the money to spend. Tom Ricketts treated budgets like he was the head of a family hardware store, not a major-market baseball team. The budget was made up of all expenses—from the pricey expansion of Wrigley to the entire baseball operations department. The Cubs had spent plenty of money and would spend for years to come, but there wasn't going to be a big-ticket expenditure after the 2018 season. They did add pieces, however.

The Cubs first picked up Cole Hamels' $20 million option, the last payout on a $144 million extension he signed during the 2012 season—Epstein's first season with the Cubs. They had to trade pitcher Drew Smyly, whom they paid during the 2018 season to rehab as a gamble, to do it. The Cubs also added utility man Daniel Descalso and traded away Tommy La Stella to make room.

While La Stella is most remembered for his boycott of Triple-A Iowa in 2016, he had become one of the most influential members of the clubhouse as some players flocked to his chilled-out Eastern philosophy attitude. Some in the organization thought he was too influential, and the Cubs needed edgier players.

The Cubs also signed relief help in Brad Brach, among others.

Ricketts didn't do himself any favors with a brief media tour before January's Cubs Convention. He and his family decided not to hold a family panel at the convention, as they had done in every year of their ownership, because of "low ratings" in a fan survey. Most felt it was because they didn't want to face fans' angsty, if not angry, questions. In his interviews with both sports radio shows in town, he tried to shield himself from blame for not freeing up the dollars to pursue Harper or Manny Machado by talking about how much the Cubs pay in local taxes and revenue sharing. (None of these figures were verified.)

"I think a lot of people don't appreciate that the Cubs, unlike most professional baseball teams, have to pay all their own expenses for the stadium," he told ESPN 1000's David Kaplan. "We have to pay all the costs that go into that, we pay about $20 to $30 million a year in local taxes that no other team does and also as we raise revenue, as we add incremental revenue to the top line by bringing in a club or something, we pay about 40 percent of that to the league. So it's really hard to grow economics beyond where we are. But that said, we have worked hard to go from a few rungs down all the way to the top of the league and at this point, spending where we're at is about where we're going to be, but it's sustainable and it's real and we'll be amongst the top spenders in the league going forward forever."

Needless to say, fans that wanted to see the Cubs spend weren't satisfied, but what can they do? Just hope that the current core, the one that has made the postseason four straight seasons, could reverse a downward trend. That wasn't just wishful thinking. If Kris Bryant and Yu Darvish were healthy, etc. and so on.

In the fourth week of January, after Cubs Convention, I visited Epstein's office outside Wrigley Field and we talked about the state of the team. If the theme of 2015 was learning how to win, 2016 was winning it all, and 2017 and 2018 were keeping it going, what was the narrative of 2019?

"For me, it's that we have something to prove, right?" he said. "I think this, again, if you look at the post-2016 Cubs, we haven't fully realized our potential yet. We've sort of underachieved a bit since the World Series and we want to sort of get back and establish ourselves as one of the elite dominant teams in October and try to win multiple championships.

We definitely don't want the end of 2018 to be anything but a blip based on how we perform going forward and what becomes of the rest of this window and beyond.

"That can either be sort of a definitional moment, the sort of a counter to the World Series—'Here's what happened to the post–World Series Cubs'—or it can be a blip in the long run of dominance. And so, we get to, through our play, control how that narrative rolls out. And I think we know the difference between being really, really proud of how we play and how we go about our business, top to bottom, versus not being quite as proud. Such as things at the very end of last year."

A few weeks after this interview, Joe Ricketts' racist emails were leaked by Splinter News, giving the Cubs one last negative story before spring training.

The changes that were made after the season were mostly to coaches. New pitching and hitting coaches. Again. Another new bench coach. Some different faces around the team. But the names of the core remained the same—Rizzo, Bryant, Schwarber, Lester, Hendricks, Quintana, Baez, Heyward, Zobrist, Contreras, Epstein, Maddon. Addison Russell was a question mark. Other players need to prove themselves. But the Cubs had the team to make the playoffs, if not win it all.

This could be a season that might make or break this group.

"If we perform really well, and this core becomes sort of fully realized, then we're really positioned for the next several years and can sort of think about intelligent ways to affect a transition while staying on top," Epstein said. "If we underperform, then we're looking at, our starting staff mainly, we're looking at a year-plus of control left. Position players, the end of this year will be two years left. And it could go in a lot of different directions. And obviously, if we underperform this year, some change will be not just desired, but needed. So I think it's a really important year for us to feel that urgency because it's time to perform."

Hard as it was to believe, time was running out. By 2022, thanks to the contractual status of Epstein and some of his best players, the Cubs might be a radically different team. So that gave them three more years.

CHAPTER 1
CHASING GHOSTS

When the Cubs finally did it, when they won the World Series on a warm night in Cleveland in 2016, Jim Hendry was in his living room in Park Ridge, Illinois, 21 miles northwest of Wrigley Field. Like a lot of Chicagoans, he was rooting hard for the Cubs to win. He was cheering for front office executive Randy Bush, a friend of many decades who he hired back in 2005. He was rooting for Theo Epstein, Hendry's replacement, a different kind of baseball executive, but one who Hendry always liked. And Jim Hendry was happy for Joe Maddon, who Hendry knew would've gotten absolutely roasted if the Cubs had lost Game 7. He was rooting for Ryan Dempster, clubbies Tom "Otis" Hellman and Danny Mueller, Javy Báez, Matt Szczur, and Willson Contreras.

Jim Hendry was rooting for Cubs fans everywhere. After all, he still remembers the pain of 2003.

Hendry got a ring from the Cubs and he appreciated it. The Cubs held a little ceremony for him the following season in their office complex, a large building he could only dream about during his days in the cramped confines at Clark and Addison. He brought his son John, now a college pitcher, with him. It was a moment he had always dreamed about, though Hendry imagined he'd be the one passing out the rings.

So it goes. That was the famous line by Kurt Vonnegut, who spent some time in Chicago, and while Hendry doesn't seem like a Vonnegut guy, he lives his life by that mantra. He doesn't dwell on the past.

In his first season as GM, Hendry was five outs from the World Series. The Cubs could never get back to that peak.

"We were good in '04," Hendry said. "We were good in '07 and '08. Even when the things changed and it was up for sale and it was getting so at the end you probably couldn't have won, it wasn't like I ever looked at it like, 'You know, we didn't have as much as they have now, or we had a small staff.' I mean, that's not the world I'm in.

"And so I was happy for them because I grew to appreciate the [Rickettses] very well, even though I had to go. And Theo and I have been friends since he first started in Boston. And Randy Bush and I, that's about a 40-year relationship there."

The Hendry era, from 2003 through 2011, was full of ups and downs, but it also represented a sea change for the franchise, which was finally trying to be competitive on an annual basis.

After the 2003 season ended in myth and shame—that has been well-documented enough over the years—the Cubs didn't cower. That off-season, the Cubs reloaded with Greg Maddux and Derrek Lee. But first, Hendry had to get over Games 6 and 7, Moises Alou, Steve Bartman, Alex Gonzalez, and Mark Prior.

"I think it took me a couple weeks to… you never really get over it, get over it," he said. "But it took me a couple weeks. I had to finally slap myself and say, 'Okay. Yeah. That's enough.'"

On November 26, Hendry got down to the business of remaking his team, first taking advantage of the financial straits of the team that had dealt the Cubs their heartbreak by trading a young first baseman in Hee-Seop Choi to Florida for the 28-year-old Lee.

"We loved Choi at the time and the only negative about it at the time was that [Choi] was left handed," Hendry said. "We lacked left-handed power and he was our first guy in the system we thought was going to be 'the Dude.' But I was a big Derrek Lee fan. And he was only 28. And he played great against us with the Marlins. And I had a history with his father [Leon Lee], who worked for me. At the time we made the trade he was our Pacific Rim guy."

Not only that, he was the guy who recommended signing Choi, who hailed from South Korea.

"So I knew a lot about Derrek," Hendry said. "Growing up I loved him. I thought he was going to blossom, 28 to 32 is what, I think back then, prime years for hitters. And I thought he was just on the cusp of greatness. Great athlete. Great defender. Great makeup. It was like, 'I've got to do this.' Right hand, left hand, didn't matter. And I remember the difference was Derrek Lee was making $7 million, Hee-Seop was making $300,000 or $400,000. So Andy MacPhail gave me the

Derrek Lee is congratulated by Aramis Ramírez as Lee crosses home plate after hitting a two-run home run to drive in Ramírez in a game against the Rockies.
(AP Photo/David Zalubowski)

look like, 'Really dude. We just added $7 million and we need left-handed hitters.'"

Hendry can still laugh about how Lee hit .233 with two homers that April, while Choi hit nine and slugged .738 that month.

"So you can imagine the looks I was getting the first month or two," Hendry said. "But it worked out pretty good."

Choi would only hit six more homers the rest of the season and was later traded to the Dodgers.

Lee, of course, put together an all-time Cubs career, with 179 homers and a .298/.378/.524 slash line in seven seasons. In 2005, he led the NL in hits (199), doubles (50), batting average (.335), slugging percentage (.662), and OPS (1.080), and finished third in the MVP race for a losing club.

So in the span of four months, Hendry traded Bobby Hill, José Hernández, Matt Bruback, Choi, and Mike Nannini for Aramis Ramírez and Lee, who each manned the corner infield spots for nearly a decade and combined to hit 418 homers and drive in 1,380 runs over 2,048 games.

In early December 2003, Hendry went shopping for veteran pieces. He signed reliever LaTroy Hawkins to a closer's salary, but ostensibly in a role as a set-up man for Joe Borowski. A few days later he signed Mark Grudzielanek. On December 15, he traded one catcher, Damian Miller, to Oakland for another catcher in Michael Barrett. Three days later, he signed Todd Hollandsworth and, a day after that, reliever Kent Mercker. On January 21, he signed Ryan Dempster, who was rehabbing from Tommy John surgery.

Then, in mid-February, Hendry brought Greg Maddux home. Maddux, now 37, came up with the Cubs and won the first of his four straight Cy Young Awards with them in 1992. The Cubs foolishly screwed up his free agency and he wound up in Atlanta, which was probably for the best. Okay, definitely for the best for him, not so much for the Cubs. After winning 194 games (in 363 starts) with a 2.63 ERA with the Braves, he wasn't exactly at his peak in 2004 (he finished with a 4.02 ERA, his worst since his first full season in 1987). But the Cubs didn't need him to be.

Mark Prior and Kerry Wood were the top two pitchers, in any order, while Carlos Zambrano was the No. 3 and Maddux four. Matt Clement was slated to be the fifth starter.

In 2003, the Cubs surprised people behind Dusty Baker's leadership. Before the 2004 season, Wood was on the cover of *Sports Illustrated*

Greg Maddux answers questions during the press conference to announce his signing with the Cubs, as manager Dusty Baker and GM Jim Hendry look on. (AP Photo/Roy Dabner)

with the headline: "Hell Freezes Over, The Cubs Will Win The World Series."

The Cubs would spend all of two nights in sole possession of first place: April 25 and April 28. The last time they would finish a day tied for the NL Central lead was May 23.

Injuries started to pop up, the kind that would decimate this group's run before it really began. In Wood's first six starts he put up a 2.52 ERA with 50 strikeouts in 42⅔ innings. He was second in the NL in strikeouts to Randy Johnson.

Fifteen years later, a starter with a history of elbow problems, who had just pitched deep into the postseason, would never be allowed that kind of workload so early in the season. He pitched seven innings three times, eight innings once, and 8⅔ once. But in his seventh start, May 11, he only lasted two innings, leaving with a tender right triceps that would sideline him for two months. He would make 15 more starts that season, but with a 4.14 ERA and 92 strikeouts in 95⅔ innings. Wood's days as a premier starter were over, though no one knew that quite yet.

Mark Prior, meanwhile, didn't pitch that season until June 4. He had his moments—eight strikeouts in five scoreless innings in Houston on June 14—but was otherwise very human. By the end of July his ERA ballooned to 4.69. It hit 5 after giving up seven runs to the Padres on August 10. A solid September (2.17 ERA over 37⅓ innings) saved him from a truly unsightly line.

A team built on Prior and Wood looked incredible going into the season. But midway through, the cracks were evident. That season was the first full season in which I covered the team as a freelancer for both the Associated Press and MLB.com. I remember a heaviness of press conferences with no easy answers and an undercurrent of tension. Dusty Baker, a hero before that foul ball drifted into the stands in the eighth inning of Game 6 of the NLCS, was now morphing into an embodiment of the goat itself.

Pitch counts weren't quite the warning sign they are by this era, but Wood's in 2003 were alarming.

He threw 120 or more in 13 starts, including four times in September. In four playoff starts, he threw a combined 462 pitches, starting with 124 pitches in the NLDS opener.

While 100 pitches is an arbitrary number, he only went under 90 in five starts in 2003, and three of those starts were four innings or less.

Prior went over 120 pitches in nine starts and threw fewer than 95 in just one of 30 starts. He threw between 129 and 133 pitches in four of his six September outings, and the other two he threw 124 pitches and 109. In three playoff starts, he threw 368 pitches. These two threw hard, putting a bit of strain on their arms, from shoulder to forearm.

In 2003, the Cubs led the NL with starting pitchers averaging 104 pitches and a little more than 6⅓ innings per start. (In 2004, the Cubs tied for the NL lead, averaging 99 pitches and more than six innings per start.)

To blame this on Baker would be too simple, as the Cubs weren't a sophisticated operation quite yet—these days front offices have a bigger say in pitching limits—but Baker was the face of the team and was sensitive to criticism, which only made it worse.

Throughout all these issues, the Cubs were safely above .500, but out of contention for the division. It would likely be Wild Card or bust. On July 31, they lost to Philadelphia to fall 10½ games back of St. Louis, but Hendry pulled off a major trade.

Epstein and Hendry were part of a massive four-team deal with Montreal and Minnesota that launched Nomar Garciaparra to Chicago and landed the Red Sox Orlando Cabrera to play shortstop and Doug Mientkiewicz to play first base.

To jettison a big name like Garciaparra for two pluggers was a risk, but one that was backed up by analytics, a newfangled word in baseball circles, which was only just waking up to the "Moneyball" revolution that was slowly but surely taking over front offices.

While Epstein and his crew, whose team was 8½ games back of the Yankees at the time, celebrated trading "Nomah" in Boston, for Hendry, landing Garciaparra was a coup and the move was celebrated across the city.

"Trade deadline day in '04, hell, people would have thought we were having the parade already," Hendry said in a phone conversation in December 2018.

"The deadline, to my recollection, back then was 3:00 Central," Hendry said. "And I'd worked on some things with Theo earlier in the week. And I was really hammering Nomar. And then, I think, about Thursday—I think it was Saturday, the deadline—I think at Thursday when I went to bed that night I didn't think I could get much done. My recollection was we didn't even get into a three-way until 1:00, 1:30.

"The four-way thing all happened in the last one to two hours and it came right down to the last second, to be honest. We were just wheeling and dealing. I've got to have Matt Murton too. And Omar [Minaya] had to have somebody else. And I think Terry Ryan kind of felt like he got left out. He deserved another guy because he and Theo had been working on some other deal the day before. So he thought they were all tied together and they weren't. There was some explaining to do and smoothing over after it was over too. It was just crazy. It was good. It was good."

After that deal, the *Chicago Tribune* Cubs beat writer Paul Sullivan wrote: "After turning the Cubs from pretenders to contenders last July by stealing Aramis Ramírez and Kenny Lofton from Pittsburgh, Cubs general manager Jim Hendry knew an encore performance would be difficult as this year's trading deadline approached. But in a move that rocked Wrigleyville Saturday afternoon, Hendry reached into his bag of tricks and pulled out Boston shortstop Nomar Garciaparra."

"The only way this could have been a more lopsided trade is if the Cubs had drunk the Red Sox's rum and carted off their women. Maybe there's some rum to be named later," *Tribune* columnist Rick Morrissey wrote for the August 1 edition.

The next year, in 2005, Cubs blogger Andy Dolan recapped the premature jocularity: "Do you remember where you were on July 31, 2004? Of course you do. The reason you remember is that was the day the Cubs acted like a real baseball organization and traded for a superstar. Not a washed-up superstar, but one who was only 31 years old, played the position the Cubs were weakest at, and the trade cost them pretty much nothing.

"You were giddy. You had dreams of another run through the National League playoffs. And you, and I, were wrong. Dead wrong."

Garciaparra was fine, actually. He played 43 games in August and September, slashing .297/.364/.455. But he only played 62 games in 2005 because of a nasty groin injury. His Cubs tenure was short and not particularly meaningful beyond the details of the trade itself. Naturally, he signed with the Dodgers in 2006 and made the All-Star team at 32. You can still see Cubs fans wearing worn-out Garciaparra shirseys at games.

But Cabrera and Mientkiewicz were difference-makers for the Red Sox and that trade helped cement Epstein's reputation as a gifted dealmaker at the beginning of his career. Winning the World Series in Boston certainly helps one's legacy, as you might imagine.

"I knew Theo did awfully well too," Hendry said. "Because I tried to get Cabrera for two or three weeks before that. So, it took that four-way thing at the last minute to pull it off. But we were happy with Nomar too. And he did fine for us. The next year he got hurt again and all that, but yeah, he wasn't the reason why we didn't win."

If the 2003 Cubs were a revelation, the 2004 edition was more proof that the organization was incapable of sustaining success.

The Cubs finished with 89 wins that season. They looked poised to make the postseason for consecutive seasons for the first time since 1907–08, until a 2–7 finish, which began with a walk-off loss in New York against the Mets. The Cubs lost two of three in Queens, three of four at home against Cincinnati, and two of three at home against the Braves.

"We're playing with a lot of confidence now," reliever Mike Remlinger said the day before Diaz's heroics, according to the *Tribune.* "No matter who we're playing, we feel good about our chances on that given day."

"We were good enough to win it again," Dempster said, 14 years later. "At least to have a chance to win it and we really struggled offensively the last 10 days of the season, especially with runners in scoring position."

Dempster was already a veteran with 156 starts under his belt when Hendry signed him in January 2004, only months after Dempster had Tommy John surgery in August. He was able to work out an enviable situation once his rehab turned into minor-league work. He would rehab in Chicago; pitch in Lansing, Michigan; and return to Chicago.

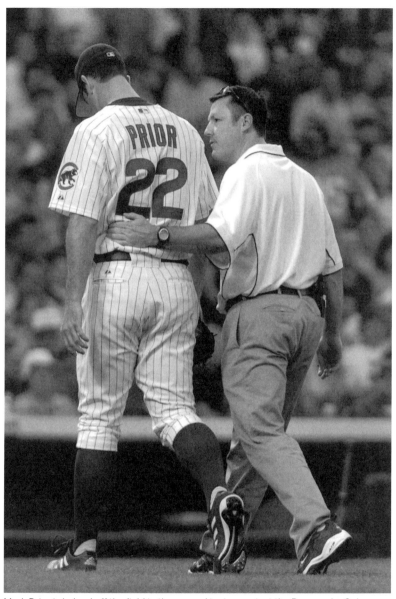

Mark Prior is helped off the field in the second inning against the Brewers by Cubs head athletic trainer Dave Groeschner on July 15, 2004. (AP Photo/Jeff Roberson)

One day Mark Prior was making an injury rehab start and Dempster had a little fun. There were actual posters around the ballpark advertising Prior's appearance, "So I put up like little pictures of me. 'And also, Ryan Dempster.' I was like the follow-up act."

While he only pitched five games for the Class-A Lugnuts, it seemed like he was there for an entire season.

"Jim Hendry was hilarious," Dempster said. "He actually made up a fake press release that I made the Midwest League All-Star team because I had been with Lansing for so long. I went back and forth. I'd go pitch and then I'd come back here and throw my bullpens, then I'd go back there."

As Dempster got healthier and ready for action, he had an idea.

"Our rotation was good," he said. "It was great. Guys were throwing the ball great. And then, I think, everybody was healthy and I was like, 'What do I do?' So I called up Jim and Dusty and was like, 'Why don't you put me in the bullpen, so I can help out of the bullpen?' So then I just came over in August and pitched out of the bullpen in August and September."

The bullpen was a hot-button issue in Chicago, as it is most years. Young flame-thrower Kyle Farnsworth had a 4.73 ERA, a 1.50 WHIP, and a regular shift at the late-night bar Tai's Til 4. Borowski didn't last in the closer's role and Hawkins, typically a media favorite in most cities, was unpopular with reporters and fans.

After he got the closer's job, Hawkins asked Cubs PR to call a press conference for him in the dungeon-like media room. When everyone was there, he told the media he wasn't going to talk to them. "I can do what you guys do, [you] can't do what I do."

Hawkins, a native of Gary, Indiana, was actually a very personable guy who finished a proud 21-year career in 2015, but he bristled with the over-the-top coverage and just the regular ol' coverage in Chicago. It happens.

What fans cared about was that he went 25-for-34 in save opportunities in 2004, with some high-profile blown ones, both in the tinderbox of Wrigley Field and on the road.

His eighth blown save came at Shea Stadium and it's one that would live in infamy for the Cubs: the Vic Diaz game.

The Mets were down 3–0 with one out in the ninth when Dempster, who had taken over Hawkins' role as closer, walked two hitters in a row. Baker pulled Dempster for Hawkins, who had to get ready in a hurry and who had worked six games in seven days. He got another out, before "Diaz-ster" hit. Diaz hit a 2-2 pitch for a homer to tie the game. Kent Mercker wound up taking the loss in 11 innings. Mark Prior's 7⅔ scoreless innings were wasted and the Cubs' Wild Card lead was cut to a half-game over San Francisco.

To make matters worse, it was in Shea Stadium, the site of the Cubs' 1969 collapse and Diaz was a Chicago native, by way of the Dominican Republic, having gone to a West Town high school named after Roberto Clemente.

The next day, Chicagoans woke up to this lede from the *Tribune*'s Paul Sullivan:

"There was no evidence of a black cat strolling in front of the Cubs' dugout late Saturday afternoon in Shea Stadium, as happened in a September loss one day before the Cubs dropped out of first place during the fateful summer collapse of 1969.

"The Cubs didn't need any supernatural occurrences to haunt them on an otherwise perfect afternoon in Queens.

"A juicy fastball from LaTroy Hawkins did the same job as the black cat, as the New York Mets handed the Cubs a heartbreaking 4–3 defeat in 11 innings."

"Opposite-field home run off of LaTroy," Dempster said 14 years later, the memory as clear as day. "I remember we had so many chances to score, it never should've been that way in that whole series. We just couldn't get it done. We just… I don't know if it was like the pressure became so much because we were following up on '03. I don't really know the reason why. Teams always get up for the Cubs—it's funny. Especially then, teams were really getting up, we got the best [shot] from them, the Mets, and couldn't get it done. Then we came home and got eliminated that last Saturday."

The Cubs actually went 13–3 from the second game of a double-header on September 10 through the first game of that Mets series on September 24. They didn't actually fall out of the Wild Card lead until a 2–1 loss to the Reds at home on September 30. They were eliminated from the playoffs on the next-to-last day of the season at home where a miserable crowd of Cubs fans wallowed in defeat. In the October 2 game that officially knocked the Cubs out of the playoff race, Remlinger blew the team's 24th save of the season, which was nine more than in 2003.

"When things started to go rough in '04, it was like 'Here we go again. It's never our year,'" Dempster said. "From the fans' standpoint, something bad's going to happen. We were always waiting for something bad to happen."

What you might remember from the final day of the season is Sammy Sosa leaving early—and the fact that his boom box was destroyed after he left.

Sosa was no longer the headliner of the Cubs, but he still hit 35 homers in 126 games. In 2003, Sosa was busted corking his bat, a clumsy metaphor for his other suspected cheating. In mid-May 2004, he injured himself… sneezing?

That was the story, anyway. According to the Cubs, he sprained a ligament in his lower back after suffering back spasms for a pair of "violent sneezes." Interestingly enough, for how hard Sosa swung and, um, how unbelievably muscular he became, he only had four DL stints for his entire career before this happened. For whatever people wanted to criticize him for, Sosa was a gamer.

Sosa was slashing .291/.385/.590 with 10 homers through May 15. He returned on June 18 and his numbers dropped precipitously to a

.238/.311/.488 slash line, though he still hit 25 homers in the last 91 games.

Sosa was on his way down, in the game and the batting order. He was used to hitting third. But in 2004, he dropped to fourth. Then to fifth, and then to sixth for 15 games.

The diva act was accepted when he was hitting 50-plus homers a season. But the Cubs had changed around Sosa, building a playoff-caliber team without him as the fulcrum.

Sammy Sosa argues a called third strike in the first inning of a game in the 2004 season, his last with the Cubs. (AP Photo/Morry Gash)

Before the last game of the season, he asked out of the lineup, a not-unreasonable request with the team out of the playoff race. Sosa arrived a little more than an hour before the game and never put on a uniform. The Cubs told reporters he was caught on camera leaving the stadium before the game ended. While Sosa told one reporter he left in the seventh inning, the *Tribune* later reported two eyewitnesses saw him take off in the first inning and that the Cubs also had footage of him leaving a game early in September.

The *Tribune* and *Sun-Times* both played up the story—and why wouldn't they? Controversy sells and Sosa was still a headliner. Sosa made excuses and instead of rolling their eyes and letting it pass, the Cubs called him out.

On January 30, he was traded to Baltimore, with the Cubs eating a significant chunk of his remaining salary.

He wasn't the only longtime employee to leave that off-season.

As the Cubs unraveled that season, they didn't get much of a break from their TV broadcasters, the acerbic duo of Steve Stone and Chip Caray, whose no-holds-barred commentary on the 2004 team was getting back to the players, as it always does.

In a September 5 story by the *Tribune*'s Paul Sullivan, he wrote: "Only a few days after suggesting Cubs fans should watch the games with the sound turned down, manager Dusty Baker insisted Saturday there's no feud between his team and announcers Chip Caray and Steve Stone."

Sullivan wrote about "an incident" that "occurred on the team charter to Montreal on August 29, when reliever Kent Mercker began loudly berating Stone in front of his teammates while Stone was reading a book. Mercker was upset that a call he made to the press box on August 27 to criticize Caray's praise of Houston pitcher Roy Oswalt found its way to the media. Mercker and several teammates have been upset with commentary from Stone and Caray that Moises Alou has termed 'negative.'"

A long-simmering dispute between Baker and Stone came to a head as the season ended, with Baker taking off his headset during a postgame interview on TV after some pointed questions following a bad loss to the Reds at the end of the season.

Hendry told reporters Stone had become too personal in his attacks on Baker. Stone had been the color guy for Cubs TV broadcasts since 1983 (he missed a couple seasons with an illness) and grew up in the business alongside Harry Caray.

Andy MacPhail, the team president, had a meeting with Baker, Stone, and Hendry, but it didn't really solve anything. Both Stone and Caray left the booth after the season, with Caray going to Atlanta and Stone doing weekly radio on Chicago all-sports station 670 The Score. He eventually returned to regular color work doing White Sox games on the radio, before returning to TV to partner with Ken "Hawk" Harrelson.

At the end of the final game of the 2004 season, Cubs fans turned to the booth, high above the stands behind home plate, and chanted Stone's name, while he waved out of the window. For sure, he was more popular than the Cubs' manager and, by that point, many of the players.

Dempster was new on the team, and has a good relationship with Stone to this day, but he remembers that kerfuffle from a very different vantage point than Stone.

"They're your home broadcasters for a reason," he said. "They shouldn't be bashing your guys and they definitely shouldn't be making comments to you when you get on the plane. Steve and Merck, and the way that all went down, I like Stoney, I get along with him well, but you know, sitting there I think my favorite comment was the next day, Mercker going up to him and going, 'Hey Stoney, you said I accosted you on the plane? Well, I do the *USA Today* crossword, I know what accost means. If you want accosted, I can give you that.' That's not what went on. All of a sudden, they were creating dissension. It's like they wanted us to lose so it could be a better story. It was really weird and it just left a sour taste in everybody's mouth and they went a different way."

When Dempster arrived in Chicago, after pitching for the Marlins and Reds, he was amazed at the level of interest in the team and anyone associated with them. This was before camera phones and Twitter and really any kind of social media.

"It was like being the fifth member of the Beatles," he said. "You'd go to a restaurant and they'd be like, 'You play for the Cubs? Whoa.' You were like a rock star. I was like, I haven't even pitched yet, by the way. But it was just incredible to see how the expectations for the team were so great. Probably for the first time in a long time, the expectations were there."

The attention could be suffocating, even to the veterans.

Early that season, Moises Alou revealed to an ESPN reporter he peed on his hands to make them tougher. Needless to say, this became a popular story in a town that was crazy over the Cubs. Alou was annoyed reporters asked him about the concept, which had some backers among other Latin players. At least some people could laugh about it.

"I notice guys don't want to shake his hands now," Dusty Baker said. "Everybody just gives him the fist."

"It was tough to watch a team—for me anyways, guys were doing so well, the team was doing so well—to watch it unravel at the end, it was a bummer," Dempster said. "Because we were good enough to compete for the World Series. We were as good as the Cardinals, they went to the World Series.

"That year, I don't know, especially after they beat the Yankees, nobody was going to stop the Red Sox. But we had starting pitching, we had relief pitching, we had good balance in our offense. It was just like watching a poker game on tilt. 'Lose another one, lose another one, lose another one.' Then everybody started to feel it. I think for me it was a little bit harder because I wasn't there in '03. I didn't feel the collapse, being up 3–1, I didn't feel that. I was like, 'C'mon guys!' Meanwhile, everybody else was taking it on a little more. It was a lot for Dusty to take on. A lot for Woody and Prior to take on. Zambrano and those guys, after living through it in '03."

After the 2004 season, Sosa and Alou left. Mercker was gone as well. The Cubs re-signed Nomar Garciaparra, Todd Hollandsworth, and Todd Walker. They traded Kyle Farnsworth, signed Jeromy Burnitz. Not exactly blockbuster moves to shake up a franchise.

With those moves in mind, in 2005, the Cubs hovered around the .500 mark, finishing with 79 wins, as the White Sox unexpectedly passed them to collect the city's first World Series title in nearly a century.

It was the White Sox who threw a parade down Michigan Avenue. It was the White Sox who became the city's baseball darlings, with Ozzie Guillen and A.J. Pierzynski stirring the pot for a surprising run that saw them go wire-to-wire behind a stout pitching staff and a cobbled-together offense. It included a playoff run with plenty of drama, but no Cubs-like breakdown. No fans got their lives ruined. No reputations were forever sullied.

The White Sox made their own breaks and lived up to rising expectations.

I watched Game 4 of that World Series in Wrigleyville, on assignment for MLB.com. Some bars were packed, others less so. When Juan Uribe threw the last out to Paul Konerko, I was watching in the Cubby Bear. A disappointed young Cubs fan told me to tell Jim Hendry to improve the team.

The 2005 season was also when the Hall of Fame paths of both Prior and Wood took a serious detour.

In 2005, Prior made 27 starts and actually compiled a solid 3.67 ERA. His 166⅔ innings would be the second-most in a season of his brief career.

In late May, Prior was hit in his pitching elbow by a line drive from Colorado's Brad Hawpe. X-rays were initially negative, but later revealed a slight fracture. He had already begun that season on the DL with elbow inflammation and would wind up missing a month with the fracture.

He finished fairly strong, giving up around three runs a game in his last 10 starts from August 9 through September 28, while working between five and seven innings. The Cubs went 1–4 in his last five starts. Wood made just 10 starts from April through the end of July, and they were a mixed bag. He had a 6.15 ERA after April, missed all of May, and pitched once in June before rebounding in July with three solid starts before breaking down again.

He was shelved three times for shoulder inflammation that season and the Cubs acknowledged in July he would likely need off-season surgery. He finished the season pitching out of the bullpen to alleviate the soreness and his fastball seemed to respond. He wound up getting surgery that September.

"Every MRI we've done on him has been very consistent," the trainer Mark O'Neal told reporters in July. "There's no significant changes with any of them. There's nothing that's jumping out and saying, hey, here's our problem. Theoretically, if he had something significantly wrong, he would not be able to do what he's doing right now. Your body is not going to allow you to do that."

The confusion over Wood's injury cast a pall over the season. In April, Stone, in his regular spot on The Score, joked that Wood should "go sell cars" if he wasn't willing to change his pitching mechanics.

The Cubs expected the surgery to be minor, just a clean-up procedure to address fraying around the rotator cuff and for Wood to be ready for spring training in 2006.

The worst Cubs injury of that season, however, was to a little-known outfielder just promoted to the majors.

Adam Greenberg was a middle-of-the-pack prospect who got an unexpected promotion because Felix Pie's ankle was injured at the time when Hendry wanted to shake up the roster. In a pinch-hitting appearance on July 9, Greenberg was hit in the head by Valerio de los Santos. He went on the DL a week later with dizziness and vertigo. The next season, he was back in the minors but he couldn't hit anymore. The symptoms from his head injury hadn't gone away. He bounced around the minors for a few years, a modern-day "Moonlight" Graham, haunted by coming so close but never getting an official plate appearance in the majors.

I always linked him to Steve Bartman in a way, an ordinary individual whose fate was cursed by an association with the Cubs. In 2012, a documentary maker and Greenberg started a petition to get him a major league at-bat and the Marlins bit. Former White Sox manager Ozzie Guillen, in his one season managing the South Florida franchise, got Greenberg that AB. He struck out, but it was the most positive moment in a train wreck of a season for the Marlins.

The one positive in 2005 was the play of Derrek Lee, who led the NL in hits (199), while leading all of baseball in batting average (.335), doubles (50), total bases (393), slugging percentage (.662), and OPS (1.080), and finishing third in the MVP race. His 46 homers were five shy of Andruw Jones for the NL lead and his 107 RBIs were 21 back of the Braves center fielder. At midseason, Lee was a real contender for the Triple Crown and I remember that because I had to write about it.

I was 26 and going nowhere in the business, kind of stuck in place. The year before, I freelanced all summer for MLB.com and the Associated Press and really got to know how to work in a baseball clubhouse. But MLB.com hired a full-time intern for both teams and cut me out. Thankfully, someone recommended me to a very nice guy who was running the MLB Players Association website, which was housed now by MLB.com and had money to spend. One of my first assignments was a feature about Lee and his chances at the first Triple Crown since Carl Yastrzemski in 1967. As fate would have it, Frank Robinson, manager of the Washington Nationals and a 1966 Triple Crown winner, was in town while I was doing the reporting.

While Robinson, who passed away in February 2019, was a baseball legend, at that point, he was just a grumpy ex-big leaguer who would rather be golfing than sitting in the claustrophobic visiting manager's office at Wrigley Field.

"I don't talk about other teams' players," he told me in a crowded room of reporters. Undeterred, I asked at least two more slightly different questions, desperate to get an answer. I learned that day I could not break the will of one Frank Robinson.

The 2005 Cubs weren't horrific and they weren't good. They were still drawing fans, still getting a lot of attention, but a dark cloud seemingly hovered over Wrigley Field. Could things ever go right again?

They would, but first they would have to bottom out.

That off-season, Hendry added veterans like Juan Pierre, Neifi Pérez, Scott Eyre, Bob Howry, Jacque Jones, and Wade Miller. It was Baker's last season under contract. No extension was forthcoming.

And it got worse. The injury-plagued Cubs lost 96 games, making it the fifth time in a decade the team had lost 90-plus games.

"Oh-six was miserable," Dempster said. "We weren't a good team, I was closing and having a save opportunity once every five or six games. And then struggling in that role, not really having a consistent role, not knowing how to do that. I battled a little bit of depression that year. Not fun. Work not being fun to go to was tough."

Lee only played 50 games because of a recurring wrist injury. At one point, the Cubs replaced him with Phil Nevin, who was particularly unpopular with reporters.

Prior started nine times that year and gave up a whopping 35 earned runs in 43⅔ innings. I'll do the math for you, that's a 7.21 ERA. The last start, and appearance, of his major league career was on August 10 in Milwaukee. He left after giving up five earned runs (six total) in three innings. The previous start, at home against Pittsburgh, he pitched 5⅔ innings and got the 42nd and final win of his career.

Kerry Wood only started four times that season, all while Prior was on the DL. The last start of his major league career came on June 6, when he pitched 3⅔ innings in Houston. Like Prior, he got a win in his penultimate start, lasting six innings in a home victory over the Reds.

It was his 71st win. He would tack on another 15 as a reliever through 2012.

The rise and fall of Wood and Prior was the story of 2004–06. It was a sad story, one that recurred years later with the Bulls and Derrick Rose. These were stories of untapped potential and the fragility of the human body.

"They were different in their own ways," Hendry said. "Without injuries, Kerry Wood, who knows what that would have been like. From '82 on, the best people I ever saw pitch at high school, prospect-wise, was Doc Gooden and Woody. And then Prior in '01 was unbelievable. And I don't know if anybody's come on the scene in a market like this, in a pennant race and pitched better than he did in '03 since Gooden did it with the Mets.

"You had to think Prior was going to pitch great for 10 years. So it happens. And so, it is what it is. We recovered and then the club went up for sale and we redid it the best we could and went for it for a couple of years."

While the 2006 season was a lost one, there was at least one good story that came out of it.

In mid-August, the Cubs needed an emergency starter and Ryan O'Malley, an undrafted 26-year-old from Springfield, Illinois, who was an outfielder at the University of Memphis, got the call from Triple-A Iowa. He was a recent addition to the Iowa Cubs' rotation and had a 4.08 ERA at the time. But it was his turn to start.

All he did was throw eight scoreless innings in a 1–0 win over the Astros in Houston, despite six walks and just two strikeouts.

"Oh man, that was sweet," Dusty Baker said.

"It made sense to give O'Malley a call because it was his turn to pitch," Hendry said, according to the *Tribune*. "But at the same time, he deserved it too. He has been pitching better than some of the guys on the roster. It's good when somebody like that gets a chance."

O'Malley got one more start, but sadly, this one ended his career. He gave up three runs in 4⅔ innings against Jamie Moyer and the Phillies, but he felt something awry in his elbow. He tried to pitch through it, as he shared more than a decade later to the *Sporting News*, but his catcher Henry Blanco knew something was up. He pitched two more seasons in the minors for the Cubs and White Sox, and that was it. But he'll always have 2006.

After the 2006 season, Dusty Baker was fired, as expected, and looking at dwindling attendance (the Cubs still drew more than 3 million, but empty seats were noticeable that season) the Tribune Company went about remaking the organization, knowing that the publicly traded company was going to be sold.

Andy MacPhail resigned at the end of the season as well, ending his 12-year run with the club.

"The clock on the MacPhail-o-meter has run down to zero," MacPhail told reporters. "It's not just that we had a terrible season. I've been here 12 seasons and only two postseason [appearances] and to me that's not what I came here to do. Obviously, I've not been as effective as I wanted to be."

Hendry had been the face of the baseball operations department since 2003, when MacPhail was bumped up to a president/CEO role, but this change meant the Cubs were promoting their marketing whiz John McDonough to the president's role, while Tribune Company executive Crane Kenney continued to take on a larger role with the team.

When MacPhail stepped down, Tribune Company chairman Dennis FitzSimons said the company had no plans to sell the Cubs, but behind the scenes, the Trib wanted to fatten up the Cubs for sale or slaughter.

CHAPTER 2
ONE LAST RUN AT THE BRASS RING

After the 2006 season ended, there were big changes for the Cubs, and Jim Hendry was given more power and more money. "There were tough times for the [Tribune] Company, and Dennis FitzSimons, he treated me great," Hendry said. "I felt bad for him. And he stuck with me after the '06 season. Dusty left and Andy left. And Dennis called me in and says, 'You're staying. You get another shot.'"

The Tribune Company wasn't interested in a gradual rebuild. On September 21, 2006, the company was officially for sale and 12 years later, Hendry remembers a "directive to win now." If the Trib was sold, that meant the Cubs would get spun off, because the type of person or group willing to buy a huge publicly traded media company wouldn't be interested in a sports team.

Future Cubs owner Tom Ricketts explained that logic to me years later.

"When the Tribune was looking to sell to a private equity, it was likely it wouldn't be able to keep the Cubs asset because the Cubs, and sports teams in general, don't have a profile that lends itself well to private ownership," he told me in his office in 2010. "There's not a typically short-term payoff, a five- or seven-year payoff, and not a lot of cash flow. It doesn't fit into a portfolio nicely. It was logical if the Tribune went to a private-equity firm, they would have to sell. There were no guarantees, but we had a hunch that wouldn't fit. So we got all of our ducks in a row and got our bankers and lawyers and other advisers teed up and waited for it to come on the market."

All Hendry knew or cared about was that he was going to have a bigger budget that winter. He went into that off-season with his eyes wide open.

"So, at the time," Hendry said. "You knew some of the things you were doing, if they didn't work, three or four years down the road you're going to have a high payroll with the back end of some contracts. So there's a price to pay for that too. And I just wish we could've won in '07 or '08. We were good enough obviously. Certainly in '08 we were. And it just doesn't happen."

So with money to spend and a clear directive to win, he hired Lou Piniella to replace Baker. Piniella had been out of the game after an unsuccessful stint as manager of his hometown Tampa Bay Devil Rays. Some no-name coach from California named Joe Maddon replaced him.

There were two signings that defined Hendry and the Cubs that winter: breaking the bank to sign Alfonso Soriano to an eight-year, $136 million contract and Hendry finalizing the Ted Lilly deal on a gurney.

Let's get the Soriano deal out of the way. To this day, Hendry hasn't blamed his bosses for the excessive length and money of the Soriano deal and he wouldn't do it with me, despite my prodding. But it's well-known in Chicago the deal was a year or so longer than it needed to be

GM Jim Hendry speaks with All-Star Alfonso Soriano at the Wrigley Field press conference announcing Soriano signing with the Cubs on an eight-year deal.
(AP Photo/Jeff Roberson)

because his bosses, Crane Kenney and John McDonough, got involved while Hendry was traveling. It was a clear win for Soriano's agents, who took advantage of less-experienced negotiators.

Hendry wore it, taking the heat for overpaying Soriano once his play declined. The deal was clearly going to be an albatross for whomever bought the team. Soriano had a base salary of $9 million in 2007 and just $13 million in 2008. Then it went to $16 million before bumping up to $18 million per year from 2010 through 2014.

He outearned his deal in 2007 and 2008 and after that, it wasn't the Tribune Company's problem. But Hendry had to grin and bear it whenever people brought up the length and extravagance of Soriano's deal. And certainly neither McDonough nor Kenney ever took that heat.

But that's part of the job. Hendry could vent with the best of them, but he understood the demands of a job like GM of the Cubs.

As for the Lilly story, which unfolded while the 2006 winter meetings were going on in early December at the Swan and Dolphin Resort at Disney World, well, like most stories, it's better to let Hendry tell it himself.

"It's a little bit, I wouldn't say embellished," he said. "It all happened. But I didn't feel good for [the first] couple of days down there. I got these real bad chest pains that I probably should've gone in for a couple of days before. And then finally [Lou] Piniella and Scott Nelson took me to the doctor. But the story is true. I was on the gurney getting another EKG at the regular hospital near Disney World because they didn't like the first one. I was getting ready to go put my clothes back on and go do the Scout of the Year Awards. Timmy Wilken was getting a big award and I was doing the speech.

"And I was like, 'Hey Doc. I'm better now. I'm good.' The first EKG didn't really look that bad. It was an intern that gave it. So I started to leave and get my clothes on, then the nurse comes and says, 'Doc needs you to do another.' So he comes in. He said, 'Where are you going?' I said, 'Well, I'm going to…' He said, 'We need another one.' This and that. So I go in for the other one and I didn't know what was going to happen yet. The story, as it's [been] told over the years, it's like I was getting wheeled into surgery. But I didn't know for sure I was getting the surgery yet.

"What I don't realize is why I had the phone in my hand on the gurney. I did. So Ted's agent called. He said he's coming with us. So I didn't want to tell him where I was. I didn't want this news getting out. I got two young kids at home in Chicago. So he said, 'Okay. Let's get the paperwork done. Over here. We'll go over it and have a drink.' I said, 'Well, Scott Nelson's in my room. Just go do it with him. I got some other things going.' So I get off the phone and then Ted called and thanked me.

"So then I get done with EKG, so I go back to where my clothes are and I'm thinking I'm going. I've got to hustle up, go put a suit on. So I'm getting dressed and here comes the doctor. And he said, 'Where are you going?' 'I'm going back to the banquet.' And he said, 'No, no, no. No you're not. You've got some problems.' I said, 'Doc I'll go do this. If I get any more pain, I'll be back tomorrow.' And he goes, 'Dude if you walk out that door, there might not be tomorrow.' Ooooh. Okay.

"Then they took me to this heart hospital 30 miles away in an ambulance. So, anyway, I guess over time, I think people thought I was actually getting wheeled in for the surgery. So I actually got the phone call when I was getting the second EKG. I didn't know how bad it was. But I still don't know why I had my phone in my hand. Anyhow, that was it. I think it's been magnified a little bit over the years."

Hendry wound up getting an emergency angioplasty and in a 2017 story by Carrie Muskat, then of MLB.com, he said he called his kids, who were in elementary school, to let them know they might hear about it on the news.

Hendry told Muskat that his 10-year-old daughter asked if the surgery meant they wouldn't be traveling to Florida to meet him at Disney World. Hendry got four stents that day, but recovered quickly and got back to work. The Cubs were coming in 2007.

"We knew what the lot was," he said. "We were going to have to win the next couple of years, two or three max, or it wasn't going to be pretty after that for a while. And that's what happened."

The Cubs had already re-signed Aramis Ramírez and brought on Mark DeRosa, Jason Marquis, and Cliff Floyd as free agents. They committed $297,500,000 in total contracts that off-season, mostly with Soriano's $136 million deal and Ramírez's $75 million extension.

Lilly's four-year, $40 million deal was a relative steal, as was DeRosa's three-year, $13 million deal.

In 2007, the Cubs got plenty of attention—Remember the *Sports Illustrated* cover with Lou Piniella and Alfonso Soriano?—but they started slow and were still under .500 in August.

Piniella was grouchy. In spring training, he declared the Cubs were "no push-button organization." But he sure knew how to push buttons.

"The way I looked at Lou, he was old-school, he was harsh," Dempster said. "And all you had to do was stand up to him one time and you earned his respect."

For Dempster it came in his first save opportunity of the 2007 season. The Cubs lost their season opener at Cincinnati and then were up 4–1 going into the ninth.

"I came in and I walked Edwin Encarnacion with one out and then I went 2-0 on Griffey and here comes Lou," Dempster said. "He said, 'Son, what's the problem?' I said, 'What do you mean?' And he's like, 'It's 30 fucking degrees out. We're winning 8–1. Throw the fucking ball over the plate.' And he turned around and he walked away.

"I got out of it and then I went to his office the next day and said, 'Hey Lou, can I talk to you?' He goes, 'What's up?' I said, 'I'm your closer, right?' He goes, 'Yeah, of course.' So I go, 'I don't need a pep rally. The only time you should come out to the mound when I'm the closer is to set up a bunt play or take me out of the game because I blew the save.' He said, 'Oh, alright.' He never came out again unless he was taking me out after I blew a save. We just had that relationship, like, 'You give a shit, you're going to stand up for yourself, and I respect that.'

The guys that didn't, he kind of walked all over, but the guys who did, it was a good relationship to have."

Soriano took a lot of heat for not playing well in the cold—and playing outfield like, well, someone who had just started playing outfield the previous season—but he caught fire in June, hitting 11 homers and slugging .697. He cooled off in July and got got injured in August, tearing a muscle in his leg that all but ruined the speed part of his game (he joined the 40-40 club, 40 homers and 40 stolen bases, in his contract year with the Washington Nationals in 2006) for the rest of his time in Chicago.

While Soriano got criticized thanks to the excess of his deal and his curious weaknesses (he struck out a lot as a leadoff hitter and hopped when he caught the ball in left field), he willed himself back onto the field in September and had a record-setting month, hitting 14 homers and slugging .754 in 28 games. Soriano drove in 27 runs as the Cubs' leadoff hitter that month. He wound up hitting 33 homers that year with an .893 OPS. He finished 12th in the NL MVP voting, ahead of Aramis Ramírez for a team that won the NL Central with just 85 victories.

Soriano wasn't always appreciated outside of the team, but the Cubs players loved him. (A famous, possibly apocryphal story from later in his career was when a teammate asked Soriano if he had change for $100, he replied "Hundreds are change, babe.")

"It's always interesting to me when a guy goes 40-40 [and after that] people go 'He's not the guy!'" Dempster said. "He never was going to be the guy. How many guys go 40-40 every year? It's like you're paying him for his best performance, so if you can get 80, 90 percent of that you're going to be happy. And I felt like we got that out of him. He was a great teammate. The way he was, if he hit three homers and we lose, he's pissed. Winning meant everything to him, you know, and he had a little bit of a style, flashy. He became a better outfielder. He learned how to drive runs in. Sure, he swung and missed a lot, but he was a great teammate and a great addition to our ballclub."

While Dusty Baker press conferences were often tense and awkward after 2003, Lou Piniella's meetings with the media always had the chance for a Lou eruption.

Early in Piniella's first season in charge, the *Tribune*'s Dave Van Dyck ran a postgame story with this lead: "You could sense it coming, like an agitated volcano just waiting to blow built-up steam and lava."

"What the hell do you think isn't working?" Piniella yelled at some reporter who had the temerity to ask about the pitching. "You see the damn game."

Carlos Zambrano and reliever Will Ohman combined to blow a game. Of Ohman, Piniella offered this famous line: "And then I bring in the reliever who's throwing 30- or 40-foot curveballs to boot."

"I can start to see some of the ways this team has lost ballgames," he said, according to Van Dyck's story. "I can see it. We have to correct it."

That series is mostly memorable for two reasons: Lou Piniella pulling Carlos Zambrano early from Game 1 to save him for a possible Game 4 and Ted Lilly's glove spike.

Before the NLDS started in Arizona, Piniella said he'd like to use Zambrano on three days' rest for a possible Game 4, so he'd limit him to something around 100–110 pitches. He pulled Zambrano in a 1–1 tie after 85 pitches and six innings. Talented reliever Carlos Mármol started the seventh and promptly gave up a leadoff homer to Mark Reynolds, before allowing an insurance run as well. The Cubs lost 3–1.

In 2018, pulling a starter after 85 pitches in a playoff game to go to your bullpen is almost expected. But in 2007, Piniella was accused of looking ahead, thanks to his pregame comments.

"I'm not accused of anything, sir." he said after the game. "I've got a good bullpen here, okay, and I trust my bullpen. I'm bringing back a pitcher on three days' rest on Sunday, and I took a shot with my bullpen. It didn't work today. They've done it all year. I've got confidence in them. Period, end of story."

Lilly started Game 2 and didn't last long, giving up six runs on seven hits and four walks in 3⅓ innings in an 8–4 loss to put the Cubs in a 2–0 hole in the best-of-five series.

The Cubs were up 2–0 when Lilly shook off rookie catcher Geovany Soto, who wanted a curveball to outfielder Chris Young with two men on. Lilly wanted a fastball. So did Young, apparently.

Lilly watched the ball sail out and then slammed his glove to the mound with considerable oomph. That kind of reaction was expected from Lilly, who was a touch intense, but it still was quite a moment to witness.

"I've never seen a pitcher throw their glove like that on the mound," Piniella said after the game. (Piniella got a kick out of Lilly's comportment and took to calling him by his full name: Theodore Roosevelt Lilly.)

"No one will ever top the Lilly glove spike," Dempster said. "That's so great. I think even better was the next year. So the pitch to Chris Young was a heater in that Soto did not want to throw. The next year, we're facing Arizona early in the season. Soto goes heater away, no. Backdoor slider, no. Curveball, no. And you watch Soto literally go [puts down the sign for a fastball] and Ted go, 'Yeah,' and he took him deep again! It was pretty funny. That's what I say about Teddy, though, he's bound and determined and I admire that."

Dempster, one of Lilly's closest friends, has a good memory. With two outs in the first inning of a home game against Arizona on May 9, 2008, Young indeed homered again off Lilly.

* * *

While the Cubs spent big to win in 2007, the draft should've given them a chance to get better as well.

In 2007, the Cubs drafted third. After David Price and Mike Moustakas were taken in the first two spots, the Cubs selected high schooler Josh Vitters. Vitters, a power-hitting third baseman, would finally make the major league roster during Theo Epstein's first season in 2012, where he struck out 33 times in 99 at-bats. It was his only big league action.

While the Cubs allocated most of their budget to major leaguers—this was a win-now situation—Vitters didn't come cheap. He signed for a $3.2 million signing bonus. Price signed a six-year contract that summer that included a $5.6 million bonus while Moustakas got $4 million.

Tim Wilken came over from Tampa Bay in the winter of 2005, just after the winter meetings, to run the Cubs' scouting department, which had between 21 and 30 scouts and supervisors, he said. It wasn't a large operation.

"With the Cubs, it wasn't smaller than Tampa's—that was bone thin—but it was pretty small," Wilken said. "We tried to increase regional supervisors at that time with a couple national guys we brought over in 2008. Jim gave me the full boat, and other than trying to wrestle more money from the Tribune Company—I can still remember, in Toronto and Tampa Bay, we would send out flowers on Easter and Mother's Day to all the scouts' families and the Tribune Company wouldn't allow it. It was little things like that. It was a smaller scouting department, but not the smallest. A lot of guys had double roles as pro and amateur scouts. I think I was the last guy to be the head of both departments."

When Wilken arrived, the Cubs' drafts improved significantly, starting in 2006 when they took a Notre Dame wide receiver/pitcher in the fifth round.

While Vitters didn't work out, the 2007 draft did pay dividends for the Cubs, who took future All-Star Josh Donaldson with the 48th pick. He was traded in 2008 to Oakland for starting pitcher Rich Harden. The Cubs also drafted future major leaguers Darwin Barney, Brandon Guyer, and James Russell that season.

More importantly, the 2007 draft produced several future Cubs of varying importance. Jason Heyward went 14th overall to Atlanta, Jake Arrieta was taken by Baltimore in the fifth round, Steve Cishek was taken seven picks after Arrieta, and Anthony Rizzo was drafted in the sixth round by Epstein in Boston.

In 2008, the Cubs drafted pitcher Andrew Cashner with the 19th pick and Ryan Flaherty at No. 40. Future Cardinal Chris Carpenter was drafted 97th, Josh Harrison at pick 191, Tony Campana at 401, and Casey Coleman at 461.

In 2009, the Cubs took Brett Jackson at the end of the first round, but also DJ LeMahieu in the second.

The next year's draft saw a curious pick at No. 16. Hayden Simpson, a right-hander out of Southern Arkansas. What was that about? Simpson didn't pitch in 2010 and never got higher than A-ball in the next two seasons. He was out of pro baseball at 24 after a year in the independent Frontier League. He pitched in 56 games and compiled a 6.42 ERA. Most figured he was drafted because of budgetary reasons, but even that didn't make much sense.

Cubs closer Kerry Wood celebrates with Carlos Mármol, Ted Lilly, and Daryle Ward after the Cubs defeated the Cardinals 5–4 on September 20, 2008, to clinch the NL Central. (AP Photo/Nam Y. Huh)

"It wasn't a budget thing," Wilken said. "We thought he could be Roy Oswalt. He threw 93–97. If you look at his college career, he went 35–2 in Division II. Just a great arm. We saw him really well before the draft; three different guys, including myself. All of a sudden he signs and he's got mono. He lost roughly 35 pounds, went from 185 to 150. I don't regret the Simpson one. It is what it is."

The 2010 draft was a bust for the Cubs, but they did draft another football player in the fifth, a speedy Villanova Wildcat named Matt Szczur.

Hendry's love of two-sport athletes showed with their picks of Szczur and Samardzija.

Hendry was close with Samardzija's college coach at Notre Dame, but just him being local was a boon for the Cubs, Wilken thinks. He didn't get to pitch a ton in college because of his football commitments and given the lack of a minor league in football, some people assumed Samardzija would go to the NFL. And indeed he was asked about going to the NFL until he became an established major league starter in his mid-twenties. Now, after signing a $90 million contract with San Francisco before the 2016 season, he's probably the highest-paid Notre Dame athlete in school history. He got a $7.25 million signing bonus and if his career ends when his contract is up after the 2020 season, he'll have earned nearly $130 million.

"I don't think a lot of people did their homework on him," Wilken said. "He was a first-team All-American in football. I talked to three different NFL personnel people and they said this is Joe Jurevicius. He'll probably go in the first round or the top of the second. If Samardzija was from the Deep South or out West, I don't know what would've happened."

Wilken and Hendry could see the potential in Samardzija if he ramped it down a little and quit football. He debuted in 2008 in the pennant race as a hard-throwing reliever. A mistake, in retrospect.

"I think it stunted his growth as a starting pitcher," Wilken said. "He had to go back to Triple-A and become a starter again and I didn't think it was good for him. He's had a good career, but it could've been even better. He's still got time left."

As for Szczur, his career never really took off either. But he made it to the majors, which is an achievement for any minor leaguer, let alone a fifth-rounder. How did they get on Szczur, who played in the East Coast, not typically a fertile recruiting ground for baseball players?

"Jim is very good friends with the Polian family," Wilken said. "Jim got a pass to go to the NFL WRs/RBs camp in Fort Lauderdale during the winter, I want to say January. Jim went down to watch Matt Szczur, who ran a 4.36 and a 4.4 [40-yard dash] at that camp. Once again, like Samardzija, he was a great football player. I think he was the I-AA player of the year his junior year. They thought he was going to be like one of those New England slot guys or a running back.

"He came out that junior year to Florida. Villanova was playing in a tournament in the Clearwater/Tampa area and we saw him play. One of our area scouts, Tim Atkins, was told, 'Tim, stay on this guy. This guy's never played in the summer. His experience level compared to other people, he just hasn't had the at-bats.'"

Szczur missed time his junior year, a month before the draft, after donating bone marrow to a needy girl from the Ukraine. He returned to football the fall after being drafted and the Cubs redid his contract that January to keep him from entering the NFL draft. He initially got a bonus of $100,000, but the Cubs gave him another $1.4 million.

"We thought he'd be a true center fielder," Wilken said. "He's been good enough to play in the major leagues, so we did a pretty good job."

Those 2007 and 2008 teams weren't all built on free agents or trades, either. Mármol came up through the system, first as a catcher and then as a pitcher. Ryan Theriot was a homegrown shortstop and Geovany Soto emerged late in 2007 as a budding star at catcher. Of course, Carlos Zambrano was a major scouting victory for the International team. While other prospects like Felix Pie would go on to disappoint, *a la* Corey Patterson, the Cubs did strike gold on occasion.

* * *

After bowing out quickly in the 2007 postseason, the team was still primed for 2008, the 100th anniversary of their last World Series title. The Cubs had to rally to make the postseason in 2007. In 2008, they were expected to win it all.

They re-signed Kerry Wood, who was successful in relief in 2006 to serve as the closer and let Mark Prior walk in free agency. On the same day Prior was granted his freedom, the Cubs signed a major free agent that was in high demand: Kosuke Fukudome. The left-handed hitting outfielder from Japan got a four-year, $48 million contract. The Cubs needed his contact hitting skills from the left side of the plate and early on it looked like he was going to have a serious impact.

In his first game, the season opener against the Brewers, Fukudome had three hits, including a three-run homer in the ninth that cut a four-run deficit to one. He had 11 multi-hit games in April and a four-hit game to kick off May.

"It's like he became a legend here," Ryan Theriot told *SI*. "In one day."

That week, he was on the cover of *Sports Illustrated* with the inevitable "It's Gonna Happen" headline, written also in Kanji.

Unlicensed Fukudome memorabilia sprung up, including mildly funny "Fukudome is My Homie" shirts and straight-out racist "Horry Kow" T-shirts.

(Cubs T-shirt sellers borrowed the similarly racist "Zambrano mows my lawn" T-shirt idea and adapted it to Albert Pujols and Ozzie Guillen. Guillen, of course, loved the "Ozzie Mows Wrigley Field" shirt and went and bought one and wore it for years before games. "I might cut lawns, but I don't stand in the rain selling T-shirts," he told reporters.)

But Fukudome cooled off. Every month that season, his numbers dropped. In March/April, his OPS was .915. By July, it was .688. Early on, it was theorized that Fukudome's patience at the plate was contagious. In the first month of the season, he walked 19 times in 117 plate appearances. In July, he walked nine times in 99. In August, his slash line was .193/.293/.253, though the Cubs were still getting on base ahead of him and he drove in 14 runs. He only started nine games in September.

The 31-year-old wasn't the first Cubs newcomer to get overhyped. Cubs fever was at an all-time high that season, with the team drawing a record 3.3 million (and change), a figure they haven't eclipsed since.

The Cubs first drew 3 million fans in 2004, when the post-2003 hunger was very, very real. Wrigley Field was the place to be in Chicago, even moreso than during Sammy Sosa's heyday. The Cubs sold a staggering 572,205 tickets on the first day tickets went on sale in early 2004, effectively selling out the single-game allotment for the season. It was believed to be a major league record.

"All signs have been pointing that way since December," Frank Maloney, the director of ticketing for the Cubs, told me when I wrote about sports business for Team Marketing Report. "But those numbers just shocked us. I can't believe you can sell that many tickets in one day."

The 3 million attendance streak lasted until 2012 and started back up in 2016.

And with demand came commensurate price increases. By 2008, the average Cubs ticket (not including the small pocket of premium seats near the field) was $42.49, a 24 percent jump from the previous year. Only the Red Sox had a pricier "average" ticket. The Cubs had been using a tiered pricing structure for years, but in 2008, 50 of the team's 81 home games were slotted into the highest of three tiers, while only six were at the lowest.

The Cubs went 17–9 in April and 18–11 in May. The mood was ebullient around the city. Eight Cubs made the All-Star team, with Alfonso Soriano, Geovany Soto, and Kosuke Fukudome all starting. Ryan Dempster, Carlos Mármol, Carlos Zambrano, Kerry Wood, and Aramis Ramírez joined them on the NL roster.

On July 9, one day after division rival Milwaukee landed C.C. Sabathia, Hendry made his big move. He traded Sean Gallagher,

Matt Murton, Eric Patterson, and some young catcher named Josh Donaldson—who was hitting .217 with six homers at the time of the deal—to Oakland for pitchers Rich Harden and Chad Gaudin.

Harden had filthy breaking pitches and looked like the missing piece to the puzzle. He would go on to make 12 starts for the Cubs that season, giving up just 14 earned runs in 71 innings for a 5–1 record and a 1.77 ERA. It was a perfect deadline trade, another Hendry masterpiece.

Sabathia was even better, going 11–2 with a 1.65 ERA, pitching 130⅔ innings in just 17 starts, essentially going 7⅔ innings every outing.

But the Cubs got hot later that month and the Brewers chilled out a little, and the Cubs went from being tied with Milwaukee atop the NL Central to leading by five games in the span of a week from late July to early August.

"It's Gonna Happen" signs and T-shirts replicated themselves all over the park. My joke about covering that season was that every day we found a new way to ask Mark DeRosa what it was going to be like to win the World Series.

DeRosa was the de facto spokesman of that team, even though Derrek Lee had the gravitas and tenure. That was how they liked it, Dempster told me. DeRosa's personality, mixed with his talent, made him a popular major leaguer, and now it makes him a managerial candidate, perhaps with the Cubs in 2020.

"Mark DeRosa, what he brought to the locker room was unmeasurable," Dempster said. "He was as good at bringing a clubhouse together as anybody I've ever been around."

Dempster said that on the 2007 Cubs' first flight, Lee was wearing a checkered suit and DeRosa started yelling something like "Pawn to Rook 9!" It cracked up everyone, including Lee.

"It matters, it matters," Dempster said. "You play 162 games over 187 days or more. You need those guys to keep things light. You need those guys to be able to motivate those superstars when they're feeling a little bit of pressure because they live on a different world than we live. The requests, the demands on their time are different. How do you bring levity to those guys, keep them loose, keep them relaxed? Make sure guys are doing well. Sure, I'm going to push you and yell at you to get out to batting practice, but I'm also going to be genuinely interested in how you're doing how you're family's doing. Those kind of guys matter.

"For sure, for some guys, that's not their jam. Just because you're good at baseball doesn't mean you have a good personality."

Lilly and Dempster became fast friends in 2007 and then were rotation mates in 2008. They would go on long bike rides and runs along Lake Michigan before games and sometimes play cards in the Wrigley Field laundry room ("Me and Ted playing gin on the top of a laundry hamper that we put a towel over top of while the laundry machines are going and Gary Stark is throwing in towels. Because there's nowhere in the clubhouse to play.")

Why run along Lake Michigan?

"I remember being a kid and going to a Seattle Mariners game, I was like 14, 15 years old and I was waiting for autographs where the players went in and here comes Dennis Eckersley with his incredible flow of hair, sanitary sock tied around like a headband, shorts, and cutoff shirt," Dempster said. "He went out and he left. I asked a security guard, I'm like, 'Where is Dennis Eckersley going?' He goes, 'Every time he comes, he goes for a run here.' I used to always remember that. So when I got here, you're living in the city and there's a beautiful lake right here, like let's get out and go for a run.

"Me and Ted, we'd ride our bikes down to Soldier Field and go do the stairs at Soldier Field. We'd ride down to U.S. Cellular instead of taking the bus or fighting traffic and guys would make fun of us. 'You guys are idiots. You guys like riding your bikes?' We're the idiots? When we're back in the clubhouse having a beer you're still sitting in traffic on I-94. We're not the idiots, you're the idiots.

"It was a tremendous way to bond. Ted, he was the best teammate I ever had for pushing me to get the best out of me, and pushing each other. He'd throw eight shutouts, he'd walk by your locker and you'd be like, *I've got to go nine tomorrow.* And competitive motivation was awesome. Friendly competitiveness to really push each other and see how good we can be."

Those two each won 17 games that season and each threw over 200 innings with almost the exact same number of strikeouts. Why did Dempster have a 2.96 ERA to Lilly's 4.09? The long balls. Lilly gave up 32, while Dempster allowed just 14.

Documentaries were being filmed, books were being written. Everything was focused on the Cubs making it to the World Series. Could the City Series finally happen to boot?

The White Sox needed a Game 163 to win the AL Central, but by that point, they had already lost emerging slugger Carlos Quentin to a self-induced broken hand. Still, they both made the postseason for the first time since they faced each other in the 1906 World Series.

As it turned out, the White Sox were the only team in town to earn a postseason win 102 years later, taking one game from new Tampa Bay manager Joe Maddon in the ALDS.

The Cubs, again one of the playoff favorites with the narrative of the 100-year anniversary of their last title, were unceremoniously swept by the Los Angeles Dodgers.

With all the hope and hype on his shoulders, the gregarious, built-for-this Dempster walked seven hitters and gave up a grand slam to James Loney in the fifth inning of the NLDS opener at Wrigley Field. He folded and the Cubs followed suit, losing 7–2. The crowd was funereal. The black cloud had returned.

"I made it too big," Dempster would say 10 years later while we ate lunch in Lakeview. He had his newborn baby daughter with him. He is happily remarried now and his other three children live with their mom just down the street from him. Dempster works for MLB Network and serves as one of Theo Epstein's advisors. A lot of time has passed and life has chugged along, but if you bring up the first game of the 2008 NLDS, the memories flood back.

"I made it way bigger than it needed to be," he said. "It meant so much to me. I loved being here. I wanted to win a World Series for the Cubs so bad that I was trying to be too perfect. My stuff was so good, I was throwing 94, 96, nasty split, nasty slider. I was getting ahead of guys and trying to strike everyone out. It's like I wanted it so bad, I wasn't just relaxing and doing what I needed to do.

"If I could look back and tell my younger self what to do in that situation, it would be just relax and don't make it bigger than it is. I literally did. I wanted it so much for everybody I tried to do so much."

When he said everybody, he meant it. Dempster made friends with fans when he sat in the old bullpen along the left-field line. He made friends in the neighborhood, on trips to the park with his kids. Dempster made friends with everyone. I am guilty of making fun of his Harry Caray impression (which is really just an impression of Will Ferrell's impression), but no one can argue that Dempster is one of the best guys the Cubs have employed over the years. And he wanted to win for the ushers and diehards just as much as for himself and Ted Lilly.

"Years of knowing season ticket holders, people in the bleachers, security guards," he said. "You get to know all of these people and then you start to really feel it and you really feel the intensity of it all. When something goes so long, as it gets closer and closer to the reality of it… it gets more and more intense."

Dempster held the Dodgers scoreless through four innings, but walked four in the process. Mark DeRosa hit a two-run homer off Derek Lowe in the second. In the fifth inning, Dempster's wildness continued, but this time he couldn't save himself. He walked the bases loaded while getting two outs to bring up Loney. He got two swinging strikes and then Loney fouled off a nasty splitter.

"I don't even know he fouled it off," Dempster said. "It like barely got a piece of it."

One ball later, homer.

"And it bummed me out because even as bad as I was, it was still just a two-run game when I left," he said. "It was a 4–2. A bloop and a blast. I felt like that grand slam sucked the life out of Wrigley Field."

"Yeah, I'm still convinced if we win the first game, we win the series," Hendry said. "The Phillies won the whole thing that year and were very good. The Phillies and us were the best two teams in the National League. We really felt we'd be playing each other to go to the Series."

(Cole Hamels was the NLCS and World Series MVP that season and wound up pitching for the Cubs a decade later. Matt Garza was the ALCS MVP and was acquired by Hendry before the 2011 season.)

In Game 2, Carlos Zambrano gave up five runs in the second inning, thanks to consecutive Cubs errors, en route to a 10–3 loss that stunned the Wrigley Field crowd into silence.

I remember walking around the upper deck, looking at the sullen faces in the crowd. This was not the year, was it?

It wasn't.

Rich Harden pitched Game 3, a 3–1 clinching loss in Los Angeles. The dream was dead. The World Series drought would officially enter a new century.

In the three-game series, the Cubs scored just six runs, four of which were driven in by DeRosa. The Cubs struck out 24 times and walked only six. The only thing the Cubs hit was a water pipe in the visitors dugout on their way into the clubhouse.

"That was pretty funny, though," Dempster said. "It kind of summed up the season right there, walk through a puddle of sewer water to get to the clubhouse afterward.

"If you look at, you look at how well Derek Lowe, Chad Billingsley, and Hiroki Kuroda threw, all three of those guys darted down and away all series," Dempster said. "They didn't give us much over the plate to hit. Even the pitch DeRosa took Derek Lowe deep on in Game 1, that was paint, away. And he did good job hitting the ball the other way."

DeRosa couldn't do it by himself. The team built for October just didn't show up.

CHAPTER 3
THE HANGOVER

While it took Hendry weeks to get over the collapse of 2003, this playoff ouster wasn't quite as emotionally draining on him. The Dodgers were just better. Getting Manny Ramirez at the deadline was a definite boost, but like Dempster said, the Dodgers' starting pitching came through in the clutch.

"It was great," Dempster said of the 2008 season. "We were the best team in baseball all year. We picked the wrong time of the year to have a three-game losing streak. You know, we were confident we were a great team, we traveled together, we hung out together, always 10 guys in a hotel room, 15 guys for dinner. We got along together. It was really unfortunate because we had the team to win the World Series that year."

The Cubs were seriously for sale now with a host of interested groups willing to buy the team for just shy of a billion dollars. The Tribune Company was also in bankruptcy court, thanks to Sam Zell's machinations. The Cubs were an asset being sold, so while they weren't technically bankrupt, there were levels of complications to everything.

Still, Hendry got his contract extended in 2008 and he had a budget for 2009. So he got to work.

At the GM meetings in November, he met with his good friend Padres GM Kevin Towers about Jake Peavy. The Padres' ace, just one year removed from sweeping the Cy Young voting, was owed $63 million over four seasons and the Cubs weren't the only team with money problems. San Diego owner John Moores was going through a messy divorce and asked Towers to lop off nearly $34 million from a $73.6 million payroll.

Hendry had the advantage in that he and Towers, two old-school types, loved to work on deals. So they talked at the GM meetings in Dana Point, California, and it got so serious that Towers had Peavy's agent, Barry Axelrod, drive over from San Diego.

"I typically didn't go to the GM meetings," Axelrod told The Athletic's Dan Hayes in 2018. "Kevin said, 'Hendry's going to be here and we'll sit and talk.' We did. We sat down and talked for a while. That was a memorable night in its own right. Any time you had Kevin and Hendry and a few other GMs in the bar, it was a memorable night."

The discussions continued over the next month and into the winter meetings in Las Vegas. Peavy was in town to go to the rodeo with ex-Cub Rick Sutcliffe and this potential trade became the talk of the baseball world.

"It's one club we're talking to," Towers told reporters that week. "There's no secrets there."

Hendry and Towers hashed out the deal, which was more fun than work.

"The conversations between Jim and Kevin were always entertaining," Padres assistant GM Fred Uhlman Jr. told Hayes. "There was nothing off the table when you talked about players between those two guys. They would try to work through any scenario that one of them threw out. They were both very creative and both very bold."

Cubs prospects like Josh Vitters, Felix Pie, Kevin Hart, Sean Marshall, and Angel Guzman were rumored to be in the mix at one point. The Padres wanted Mark DeRosa and Hendry knew if he pulled this off, he'd have to trade his veteran leader, along with pitcher Jason Marquis.

Peavy was worth it, Hendry thought. While he still needed a left-handed bat, an ace-caliber pitcher like that was too good to pass up.

"I was a Peavy fan like everyone should have been at the time," Hendry told me. "He's a gamer, a winner, a Cy Young guy, and a ballsy guy. He would have fit right in.

"We were back on a roll of winning again and just couldn't get past the first round for two years in a row. But no reason to think we still weren't going to be good if we added a pitcher and maybe another hitter and kept our other guys."

The deal was there for the making. The Padres front office thought it was done.

"Real close, real close," Hendry said. "And at that time, the club was not sold. And there was still four or five people in the possibility of owning the club. Maybe it was down to two or three by then. But it was not done. There were a lot of moving parts. And it was the first time, all of a sudden in Vegas, we got the message that everything's frozen until the sale's done. So we were still in the mindset of, 'We won 97 games. We need one more better pitcher. A little more this and that.' But that Peavy deal was probably three or four hours from getting done."

Then Hendry heard from his bosses at the Tribune that he couldn't do it. The money owed to Peavy was too much. Hendry had to make a walk of shame to Towers' suite at the Bellagio.

When I asked Crane Kenney, Hendry's Tribune overseer, about this deal 10 years later, he claimed it wasn't as close as Hendry and the Padres thought it was to being done.

"I don't want to throw cold water on any stories being told, but we weren't that close to a deal," he told me. "I don't remember exactly, but I believe Peavy was owed [$63 million]. I believe he really wanted to come here and that had a lot to do with Rick Sutcliffe. He and Peavy were really close. There was a true desire from that player and there was a desire on our part to have him here. But it never got that close in my mind. The team was for sale and it was just too much money. Really it was a budget issue. We were operating a business, like we do now with Theo."

Free-spirited rookie Randy Wells, who aspired to live and pitch like Peavy, wound up making 27 starts for the Cubs and doing pretty well, compiling a 3.05 ERA.

Hendry still traded DeRosa and Marquis a few weeks later. But instead of making space for Peavy, those deals cleared the decks for the Cubs to acquire that left-handed hitter they needed: Milton Bradley.

Bradley, a switch-hitter with on-base skills, charmed Hendry in a dinner meant to assuage Hendry's nerves about signing the mercurial player to a long-term deal. Bradley was coming off his best year in Texas, where he blossomed under manager Ron Washington, finishing the season with a .436 on-base percentage and a .999 OPS, both of which were the best in the American League. Sure, he had to undergo anger management counseling in 2004 while with the Dodgers. Yes, he flipped out on reporters from time to time. Of course, you remember that time he tore his ACL in 2007 while arguing with an umpire. He had one of the worst reputations in baseball and as we found out later, we didn't know the truly awful things he was doing off the field.

Bradley had changed, according to Bradley. Just look at how he performed in Texas. So Hendry crossed his fingers and invested about half of what it would've taken to sign Peavy: three years, $30 million.

As Hendry would joke to reporters over the ensuing years, that contract would one day wind up on his tombstone. If DeRosa were the best clubhouse guy in baseball, Bradley was the worst.

The Cubs clubhouse, the actual physical clubhouse, was too small for his negative energy. Perhaps if Bradley had got off to a hot start, things would've been different for him, but he started slow and he quickly came to resent the wall-to-wall coverage of the Cubs media.

He only started in 10 games that April and collected just four hits, two of which were homers.

In his first at-bat at Wrigley Field as a Cub, he got a standing ovation. Then he got called out on strikes and argued with home plate umpire Larry Vanover, who ejected him.

A week later Cubs fans booed him for not running out a ground ball and he refused to talk to reporters. There was the time he threw the ball into the stands with two outs. Through it all, he blamed reporters. I must confess, we can be an overly inquisitive bunch. But what I've long said about the Chicago sports media is we're not tough or mean-spirited—aside from Jay Mariotti, who had already left the *Sun-Times*, there aren't many angry writers—but we do ask a lot of questions. And that can rub people the wrong way.

"I need a stable, healthy, enjoyable environment," Bradley told beat writer Bruce Miles at the end of his season. "There's too many people everywhere in your face with a microphone asking the same questions repeatedly. Everything is just bashing you. It's just negativity."

His numbers improved over May and June, but not to any appreciable degree. From May to June 21, he hit .283 with a .784 OPS, but the Cubs were just 18–20 in games he played. It wasn't his fault, to be sure—Soto went from Rookie of the Year to a .218 hitter, Aramis Ramírez got hurt, Soriano slumped, the bullpen scuffled—but it felt like Bradley's arrival was the harbinger to the end of this group's abbreviated run.

Bradley's uneven season lingered on through the summer until late June when the Cubs traveled to U.S. Cellular Field for the always-entertaining city series with the White Sox.

Before the first game of the series, Bradley opened up to the *Tribune*'s Paul Sullivan about feeling alone on the team.

"This isn't me," Bradley told Sullivan. "I've always excelled at playing baseball, and to come here and suck like I have, it's just not a good feeling. And there's really not one guy who I can sit and talk to. I've been on teams where I have guys I know, or somebody I can just vent to."

In the sixth inning that day, he hit a fly ball with one out and nobody on and returned to the visitors dugout and threw a tantrum, tossing his helmet and busting up the water cooler. Piniella told him to leave, while following him through the tunnel to the clubhouse, calling him a piece of shit.

"What led up to it was the fired helmet and the smashed cooler," Piniella told reporters. "This has been a common occurrence, and I've looked the other way a lot. And I'm done with it."

The Cubs players didn't know what to expect going forward.

"I hope he comes back and he can help the team to win," Soriano told reporters. "If he's not that way, we don't need him. We have 25 players, we have to be on the same page. If he's not 100 percent to help the team to win, we don't need him."

Bradley did come back, but in late September, after telling a reporter, "You understand why they haven't won in 100 years here," Hendry suspended him for the season. Supposedly, the team cheered when Hendry broke the news in the clubhouse. In his lone season with the Cubs, Bradley hit .257 with 12 homers and 40 RBIs.

"Jim made the decision and I support it," Piniella said. "I really do."

Bradley often brought up his poor treatment from Cubs fans, and insinuated he was the subject of racism. While Bradley was known for blaming others for his failures, it was tough to argue that one. Manager Dusty Baker, LaTroy Hawkins, Jacque Jones, and other black players had similar complaints and even had racist letters sent to them at Wrigley Field to prove it. Ozzie Guillen would sometimes show reporters the racist mail he would receive, though Ozzie being Ozzie, he laughed it off. (Guillen gave out his email address and would write his critics back.)

At one point, Bradley said someone called him the "N" word from the bleachers. No one was ever arrested, but I didn't doubt it was true.

Bob Brenly, the former Diamondbacks manager who started calling Cubs games in 2004, said that kind of ugliness was brought up by Hendry to Bradley before he signed him. "I remember talking to Jim about the signing of Milton Bradley, now that you've mentioned it," Brenly said, "and I don't even know if I should say this, but Jim asked him, 'What are you gonna do when someone calls you the 'N' word out in the bleachers? Because it's probably gonna happen,'" Brenly said. "And whatever Milton's answer was, it was good enough for [the Cubs] to feel like he could do it. He could come in here and be strong enough, have tough enough skin to put up with the naysayers. And given his history there were a lot of naysayers."

But were racist fans, as abhorrent as those people are, Bradley's biggest problem in Chicago? No.

That off-season, Hendry was somehow able to offload Bradley to Seattle—his eighth team in 11 seasons—for pitcher Carlos Silva, another problem child. At least Hendry got a year of passable starting pitching for Silva.

But Bradley's problems off the field were more serious than anything that happened between the white lines. The postscript of his career was tragic, but not for him.

In July 2013, he was sentenced to nearly three years in jail for abusing his wife, Monique, during their marriage.

The case was covered in detail by *Sports Illustrated* in 2015, shortly before he was ordered to start serving his sentence. (He was out on appeal.) The details of the physical and emotional abuse, some of which happened while he was with the Cubs, were horrifying. His ex-wife died in September 2013 of cirrhosis of the liver. They had two kids together.

Even with Bradley's dark cloud hanging over the Cubs, they were tied for first place as late as August 5, thanks to an 18–9 July, before foundering. They went from 57–48 after a win on August 4 to 61–60 on August 22. They finished with 83 wins, two fewer than they did in 2007 when they won the division.

The club's financial situation was weighing on everyone. The Cubs' only move that season was trading for left-handed reliever John Grabow. Minor league infielder Josh Harrison was part of the package that went to Pittsburgh. He wound up making two All-Star teams in Pittsburgh.

"We couldn't do a thing, not one thing," Piniella told his old friend Hal McCoy in 2009 about a lack of in-season moves. "The team was in bankruptcy proceedings just before the sale, and we couldn't spend one cent. Not one penny. And we haven't hit all year."

The Ricketts family took over after the 2009 season, which was one positive. But it wasn't like they came in with a bag of money or fairy dust to get the team back into contention in 2010. The Cubs payroll was $146 million and Ricketts had to eat $10 million for Bradley.

Hendry's big signing in 2010 was Marlon Byrd, who put up an above-average season.

Most importantly, 20-year-old shortstop Starlin Castro came up, driving in six runs in his MLB debut on May 7, 2010. He became the first MLB player born in the 1990s. Castro, the team's best position prospect in some time, put up a .300/.347/.408 slash line in his rookie year. While he only hit three homers, he did have 31 doubles, 10 more than Aramis Ramírez.

It was promising, but the Cubs needed a lot more than one Starlin.

On July 20, Piniella announced 2010 would be his last season. A month later, he decided to retire immediately to return to Florida to take care of his mother. In his recent book, co-authored with writer Bill Madden, Piniella recounted a funny story that encapsulated the state of the Cubs in 2010.

In the previous off-season, the Cubs made Rudy Jaramillo the highest-paid hitting coach in baseball. But the Cubs offense wasn't clicking. After a 2–9 stretch in May, Hendry met with Piniella and Jaramillo. Hendry wanted to know what was wrong and how the Cubs could fix it.

"This is a three-year program," Jaramillo told Hendry.

"Three years?" Hendry said. "I'm on a three-month program!"

I do have two favorite Piniella memories from that final season. One was when he kicked Carlos Zambrano out of the visitors dugout at U.S. Cellular Field. For the second consecutive season, Sweet Lou tossed his own player for throwing a fit in the dugout. Zambrano, in the midst of a terrible season, nearly fought Derrek Lee before Piniella told him to go home. (Zambrano would make news in Chicago when he went out to dinner with White Sox manager, and fellow Venezuelan, Ozzie Guillen that night.)

The other moment was at the home portion of the city series when Piniella, out of nowhere, started ripping Steve Stone in the dugout before the game. It was 2004 all over again!

Before the June 18 game, Piniella was asked about his rookies, including outfielder Tyler Colvin. Ten days prior, Stone, now working for the White Sox, criticized Piniella on a TV show for how he handled Colvin's playing time.

"I think that means that Lou doesn't have a great grasp on what to do with young players," Stone said in the interview. "Because with Tyler Colvin, if you take a look at what he has accomplished in a short period of time, with limited play, you realize that he very well could be the one thing the Cubs have been looking for for six years. That's a left-handed run producer. Colvin could be that one guy. But he can't do it on the bench, so you make a decision that you play the guy."

In the home dugout, Piniella started ranting. "We've got a lot of people here that haven't managed and won any games in the big leagues,

Home plate umpire Mark Carlson ejects Carlos Zambrano as Lou Piniella comes to his aid. *(AP Photo/Charles Rex Arbogast)*

but they know everything, you know?" Piniella said. "They really do. I think they should really try and put the uniform on and try this job and see how they like it when they get criticized unjustly, you know? That's all I got to say about that issue."

Well, almost all.

"But you get tired of it," Piniella said. "I'm trying to do the best job I possibly can, and the only people I need to listen to are the people in my organization, that's it. I get tired of being nitpicked, and I get tired of being criticized unjustly. Why don't they talk to me first before they do it, okay? And get my viewpoints and my feelings and then make a determination.

"You know? The same way I get called 'ridiculous,' they're ridiculous in the way they report things, too.

"And another thing I'm going to say. I've won over 1,800 games as a manager, and I'm not a damn dummy," Piniella said. "There are only 13 others that have won more games than me, so I guess I think I know what the hell I'm doing."

He also named the target of his ire, in case it wasn't obvious.

"And Steve Stone, he's got enough problems doing what he does with the White Sox," Piniella said. "What job has he had in baseball besides talking on television or radio? What has he done? Why isn't he a farm director and bring some kids around? Why isn't he a general manager? Why hasn't he ever put the uniform on and be a pitching coach? Why hasn't he been a field manager? There are 30 teams out there that could use a guy's expertise like that."

Piniella then explained he had five outfielders to juggle, which was true. After he finished talking, I ran up to the press box to transcribe these quotes for an ESPN story. Then I realized other reporters were talking to Stone, so I left and headed back downstairs. Lo and behold, I ran into Stone and buttonholed him myself.

"He's right," Stone told me. "I've never managed. I've never been a general manager. I've never been a pitching coach. But I'm in my fifth decade in this game. I think I have the right to have an opinion."

I asked him if Piniella was just frustrated with his team and the likely end of his run.

"I can't look into Lou's psyche. I don't know," Stone said. "I do know he's getting $4 million a year to manage. I get paid to broadcast on Comcast SportsNet and WSCR radio. I have two TV shows and two radio shows a week. I also get the MLB package, and I watch a number of games every night. I spend my winter in Arizona watching the Arizona Fall League and seeing young kids from everybody's system. I go to all of spring training and make my way around various camps. I've seen more baseball players than Lou has. I just haven't managed them."

Piniella retired on a Sunday. His last game was a 16–5 loss on August 22 that dropped the Cubs to 51–74. They had 13 hits and struck out 13 times, while Randy Wells got rocked. It was a fitting end.

"It's a good day to remember and also it's a good day to forget," Piniella said.

After nearly a half-century in pro ball, Piniella shed more than a few tears after the game and choked up during his press conference. He went 316–293 as Cubs manager, which was nothing to sneeze at. But he couldn't win a playoff game.

"I cried a little bit after the game. You get emotional. I'm sorry, I'm not trying to be," he said with his voice cracking. "This will be the last time I put on my uniform."

Piniella was a true baseball character and reporters can't believe we had him on one side of town and Ozzie Guillen on the other for four years.

To this day, the media relations staff still cracks up when they recount Piniella stories, particularly the ones he told about his days with the Yankees.

To replace Piniella, Hendry gave the job to the interim manager, Mike Quade, a Chicago native who worked his way up the old-fashioned way. He was popular with the veterans in 2010, giving them a little more attention than a tired Piniella.

The end of 2010 was a sad time for a different reason. Ron Santo, the voice and soul of the Cubs, died on December 3. Santo, the ex-Cub, "This Old Cub," was the radio color man of the team. A third baseman, he was a perennial borderline Hall of Famer, making it posthumously a year later. Santo wore his fandom on his sleeve and oftentimes it was more enjoyable to listen to him when the Cubs would blow a late lead. You would be stuck in traffic on the Kennedy, cursing your life, but there would be ol' Ronny croaking out, "Nooooooo!" as some Cubs reliever reliably coughed up a lead in the ninth. He was perfectly paired with the buttoned-up, sardonic straight man Pat Hughes, who used to tee up Santo with a wink and a smile.

Santo, who struggled with diabetes from his playing career until he passed away (he lost parts of both legs), was beloved by the fans. His work with his diabetes charity linked him to a fanbase that ranged from the cradle to the grave.

His church service was shown live on TV and attended by ex-Cubs of every generation. When the Cubs finally won, hundreds of thousands of Cubs fans thought of Santo clicking his heels in heaven.

Hendry got one more shot to make the Cubs a winner. This was either a major miscalculation by Ricketts to give a dying man a life preserver or a necessary evil to get Theo Epstein the following year. But Hendry was allowed to trade several top prospects from a thin system for Tampa Bay pitcher Matt Garza. One of them was Chris Archer, who has turned into an All-Star.

"Probably my enthusiasm a few years back and my aggressiveness to finally knock my door down probably led to a couple decisions I shouldn't have made, and ended up being not good for the organization," Hendry said. "It certainly didn't turn into more wins."

The Garza trade was the final gasp. He wound up having a pretty good season (3.32 ERA), but the Cubs went 6–10 in his starts in the first half, when he had a 4.26 ERA. The Cubs had an 18-game deficit in the NL Central at the break.

Quade was an outright disaster. Everything that made him a good interim manager was seemingly forgotten once the pressure of the regular season got to him. One reliever told me after that season that Quade didn't talk to him all season. As in, when Quade would pull him from the game, he would just take the ball. No "good job" or "thanks." Literally, not a word.

In early July, Dempster yelled at Quade in the dugout after he was told he was being pulled after five innings. The bullpen had been used a lot in recent days and Dempster thought it was his duty to keep pitching as the Cubs had the lead.

"I said something and then he said something to me that I didn't like very much and then I kind of lost it," Dempster said. "I think I lost it a lot too, because a lot of people stuck up for him about getting the job and I was one of the guys who was very vocal about it. There's no excuse. I just took it really personal in the heat of the moment. I didn't like how it looked, I didn't like being in front of the other guys while I did that. I don't regret a lot of things about my playing career, but that was one of the moments where I regret how I handled that, for sure."

What happened to Quade? The pressure of managing the Cubs.

"A lot of guys felt like a lot of things he did to get the job, they stopped," Dempster said. "And at the same time, I don't know what it's like to manage the Chicago Cubs, especially one that hasn't won the World Series in all that time. I'm sure it's pretty intense and to be able to balance that takes a pretty special person."

Hendry was fired early in the second half, but the move somehow remained a secret for nearly a month as he worked through the culmination of the draft pick signings.

"It may be one of the best-kept secrets in Cubs history," he said at the time.

One of those picks was Javier Baéz, a Puerto Rican–born infielder with an explosive bat. As someone in the room for the draft told me at the time, Hendry was so happy to get Baéz, he "acted like this guy would be playing third base for him for the next 10 years."

That season, 2011, a 19-year-old prospect made his U.S. debut with the Boise Hawks. Of the 60 games Willson Contreras played that summer, 45 were starts at third base. None were at catcher. Contreras didn't hit that much in 2011—he was one of the youngest players on the short season Class-A team—but the next season, the first of the Theo Epstein regime, he was switched to catcher. Four years later, he was in the majors.

* * *

Days before his firing was public, Hendry suspended pitcher Carlos Zambrano, putting him on the disqualified list for throwing a temper tantrum after a bad start in Atlanta and telling team officials that he was retiring. Hendry suspended Zambrano for 30 days without pay.

"His actions last night were totally intolerable," Hendry told reporters. "This was the most stringent penalty we could enforce without a release."

During the game, in which the Braves were honoring former manager Bobby Cox, Zambrano threw at Chipper Jones after giving up a pair of homers. The Cubs, players and staff alike, were tired of Zambrano's volatility.

"If he changes his attitude, he's more than welcome," to return, Aramis Ramírez told reporters.

Zambrano never returned to the Cubs, as Epstein got him to waive his no-trade clause to finish his career with a season in Miami under Ozzie Guillen's watch. Zambrano was only 31 when he last pitched in the majors.

His decline started in 2010, the season when Piniella tossed him from the dugout. Earlier that year, the Cubs moved him to the bullpen for a bit in April and May. What did it say about the Cubs' feelings about Zambrano, who had a 7.45 ERA in his first four starts, that they moved him to the 'pen and kept Tom Gorzelanny in the rotation? Zambrano was told the Cubs needed an eighth-inning guy and the move was temporary. At the time, he was the fifth-highest paid pitcher in baseball.

"Like Schwarzenegger says, 'I will be back,'" Zambrano said.

Most saw it as a wake-up call for the mercurial pitcher. The Cubs were tired of coddling him. With the exception of three relief appearances in late July and early August, he started 16 times from June through the end of the season and put up a 2.40 ERA. But his 2011 season never got on track, and like Hendry and Aramis Ramírez, who left for free agency, his time with the Cubs was over.

Zambrano made his debut in 2001 and in his 11 seasons on the North Side compiled a 3.60 ERA and made 282 starts. He finished his Cubs career with 1,826⅔ innings and 1,542 strikeouts, winning 125 games. From 2003 through 2007, he worked at least 200 innings every season.

Beyond being reliable—aside from sporadic cramping issues from a lack of hydration—he was also entertaining. Zambrano would belly flop into third base like Rickey Henderson. He would break a bat over his knee like Bo Jackson. And he could hit dingers. Zambrano hit 23 homers as a Cub, slugging .395 in 659 at-bats. In 2006, his worst year for average, he hit six homers in 73 at-bats, as many as Todd Walker

(318 at-bats), Henry Blanco (241), and Ronny Cedeno (534), and three more than Juan Pierre did in 699 ABs. Zambrano is ninth all-time in homers by a pitcher, tied with Bob Gibson and ahead of Walter Johnson. Madison Bumgarner is the only active pitcher in spitting distance with 17.

In the pre-Twitter era, you'd occasionally get reports of him playing softball with friends from church in the city. During the 2005 season, he was slated to coach one of the sides in a Chicago Fire media soccer game and instead wound up playing the entire contest at forward and in goal.

"I didn't get injured; I didn't do nothing wrong," he said at the time. "I play just for fun."

Just for Fun: The Carlos Zambrano Story. Except, sometimes he wasn't very fun at all.

"Z was interesting," Dempster said. "There were two Zambranos. There was Big Z and there was Carl. Carl's great, man. He was a great teammate, you know. Funny, great person. Always trying to do good for people. But when Big Z came out, it was hard. It was heavy. It was very heavy. You felt when he was mad. You felt when he was on edge. It was not fun to be around.

"He didn't know how to lose. We all don't know how to lose, but he really didn't know how to lose. It became everybody else's fault. He automatically put up walls."

Bob Brenly, who could be very critical of certain Cubs on the air, had a soft spot for Big Z.

"He could go off the rails very quickly," Brenly said. "I mean, that was apparent. But when he was focused, out there on the mound, he could dominate. He could dominate. The biggest problem Big Z had was pitch count. It was always pitch count. You know he might be through five innings with 12 strikeouts and eight walks and be up to 130 pitches. You gotta get him out, gotta get him out. But those four or five innings were a lot of fun to watch.

"Beating the living daylights out of Gatorade buckets in the dugout, punching teammates. You know. Some of it was obviously way over the line. But I would much rather manage a player that has that kind of intensity and that kind of energy for the game, and that kind of passion for the game than somebody that kinda lets things roll off their back."

Zambrano returned to Wrigley Field with the Marlins, and eventually as a retired player. I caught up with him in August 2016.

"Oh, you know I don't like to talk about bad things," Zambrano said. "Whatever happened, it happened. I am grateful with the Cubs and I appreciate them. I am very sorry how things ended up, but baseball is a business."

He had mellowed significantly, and said he was keeping busy with his business endeavors in Miami. Later, he told the *Tribune*'s Paul Sullivan he was engaged with some amateur ministry work. That wasn't a surprise. He was very involved with his church in Chicago during his playing career.

He watched the Cubs on occasion, he told me, and he was playing a season with the Cubs on PlayStation.

"I'm doing good," he told me. "I'm in first, pitching is good. Hitting, I have Rizzo third in the National League in home runs, Fowler stealing a lot of bases."

Did he create himself to pitch and try to get that elusive World Series ring?

"No," he said. "I don't want to get mad at myself."

* * *

Hendry cried during his exit press conference, calling himself "Dick Vermeil." It was the necessary end to an era that saw the Cubs almost end their drought, but fall in poetic fashion.

"We knew what the lot was," he told me in 2018. "We were going to have to win the next couple of years, two or three max, or it wasn't going to be pretty after that for a while. And that's what happened. And truthfully the Ricketts did the right thing, because if I stood up at the podium after being there nine, 10 years and said, 'We all know this.

We took our shot. We overspent a couple of years ago. We've got to cut it back now to meet a lot of the budget criterias of the sale.' That's not going to fly without having us win it before.

"If we'd have won in '03… But we had failed the last couple of years so everybody knew what had to be done. You needed to have a Theo or a Brian Cashman or a Brian Sabean with some jewelry on and do it the way it needed to be done. And Theo did a masterful job of it. Perfect. So it just couldn't continue the way it was going and keep cutting back when you're redoing it and basically get your draft picks high for a couple of years. And Theo did a marvelous job and hit bullseyes, and great picks. My hat's off to them. Nobody could have done any better."

Hendry was the master of the off-the-record comment to reporters, but he rarely made excuses. Ten years later, he has the right attitude about his time in Chicago.

"You win the games or you don't," he said. "And I had plenty of chances. And getting close was a solid effort, but we didn't get it all the way done. So I didn't get the job and stand up and say I want to get in the playoffs every year. I wanted to be the first GM that won it since whenever. And that's how we went after it."

In his nine years as the GM, the Cubs went 733–723. The Cubs had five winning seasons, three playoff appearances, and enhanced expectations. This was a boomtime for the Cubs as a business. They drew more than 3 million fans every year to Wrigley from 2004 through 2011. They cofounded a regional sports network, won additional revenue from rooftop owners, and then, the sale. They were close to ending the curse, which just made their failure that much worse.

On the day Hendry was fired in August, chairman Tom Ricketts, in his second season as the owner, declared the race for GM was open. I wrote in a column the Cubs needed a "Theo Epstein type." Little did I know.

CHAPTER 4
A FAN BUYS
THE CUBS

Tom Ricketts' first office at Wrigley Field was not a home for an owner. Then again, nothing was special in the team offices at old Wrigley Field.

The small office was in the middle of a narrow hallway for the executives. The previous owner of the team was the Tribune Company. The Trib always had a guy on hand, but this was different. Tom would be part of the team's day-to-day life.

I spent some time in his office there in 2010, working on a story for the University of Chicago alumni magazine. Tom and two of his three siblings went to undergrad at the Hyde Park school, and both Tom and his older brother Pete also received MBAs from the business school.

Tom made his money in the corporate bond market, but it wasn't "buy the Cubs" money. No, that came from his father, Joe Ricketts. Joe, an Omaha stockbroker, founded TD Ameritrade in 1971, when Tom was in preschool. While Tom has been pilloried as a rich kid using his father's money, in truth, the family didn't have "real money" until he had been out of college for a decade, which is when Joe took the company public in 1997.

Tom had dreamed of owning a team for years. He and his brother and their friends lived in apartments around Wrigley Field. Tom was a freshman at U of C in 1984, and while Hyde Park is a ways down Lake Shore Drive from Wrigley Field, all of Chicago was in love with the Cubs in 1984. That team was as responsible for converting kids into Cubs fans as Harry Caray was for getting beer drinkers into Wrigley Field.

Just before his first game as owner of the Cubs, Tom said he found a copy of his application essay to get into Chicago Booth business school. The prompt was: What's your dream job? His answer: own the Cubs.

"He talks about that business-school essay, but I remember one day when we were living together above Sports Corner and Tom reading a story about finding out you could buy a pro hockey team for about $3 million," his friend Curt Conklin told me back in 2010. "We didn't have anything close to that. The four of us living there barely had $100 between us. But it wasn't unreasonable to think in the next 20 years, we couldn't scrape up enough money to do it."

(Amusingly enough, as Ricketts was going through the complicated purchase process, he didn't have season tickets, but he wanted to take his kids to a game, so he sat in Conklin's seats.)

Many years later, the Ricketts children had a trust set up by their father for a major purchase. Something they could buy as a family and run for generations.

In August 2006, the Ricketts family rented several rooftops across from Wrigley Field to hold a joint birthday party for the siblings. Tom used the occasion to plant a seed with his father, who is not a baseball fan.

"Tom said, 'Dad, look at this,'" Pete told me years ago. "And Dad said, 'It's a nice field.' Tom said, 'Dad, they sell out every game.' And Dad realized, 'Oh, this is a business.'"

A month later, Tom, Pete, and Joe were driving to Lincoln, Nebraska, for a football game. Pete was in the middle of an expensive, doomed Senate campaign funded mostly with his own money and Tom said he was going to get a bid ready to buy the Cubs, which weren't yet for sale, but soon would be.

So he hired Sal Galatioto from Galatioto Sports Partners, one of the leaders in the very profitable niche business of helping rich people buy professional sports franchises. Galatioto said he was approached by several would-be bidders for this historic deal.

"We wanted to pick the people with the best chance of being successful," he told me. "We thought they were the right people to own the team from the get-go."

Then Tom hired PR expert Dennis Culloton and the law firm Foley & Lardner.

Sam Zell purchased the controlling stake in the Tribune in a complicated leveraged buyout deal (one that wound up crushing the company in debt) that was finalized on April 1, 2007. On Opening Day, the Cubs were announced to be for sale and they wanted to find a buyer by the end of the season.

Early on, the most famous bidder was Mark Cuban, the outspoken Dallas Mavericks owner who liked to drink beer in the bleachers. The most obvious candidate was John "Friend of Bud Selig" Canning, a very successful private equity investor in Chicago.

"I didn't get to know the Ricketts family at all during the sale process," Crane Kenney, the Tribune's man at Wrigley Field during the process, told me. "I got to know some other bidders and I spent time with each of them during their management presentations, but I knew the Ricketts the least."

The Ricketts' interest in the Cubs became public in July 2007 and they lacked the familiar names or sports ties of some of the other groups. Unless you were familiar with TD Ameritrade, who even knew the family at all? As for Tom Ricketts, he said he wasn't focused on his competition.

"I really had no idea who was in what group or what groups were applying," Tom said. "In the end, I didn't spend much energy trying to find out. It wasn't about that. We went into it assuming it would be a fair and open bidding process and it really was. One advantage we had as just a family and not a group of businessmen was that it was easier for us than the other groups to stick together and just be patient."

Patience was needed as the process dragged on thanks to Zell's zest for negotiating and the collapse of the credit markets in 2008.

The Ricketts family was finally picked as the winning bidder in January 2009, and in February they agreed to sell more than $400 million worth of TD Ameritrade stock to help finance a deal.

This was only the start of exclusive negotiations with Zell and they wound up lasting all season. At one point, there was talk about selling the Cubs and Wrigley Field separately, but obviously that wouldn't have worked in the modern sports world. Even with the great expense of fixing up Wrigley Field, it would make more sense for the team owners to have control.

The Ricketts family (from left, Pete, Todd, and Laura) look on as Tom Ricketts talks about the family's new ownership of the Cubs. (AP Photo/Jim Prisching)

"There were certain conditions where the economics wouldn't work," Tom said. "In any deal there has to be a point where you're ready to walk away."

During the lull in action, Ricketts considered selling limited ownership stakes in the team to raise money. He tried to get celebrity Cubs fans and other rich people to fork over $25 million for a temporary stake in the team with limited appreciation. That plan didn't work (yet) and they forged ahead.

In the end the deal got done, the bankruptcy court (Zell took the Tribune into bankruptcy) approved it and so did MLB's other owners. The Cubs, Wrigley Field, and a 25 percent stake in Comcast SportsNet

Chicago (the team's regional sports network), were sold for $845 million, the most expensive purchase price in baseball history.

Their introductory press conference was held on October 30, 2009, at the Captain Morgan Club, the bar attached to Wrigley Field at the corner of Sheffield and Addison.

In the press conference, Tom Ricketts said one thing would change from the previous ownership. Well, a lot would change, but one thing that should really affect the way they'd build up the organization.

"We don't have quarterly results to worry about, or a year-end return," he said. "Our shareholders are our fans." It's a quote that was forgotten in later years, when budgetary limitations popped up.

The press conference was hopeful for some, but for others in the organization, it was tense. What changes would be made? What moves could be done? Ricketts tried to joke around to lighten the mood.

"There is no curse," he said. "There is no curse. If anybody on our team thinks he's cursed, we'll move him to a less accursed team. From this day forward, let's just get that behind us."

With all the dithering over money, it didn't seem like the Ricketts had a vault of cash to make changes and the Cubs needed an influx of money and talent to compete in 2010.

They got neither.

While Ricketts, through the media, trumpeted the money he and his family would put into the park, all the cosmetic upgrades and maintenance work couldn't pitch or hit.

The Cubs drew 3.17 million in 2009, down about 130,000 from the franchise's high-water mark the season before, but still the fourth-best number in baseball, a veritable sell-out every time the team took the field.

The 2009 Opening Day payroll was a team-record $134.8 million and with raises coming the next year, it jumped to $146.6 million in 2010. At the press conference, I remember Todd Ricketts, the youngest brother, making jokes about Jim Hendry knowing not to ask for more money. I don't remember Hendry laughing.

Ricketts spent his first season walking around the ballpark, talking to fans, taking pictures and giving away baseballs to kids. Behind the scenes, he was figuring out how to finance a massive renovation of the ballpark, while also trying to learn the business of baseball. The good thing about Tom Ricketts, the owner, is that he didn't think he knew everything. While he didn't always inspire confidence in those early days, he also didn't inspire enmity.

While a number of holdovers stuck around from the Tribune days, there was a lot of new blood in the business department with Ricketts in charge. And the new hires were hungry to add new ideas.

In 2010, the team partnered with Kraft to put a giant macaroni noodle outside the ballpark, with new Cubs marketing guru Wally Hayward calling it "noodle art." This after adding a giant Toyota sign, worth approximately $2.5 million, in left field. We joked that Hayward, a sports marketing expert, was turning Wrigley Field into "Wally's World." But he was responsible for signing the big-ticket sponsorship deals that came to be known as "legacy partnerships."

The Cubs' influx of sponsorship cash continued after Hayward opened his own marketing firm, and so did the head-scratching ideas, like the introduction of mascot Clark the Cub, who was immediately mocked both by locals and across the country. The introduction was botched by the Cubs only releasing the sillier cartoon version of Clark, which resembled the Simpsons' gag character "Poochie." That Clark, a bear of course, wore a jersey but no pants became a lightning-rod joke (even though most mascots don't wear pants). It was a perfect moment for Twitter and even the Cubs baseball operations department got in on the act. One executive wondered if he'd get busted by the IT department for googling "furries." A spokesperson railed against the online mockery, which included Deadspin making an anatomically-correct cartoon of Clark. Theo Epstein even had to address it at the team's 2014 fan convention.

"It's a natural by-product of a bit of a vacuum that's been created," he said. "I also think it shows how special this franchise is. Pick a random team, had they introduced a new character into the organization to entertain children, it may not have been met with the same attention that Clark was greeted with."

In 2010, the Cubs business department created a trophy for the annual Cubs–White Sox series for the express purpose of selling a sponsorship with it. Unfortunately for the Cubs, they signed a multi-year deal with BP at the same time as the Deepwater Horizon oil spill in the Gulf Coast. In fact, six days after the spill began.

Instead of canceling the deal, the Cubs and BP dialed down the marketing that first year, but even without the naming-rights fiasco, the pomp and circumstance surrounding it seemed small-time. It looked even worse when the Cubs tried to unveil it to the fans for the first time, which was also the day of the Blackhawks Stanley Cup parade. When a cloaked trophy was brought behind home plate before the series opener, fans roared, thinking it was the Stanley Cup. When the BP Cup was shown, they booed. (The drunken, celebrating Hawks brought the Cup later in the series.)

The Sox won the first Cup and when a couple of us asked one of their executives if we could take a picture with it, he said, "You can have it." BP's deal eventually ended and through the 2018 season, the Cubs and Sox still traded it back and forth, but without a title sponsor.

A couple weeks after the season, Ricketts made a plan—a plea, really—public.

He wanted to use city tax money to help fund the renovation of Wrigley Field. But it was complicated.

In mid-November, there was a press conference called, again at the Captain Morgan Club. Despite a perfectly good location inside the stadium, this was picked, I believed then, for the dramatics of the moment. Wrigley Field was so outdated, we had to have a moderately sized press conference in a sports bar.

Ricketts' plan was to use amusement tax revenue to help finance $200–$300 million worth of bonds to fund the improvement of Wrigley. At the time, the cubs wanted to freeze the amount of money they paid in amusement tax revenue—$16.1 million in 2009—and use increased tax money that would come with higher ticket prices and/or amusement tax bumps to fund part of the renovation through bonds to be issued by the Illinois Sports Facilities Authority, which owns the White Sox's stadium. Their plan was for this to last for 35 years.

Ricketts thought he had the backing of government in Springfield, but that fell apart. Mayor Richard Daley was wrapping up his 22 years in office. He wasn't any help.

"[Former governor of Illinois] Jim Thompson gave us good support," Cubs president of business operations Crane Kenney said years later. "So did the Illinois Finance Authority."

The amusement tax proposal, Kenney said, "came unraveled more from politics than the fiscal side."

Ricketts saw the amusement tax plan not as public money, but money the Cubs were generating that belonged to them. Needless to say, a lot of people disagreed.

"The Cubs/Ricketts are, in fact, asking for public money because any funds devoted to Wrigley renovations are dollars that can't be allocated to, or used for, any other project[s]," University of Chicago professor and sports economics expert Allen Sanderson wrote in an email to me at the time. "'Invest' is a word politicians and others who want to feed at the public trough use; it sounds so much nicer than 'blow' or 'spend' or 'divert.'"

"It's splitting hairs, extraordinarily fine to say this isn't a tax increase, because this isn't existing tax money," stadium financing writer Neil deMause told me in a 2010 phone conversation. "The tax money is not coming in yet. It's the same thing as me saying I'm only paying what I pay in income taxes now and I'm going to cut a deal with the government that any additional money I make I get to keep."

The Cubs got a new spring training stadium by using similar logic, even trying to push for a "Cubs tax" on other Cactus League games. Because the Cubs were the biggest draw in Arizona's Cactus League (by a substantial margin), they argued they needed a taxpayer-funded stadium. Given Arizona and Florida's penchant for giving away money to teams, you couldn't argue with the Cubs' demands. And by threatening to move to Naples, Florida, the Cubs got Proposition 420 passed. That provided up to $99 million from the city of Mesa. Sloan Park, which opened in 2014, is a jewel of a spring training facility, though some wonder how much of the traveling fan's money really goes to Mesa, given how popular neighboring Scottsdale is with tourists.

One benefit of the Cubs' push for public dollars is they revealed some research to back up their demands. They hired a consulting firm, Conventions, Sports & Leisure International, to do a study that claimed the Cubs and Wrigley Field generated $618 million in economic impact to the local economy in 2009, $379 million in annual "new net direct spending," and paid $59 million in taxes, a third of which went to the city of Chicago itself. The study also reported that 37 percent of Cubs fans at games came from outside of the state (not including the nearby parts of Indiana) and that these Cubs fans spent $77 million in new money on hotels and $111 million on food.

Now, no one should've taken those numbers as gospel, but at least we had a guesstimate on how many tourists were coming to games.

It was the wrong time to ask for tax dollars even if, as Ricketts tried to prove, the Cubs were producing them.

Given that Joe Ricketts' largesse funded the purchase of the team, his son was asked about his father's political activity, including a "nonpartisan" group called "Taxpayers Against Earmarks," which was dedicated to fighting "wasteful spending" in Washington. "Earmarks" refers to the much-derided government practice of appending spending on a federal bill in quick-hitting fashion. Joe was then, and is now, a major donor to the Republican Party, and in the Obama era that meant hitting at government spending. (He renamed his PAC "Ending Spending" and both Pete and Todd Ricketts became majorly involved, with Todd taking it over.)

"The fact is, what it does is it jeopardizes the integrity of the federal budgeting process," Tom said that day when a TV reporter asked him about the hypocrisy. "You can tell by the people in the room today this isn't a private process we're going through. We're trying to be as open as possible. This is a decision that will be made by elected officials and the people in this room."

(Tom brought labor leaders with him to discuss how the renovation of Wrigley would affect them in a positive manner.)

What he didn't mention was that his father's group wasn't just railing about the lack of debate for earmarks, but rather their purpose. On the website at the time, the group's mission was defined as such:

"Earmarks provide federal funding for projects benefiting only a state or local interest, or a private company, university or non-profit. In other words, most earmark-funded projects do not benefit the nation as a whole—though the 'giving' of an earmark by a Member of Congress certainly benefits that Member."

The Cubs wanted a tax break that would benefit them. It's not an earmark, but it certainly was a favor.

In the end, it didn't go anywhere. The Cubs had wasted a year. I wonder today how it would've worked out had Democratic leader Michael Madigan pushed for it. Cubs attendance cratered after 2011. In early 2019, Joe Ricketts gave the Cubs even bigger problems, as racist emails he sent and forwarded were released by Splinter News. These emails disparaged Muslims and blacks.

When business-friendly mayor Rahm Emanuel took over for Daley in 2011, Ricketts made headway in getting public money from the city. In September, they hired Julian Green as their vice president of communications and public affairs. From 2004 to '07, he was the press secretary for an up-and-coming senator named Barack Obama. This was a savvy move considering Obama's strong ties with Emanuel, his former chief of staff.

But in 2012, as Ricketts thought he was close to getting significant public money, his father's political work came back to hurt the team in a major way.

CHAPTER 5
THEOCRACY

Theo Epstein was restless in Boston. People there knew it. The Cubs knew it.

I didn't.

"Why would Epstein come to the Cubs?" I argued in conversation and in print. The Cubs wanted to be Boston, from their World Series championships after a historic drought to their renovated, historic ballpark to their bustling cable network to their money. The Cubs wanted that Red Sox cash in Chicago.

What I didn't know and what the Cubs did know is that Epstein wanted out. Everyone knew about the gorilla suit and the pressures of winning in Boston. But Epstein had tired of the circus atmosphere there, from the aggressive reporters to his own bosses' unbelievable demands.

While one of the owners, Larry Lucchino, helped raise Epstein as a baseball executive, the two had a fractured relationship. Fellow owner John Henry would email Boston manager Terry Francona every day with questions about lineups.

In November 2010, after a third-place finish in the AL East, Epstein had to sit in a meeting with TV consultants because his bosses were worried about low TV ratings at their cable network, New England Sports Network.

The consultants revealed that their market research showed Red Sox fans wanted "good looking stars and sex symbols," complained that "the games are too long with disappointing outcomes," and illustrated that "big moves, trades, and messaging in the off-season are important."

This meeting was detailed in an illuminating book co-authored by Francona and Dan Shaughnessy.

In an interview for that book, Epstein told Shaughnessy, "They told us we didn't have any marketable players, the team's not exciting enough. We need some sizzle. We need some sexy guys. I was laughing to myself. Talk about the tail wagging the dog. This is like an absurdist comedy."

Epstein partly blames what happened that winter on pressure from above.

"That type of shit contributed to the decision in the winter to go for more of a quick fix," he told the author. "Signing [Carl] Crawford and trading for Adrian [Gonzalez] was in direct response to that in a lot of ways. Shame on me for giving in to it, but at some point, the landscape is what it is."

That off-season, he traded a package of young players, including a first baseman named Anthony Rizzo, to his friends Jed Hoyer and Jason McLeod, who had recently taken over the Padres' baseball operations department, for Adrian Gonzalez, who he signed to a seven-year, $154 million extension that April.

Epstein also signed Carl Crawford to a seven-year, $142 million deal that off-season. (Amazingly, the Red Sox payroll was "only" $162 million, around $30 million more than the Cubs.)

Despite buyers' remorse and problems all over the clubhouse, including with Francona, the Red Sox were in position to make the

Cubs president of baseball operations Theo Epstein (center) watches as new executive vice president/general manager Jed Hoyer (right) shakes hands with new senior vice president of scouting and player development Jason McLeod (left) during a press conference to announce the new front office on Tuesday, November 1, 2011.

(AP Photo/Charles Rex Arbogast)

postseason again. They had a 1½ game lead in the AL East at the end of August, but a 7–20 September killed any dreams about a division title. They didn't get knocked out of the postseason until a wild last day of the season that saw Tampa Bay overtake them for the Wild Card spot. The second Wild Card, which the Red Sox would've won, was instituted for 2012.

Francona was let go and Epstein, who had a year left on his contract, wanted out. The *Boston Globe* published an anonymous, source-filled exposé on how the Red Sox season was derailed by Francona's personal problems and an unruly, spoiled clubhouse where the pitchers, like future Cubs John Lackey and Jon Lester, were drinking beer, eating fried chicken, and playing video games, instead of hanging out in the dugout.

But the collapse of 2011 didn't push Epstein out, he told me. The owners knew he wanted to leave and he was preparing Ben Cherington to take over all season. He said a decade in charge was enough. They thought of ways to keep him in the fold, like giving him a chance to run Fenway Sports Group's Premier League team, Liverpool FC, which John Henry purchased in 2010.

The Cubs had reached out through intermediaries to assess his interest and when it was allowed, he met with Tom Ricketts in his father's multimillion-dollar New York apartment. (Epstein, a devout liberal, meeting at the apartment of one of the conservative right's burgeoning fundraisers shows how we can get along, right?)

What did Epstein know, or quickly find out, about Tom Ricketts?

"I knew he was a down-to-earth dude," Epstein said. "That he didn't necessarily know what he was doing, but he had the humility to know what he didn't know. He was methodical in getting to know the lay of the land to get it right."

Epstein was used to working with big-ego owners in Boston, from Lucchino to Henry to Tom Werner, the famous TV producer. Ricketts, who grew up middle class in Omaha before his father's trading company blew up into TD Ameritrade, was different.

"When I met with him, I was really impressed about his big-picture plans," Epstein said. "He kept saying he wanted to own the Cubs for three generations. He was in it for the long haul."

What did Epstein know about the Cubs' organization? Not much.

Epstein had a good relationship with Hendry, but he didn't have an overwhelming reverence for the baseball operations department's results and they certainly did things differently. Epstein and his crew built Carmine, a vast database for their scouting operations. Hendry's baseball information department was mostly Chuck Wasserstrom, who came over from the PR department.

In a 2009 story from the winter meetings, I wrote about Twitter's creeping influence in the baseball rumor mill and Hendry told me he didn't check Twitter, but he had Wasserstrom print out stories from MLB Trade Rumors. Sure enough, Wasserstrom was in the corner of the hotel suite with a laptop and a printer.

The Cubs might compete with Boston on free agents, but the Red Sox could usually outfox them in the draft.

For instance, in 2005, the year before Tim Wilken took over, the Cubs took left-handed high school pitcher Mark Pawelek at No. 20 in the draft. Three picks later, the Red Sox drafted a college outfielder named Jacoby Ellsbury. Pawelek was the kind of pitcher Boston wouldn't dream of taking in the first round and he never made it out of Single-A.

But Epstein liked what he heard from Ricketts, and as only his close friends knew, he had been thinking about the Cubs job for a long time.

"To be honest, I started talking about the Cubs a week after we won in '04," he said.

He saw the impact that winning the World Series had on Boston. He didn't want to leave unless...

"Unless the Cubs job ever opens up," he said in jokes with his friends.

Winning a World Series in Boston and Chicago? It was a dream, not a goal.

On October 8, 2011, a Lincoln Park resident named Noah Pinzur was at a Starbucks on the corner of North Racine Avenue and West Wrightwood Avenue, a short drive south from Wrigley Field, when Epstein walked in with his wife. Pinzur, a Cubs fan, was reading a story on his laptop about Epstein possibly coming to the Cubs at the time. What are the odds? He googled around for a picture of Epstein's wife, Marie, and realized it was them. So he approached them and Epstein was so rattled he both denied he was himself and then asked who Theo Epstein was. Pinzur then emailed this anecdote to the *Tribune*'s Paul Sullivan, who published a very funny story about the tale.

Bloggers, Cubs Twitter, and talk radio hosts pilloried Sullivan for the story (Bleed Cubbie Blue's Al Yellon wrote, "Looks like Sullivan's editor told him to write 500 words about the Cubs for Sunday's paper.") But as it turned out, Pinzur was right.

At his introductory press conference at the end of October, Epstein admitted he was bad at staying inconspicuous.

"It was funny," he said. "When I'm somewhere when I don't want to be recognized and someone recognizes me, I have a couple standard lines I go to. I usually always say, 'Oh, no, that's not me, but I guess I kind of look like him. I get that a lot.' Or I say, 'Theo Epstein? Who's that?' And I was so excited to be in Chicago and so surprised to be recognized that I dropped both lines on this guy without stopping to think they really don't work very well in concert with each other. My mistake."

Years later, Epstein told me he could still walk down the streets of his neighborhood without being recognized, as long as he kept his hat low. Before the 2015 playoff run, he said he was walking behind a group of twenty-something men on Southport Avenue who were so excited about the Cubs that just overhearing their conversation pumped him up. Little did they know that dude in the Pearl Jam hat was Epstein.

It took the Cubs and Red Sox some time to work out a deal to let Epstein out of his contract to come to the Cubs. For a week he reported to a makeshift office at Fenway Park and compared himself to Milton in the movie *Office Space*.

"I keep showing up to work and it was as if somebody forgot to tell me I didn't work there," he said. "I did end up in the basement with a cubicle and a stapler."

Epstein's introductory press conference was held at the main dining club at Wrigley Field. Needless to say, the room was filled and the anticipation was intense.

Epstein read some prepared remarks, including a pseudo-ad campaign he wrote himself.

"To me, baseball is better with tradition," he said. "Baseball is better with history, baseball is better with fans who care, baseball is better in ballparks like this, baseball is better during the day. And baseball is best of all when you win."

Needless to say, I made fun of that for years, so much so that in a conversation we had before the 2016 season, he brought it up.

"I know you mock me for the 'baseball is better' bullshit, but I love Wrigley when it's packed and the fans are really getting into the game, enjoying the players," he said. "I think the genuine affection from our fans for these players is awesome. If you couldn't enjoy following the team every day last year from my role, it's time to change industries. It was so much fun and I expect it to last."

Epstein fought back on the earned cynicism some of us had that 2011 afternoon and at the same time didn't give in to the ass-kissing questions either.

This was a time for hope and honesty.

"I don't believe in curses, [and] I guess I played a small part in proving they don't exist, from a baseball standpoint," Epstein said. "I do think we can be honest and upfront that certain organizations haven't gotten the job done. That's the approach we took in Boston. We identified certain things that we hadn't been doing well, that might have gotten in the way of a World Series, and eradicated them. That's what we'll do here."

Just three years earlier, Ryan Dempster and the Cubs let the pressure to win it all get to them. Five years before that, Mark Prior, Alex

Gonzalez, Dusty Baker, and all the rest were swallowed by history. Epstein was offering a clean slate.

"When I got to Boston they hadn't won in 86 years. We didn't run from that challenge. We embraced it," Epstein said. "We decided the way to attack it was to build the best baseball operation that we could, to try to establish a winning culture, to work as hard as possible and to bring in players who care more about each other and more about winning than the people around them thought or the external expectations, the external mindset. That's something that is going to be important to us here as well.

"We're going to build the best baseball operation we can. We're going to change the culture. Our players are going to change the culture along with us in the major league clubhouse. We're going to make building a foundation for sustained success a priority. That will lead to playing October baseball more often than not. Once you get in in October there's a legitimate chance to win the World Series."

At the press conference, Epstein also said a line that is still linked to him to this day. From the very beginning, because he had the jewelry, as Hendry said, most Cubs fans didn't just listen to Epstein, they believed him. The ones who didn't were the ones hardened by years of experience being Cubs fans.

"Every opportunity to win is sacred," Epstein said. "It's sacred to us inside the organization and it should be sacred to the fans as well."

It would take three years for the Cubs to feel they had an opportunity to win, but when they did, they took it.

"Hey, go back and watch that press conference," Epstein said to me in 2016. "A lot of it has come true."

While Epstein imbued Chicago with a sense of optimism that 2011 day, he also gave a warning. He was signed to a five-year deal to start his career. Which, as he saw it, was halfway to his expiration date.

"After 10 years, no matter how passionate you are, you see the same issues day after day, you're around the same people day after day, you have the same landscape day after day," Epstein said. "Eventually, you'll benefit from a new landscape, fresh problems, and the goal for the individual is to have some reinvigoration, some rebirth."

On November 1, the Cubs introduced Epstein's top two lieutenants, Jed Hoyer and Jason McLeod, who left their jobs running the baseball operations department of the low-budget San Diego Padres to come to Chicago for Epstein's grand plan. Hoyer would serve as GM, while McLeod would be his farm system and player development guru.

McLeod and Epstein started together as low-level employees in San Diego in the 1990s. Epstein was in media relations, while McLeod worked in stadium operations. Both wanted to work on the baseball side and got GM Kevin Towers and his staff gave them scouting assignments and other responsibilities on top of their regularly scheduled work. Soon, they were on their way. Larry Lucchino brought Epstein to Boston and soon enough, McLeod followed. Jed Hoyer, who knew Epstein's twin brother, Paul, at Wesleyan University, was a Division III college baseball player looking to break into professional baseball. He got an internship with the Red Sox at 28 and was a major league GM at 35 when he got hired by the Padres, bringing McLeod over with him.

Epstein and his top guys describe their decision-making process as collaborative. While Epstein is unquestionably the boss, he invites dissenting opinions. If you can't spar with him, you can't work for him.

"We talk through every issue, every transaction, every idea, every process," Epstein told me. "Some insights you get to the right answer through a lot of debate. There's so much of the game you just don't know. We truly understand three, four, five percent. You don't really know why certain things happen.

"We spend our days talking through 50 different ideas and 49 of them don't go anywhere. The 50th might be a small insight into an issue, maybe it's the way you look at players, evaluating players, game strategy. It might give us a little insight to chip away at the unknowns by .0001 percent. Literally we might have 50 ideas and 49 you rule out and the 50th idea finds something reliable or scalable."

In Boston, Epstein took control of a successful team. He and his team had time to build their own proprietary database (named Carmine) to evaluate players, from high school and college prospects to major leaguers, and eliminate some of the guesswork involved with the job. In Chicago, they didn't have that kind of time and they certainly didn't have a lot to work with in terms of hard data. So to build their version of Carmine (named Ivy), they teamed up with Bloomberg Sports.

In their early days, the Boston front office was unusually young and collegial, in the definition of the word where the guys acted like they were still in college. (A well-respected private college, but college nonetheless.) They spent long hours at the office, building the database and batting around ideas. They'd work, work out, work some more. Most of the front office were bachelors at the time. Hijinks were involved. Pranks were numerous. That kind of behavior didn't end as the executives aged and the Red Sox started winning.

When Hoyer, who rose quickly up the ranks of the front office under Epstein, was interviewing for GM jobs, even he wasn't immune to pranks from his boss, who was, by then, one of the most famous people in baseball, but perhaps second only to Billy Beane in sports executives revered by business leaders and baseball fans alike. The difference between the two is Epstein was much too competitive to let his secrets out in a book by Michael Lewis.

On the radio one day in 2016, Hoyer recounted how he screwed up his GM interview with the Pirates at a Pittsburgh hotel by accidentally walking into an earlier interview as it was going on. What he didn't say was that during a front office outing weeks before that happened, Epstein and friends found Hoyer's phone on a party bus and texted the president of the Pirates about his very earnest interest in the job. When Hoyer got his phone back, according to one telling of the story, he threw it against a wall. Needless to say, you had to have tough skin to work with Epstein, not to mention the rest of the group.

Years later, when the Cubs were winning big, it was young executive Scott Harris who got it bad from Hoyer. They were talking in Harris' office one day when Harris' cell phone vibrated on his desk. Both looked down out of reflex and saw a name pop up. It was Harris' mother. The problem was her name was listed in his phone as "Mommy."

Hoyer and the gang got his mother to write him a long, gushy note, signed Mommy, which was read in front of a large group of Cubs employees. Harris, of course, hated that story, which was the lead anecdote in a Sahadev Sharma feature in 2018, but he understood the importance of a freewheeling front office culture, given how hard they work most times.

In an *ESPN the Magazine* feature on Epstein in 2016, the writer Wright Thompson recounted the time the Cubs execs made Harris eat prodigious amounts of bread and cake when the team needed rallies. It made it look like hazing, but Harris told me that everyone took turns doing it during the 2016 season, Thompson just caught him on his turn.

"It's important to understand how stressful these jobs are and how closely you have to work with people in a front office to be successful," Harris told Sharma. "You're talking about 15-, 16-, 17-hour days, especially during the season. If you don't like each other, it's quickly going to become dysfunctional. I think it's important for us to keep each other grounded. When people get called 'The Greatest Leader of All Time,' it's important to cut them down to size."

It was Epstein who was named "the world's greatest leader" in a much-derided *Fortune* magazine article in 2017. While Thompson's *ESPN* story captured Epstein at his most raw state—he later joked to me that after reading it, he was going into therapy—it didn't quite communicate that he is the butt of jokes as well.

The front office became the focus of fan fascination in the early years because the on-field product was so lacking. Hoyer delighted in seeing "Theocracy" T-shirts when he first got to Wrigleyville. Epstein had star power, and given Boston's success, compared to the Cubs' failures, he had a long leash to start the rebuild.

What did the holdovers think of these guys?

"Well, at that particular time, being a get-off-my-lawn kinda guy, I thought, 'Who are these smart ass, Ivy League guys that think they know baseball?'" former Cubs broadcaster Bob Brenly told me in 2018. "And over time, and then talking to Theo back then, and talking to some of our people now, it becomes a little clearer what they're trying to do. And the value of advanced metrics and all those things.

"But at the time, I think I was typical old-school baseball: 'These snot-nosed kids, they think they know everything.' You know, they'd never stood in a batter's box and faced Chris Sale or Randy Johnson. 'How can they tell us what to do?' Like I said, over time, and with more and more knowledge of myself [and] of what they're trying to accomplish, I think it's definitely—it's not even the future anymore. I was gonna say the wave of the future. It's not. It's the present."

Brenly's partner in the booth, Len Kasper, was immediately receptive to the new regime. Kasper, who now calls games with Jim Deshaies, is a numbers guy as well as an old-school broadcaster. Brenly, the former manager of the Diamondbacks, had to get used to the new ways. Both of them had to get used to losing in the short run to win in the long one.

"The only, I guess, saving grace for us as broadcasters is we knew the direction they were heading," Brenly said. "We knew that they had a pretty good idea what they were doing. They had success in Boston, turned that franchise around, obviously. Got them the ring they were looking for and the World Series trophies.

"The little bit I know of Theo, he's one of those ball players where you tell him, 'There's no way you can hit .300 in the big leagues.' Well, he's one of the guys that will find a way to hit .300 in the big leagues. Theo comes here to Chicago with a long history of losing, and no real championship since '08. And I think not only did he see that as a challenge, but I think he said, 'I'm the right guy for this job. I've done it once before with an iconic franchise, and I can do it again.' Whether that's arrogance or just confidence in your own abilities to turn a bad situation around, it's worked tremendously."

But while Brenly was an old-school type, he said he pushed for a full-scale rebuild back when he did Cubs radio in 1990–91.

"Well, I remember when I was here doing radio initially with Thommy [Brennaman] and Ron and Harry… and you know Ron, and nobody loved the Cubs more than Ron Santo, and he used to just pull his hair out, or pull his wig out, 'What can they do, what can they do?'" Brenly said. "You know, we kept signing guys and making trades. And I said, 'They need to blow it up, Ron. They need to really blow this shit up and start over again. Rebuild the minor league system. Get some players coming through your own system instead of spending all this money to bring in guys that you don't know are gonna fit or not.'

"'Well,' he said, 'they'll never do that here. They'll never do that here. They can't. These people that come out here and pay money every day to watch the Cubs are not gonna put up with that.' Well, maybe it's gonna be a long while before you see a winner out there on the field."

At the time he was hired, though, Epstein didn't know the exact direction he would take because the rules were about to change. In late November 2011, Major League Baseball and the players association ratified a new collective bargaining agreement that negated or severely limited some of the ways Epstein built up the Boston farm system— most notably limiting what teams could pay draft picks in overslot bonuses and restricting compensatory draft picks for losing free agents. International signing money was also going to be heavily regulated.

Epstein thought he would have more money to field a competitive roster early, but that panacea was unavailable. He quickly found out going from Boston to Chicago was going to be a bigger challenge than even he anticipated.

Heading into the 2011 season, the Cubs had the 16th-ranked farm system according to Baseball America, one spot above Boston, not that Epstein paid much heed to those rankings.

Epstein's first big move didn't come until the winter meetings, when he traded outfielder Tyler Colvin and infielder DJ LeMahieu to Colorado for 26-year-old veteran infielder Ian Stewart. It was a curious decision based on the Cubs' feelings, not without some basis, that LeMahieu wouldn't hit with power. He wound up winning a batting crown with Colorado and has made two All-Star teams, while Stewart slashed .201/.292/.335 in 55 games with the Cubs and was released after lobbing late-night Twitter insults at the team from Iowa.

Two of Epstein's next three trades paid dividends years down the road, with one of them landing a franchise cornerstone.

On December 23, he traded veteran swing pitcher Sean Marshall to the Reds for Dave Sappelt, Ronald Torreyes, and lefty starter/reliever Travis Wood.

On January 5, Epstein dealt Zambrano to Miami for Chris Volstad. Zambrano waived his no-trade clause to join Ozzie Guilen in Florida.

A day later, Epstein made his big move, the first of his Cubs tenure, dealing pitcher Andrew Cashner, arguably the Cubs' top pitching prospect not named Jeff Samardzija, to San Diego for Anthony Rizzo.

This trade was a clear indicator of how Epstein and his staff would approach their rebuild: focus on hitting, not pitching. Pitching prospects are enticing, but come with a greater degree of risk. Teams and pitchers can do everything right in terms of training and workload, but the human arm, from shoulder to elbow, isn't meant to throw 98 mph fastballs and wipeout sliders. And sometimes it takes pitchers years to find their control.

But you could find young hitters who could progress quickly through the system and impact the club on a daily basis.

Castro, essentially the only young talent on the major league level that Epstein inherited, was a major talent, but also a question mark. He was accused of sexual assault in January 2012, but no charges were ever filed and the case was dropped in April. He eventually signed a seven-year, $60 million extension that August.

Adding Rizzo was the first step to creating a sustainable lineup. The Red Sox loved Rizzo from the beginning, paying him $325,000 to skip college in Florida and sign as a sixth-round pick in 2007, the draft class that also produced future Cubs Jason Heyward, Jake Arrieta,

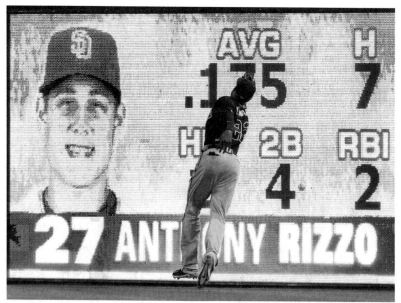

One of the new front office's first moves was trading for Anthony Rizzo from San Diego in January 2012. In this photo from June 2011, Rizzo, who was hitting .175 at the time, laces a double over the outstretched glove of Braves right fielder Jason Heyward.
(AP Photo/Lenny Ignelzi)

Steve Cishek, Darwin Barney, and Daniel Descalso, not to mention Josh Donaldson, who was traded by the Cubs in the Rich Harden deal. Rizzo was thick (or thicc, as the kids say) as a teenager, weighing 215 pounds out of high school. The Sox thought he could be a left-handed power hitter with patience, the prototype of a major leaguer.

Rizzo immediately went to the minors and started hitting. But early in his first full season in 2008, he started gaining weight, fast. Fifteen pounds on one road trip. He started swelling up, Rizzo remembered. His teammates were concerned and so were his parents. He went to a doctor in South Carolina and then flew out to Boston for a checkup. He was diagnosed with Hodgkin's lymphoma. It was a shock. Rizzo was a teenager, a kid. Epstein and the Red Sox acted like family members, not bosses.

"It really is a family when you're in an organization," Epstein said in an MLB Network special. "Our hearts were going out to him. We were panicking a little bit. And then when Anthony showed up, he was almost like the calming influence."

Young Boston pitcher Jon Lester, Rizzo's future teammate with the Cubs, not the Red Sox, had overcome lymphoma. He reassured Rizzo about treatment and how he could beat it. (Lester pitched a no-hitter days later.)

Rizzo began chemotherapy and by the fall his cancer was in remission. He went back to work in 2009 and didn't skip a beat. At 20 years old, he was the top power-hitting prospect in the Red Sox system. But the Red Sox weren't in the position to start a rookie first baseman for a team expected to win the World Series. With his bosses breathing down his neck and consultants telling him about low TV ratings, Epstein made some rash decisions to improve the major league club. One of them was trading Rizzo to Hoyer and McLeod in San Diego for Adrian Gonzalez.

"I had angst about [trading Rizzo] as we were doing it. I told Rizz we were going to trade back for him at some point—and we did," Epstein told the *Boston Globe* years later. "I just happened to be in a different organization."

Rizzo started in Triple-A with the San Diego organization and got hot enough that Hoyer promoted him a little too quickly to help a struggling Padres team. Rizzo fell flat on his face, slashing .141/.281/.242 in 49 games. He came up on June 9 and went back down by the third week of July. He returned in September and hit even worse than when he left.

In December 2011, after Hoyer had left San Diego, his replacement, Josh Byrnes, traded pitcher Mat Latos for a package of four players, including first baseman Yonder Alonso.

That meant Rizzo was expendable and for the Cubs, a safer bet to succeed in the long run than Cashner. Rizzo would start the season in the minors, but he wouldn't stay there for long.

Dealing with a losing team was new to Epstein. While he was clear on the messaging, he couldn't just say straight out he was planning on losing 100 games that season. At the Cubs Convention that winter, I asked him a question about competing in 2012.

"If we stay healthy, and one or two or three or four of the players we have actually take a big developmental step forward, I think you might look up and be surprised in the middle of the summer," he said.

Epstein would have been very surprised.

At Opening Day, Ricketts told me the Cubs would be "compelling" and could very well win some games. Ricketts curtailed his media appearances that year as the Cubs started an uncertain journey into purposeful losing—or, to be kinder, organization building.

In truth, Epstein took the job looking to compete initially. With no money or inclination to enter the high-end domestic free agent market, they were instead in on Yu Darvish, the Japanese pitcher, and Yoenis Cespedes, the Cuban outfielder. The initial plan was to speed up the rebuild with international players. The reason they didn't bid higher on Cespedes was they thought he'd need some seasoning at Triple-A, which would make a short contract less impactful because he'd be a free agent around the time they thought they could contend.

Cespedes wound up signing with Oakland for four years and $36 million, slashing .292/.356/.505 with 23 homers and 16 stolen bases. In his first five seasons, playing for four teams, he hit 137 home runs. A Cubs executive shared why they didn't sign him to me in 2014, the first year Cespedes made an All-Star team, but noted if they had scouted him correctly, maybe they don't lose as many games in 2012 and they don't get Kris Bryant in the 2013 draft.

The Cubs quickly fired Mike Quade and set about hiring a teacher who could help formulate the Cubs Way and handle an unenviable situation in the present.

The Cubs decided to make this search very public, a nice way to engage the local media. The final four managers in their search did game simulations with the front office and then real interviews with the Cubs beat.

Pete Mackanin, Mike Maddux, Sandy Alomar Jr., and Dale Sveum were the final four. In Maddux's interview, he was asked how he would deal with Carlos Zambrano, who was suspended by Hendry after an outburst in Atlanta the previous summer.

"I heard he's a big teddy bear," Maddux said with a grin. "I might pick him up and just burp him."

Maddux seemed like a good fit for the job, and he certainly had the sense of humor one needed at that juncture to manage the Cubs, but he also didn't want to uproot his family from Texas, where he served as Ron Washington's pitching coach.

Sveum, the hitting coach in Milwaukee, was a different story. He had a Red Sox connection that was important, serving as a coach under Terry Francona in 2004 and '05, which earned him a World Series ring. He was comfortable using analytics as a tool to help manage and he was known for his strong teaching work as a hitting coach.

Sveum, who was 48 when he got the job, didn't come with many airs about him. On the drive down I-94 from Milwaukee to Chicago to get introduced for his dream job, he made Epstein and Hoyer stop so he could finish an errand and so he looked presentable at the press conference.

"He had to get measurements for a tux for the wedding he's in," Epstein said at his introductory presser. "He's the best man for his [Brewers] clubbie's wedding. Then we had to stop at a Men's Wearhouse to get that sports coat.

"He came out to talk to the Cubs and Red Sox about their manager's job and didn't bring a sports coat. It's funny, we went into this Men's Wearhouse in Racine and we walked in and the kid behind the desk goes, 'Please don't leave us, Dale.'"

Epstein was convinced Sveum could teach and relate to a team that was going to be in flux for the next few years as they cycled in filler players while trying to train young ones in "the Cubs Way."

"He's a walking baseball conversation," Epstein said in 2011. "You just have to be prepared and be willing to engage with him. Players are. Players are just looking for someone to talk with them, man to man, about baseball, and have well-thought-out reasons for what you want them to do."

Sveum, along with Epstien's input, assembled the makings of a good staff, most notably his old friend from Milwaukee, pitching coach Chris Bosio, who inherited a staff mixed with veterans on their way out (Ryan Dempster), veterans the Cubs wanted out (Matt Garza), ascending talent (Jeff Samardzija), fillers (Paul Maholm and Chris Volstad), and a lot of green youth. The bullpen still had Carlos Mármol, signed to a three-year, $20 million deal before the 2011 season, and James Russell, who would stick with the team through their return to the playoffs in 2015.

Twenty-nine pitchers appeared in a game for the Cubs that season, not including position player Joe Mather. Some of those names were familiar (Kerry Wood, Randy Wells), others have faded into oblivion (Jeff Beliveau, Alberto Cabrera, Jaye Chapman, Jairo Asencio).

Seven pitchers started at least 12 games, with another four starting four or more games.

The plan going into spring training was to set up the standards for the team. Sveum implanted a much-covered, much-derided "bunt tournament." It was an inclusive, team-oriented event meant to build camaraderie and sharpen focus. Sveum, a fantasy football junkie, made it a $50 entry with the winner taking home $2,000. Veteran outfielder David DeJesus won both years, though the team's video coordinator, Nate Halm, made the semifinals in 2013. (Halm wound up coming up big in the team's wild Game 5 win in the 2017 NLDS win against the Washington Nationals.)

With the Cubs designed to lose, Sveum had an unenviable job. His job was manage them to win.

"We're not here to rebuild," he said at the start of the camp, according to a *Chicago Tribune* story. "We're here to try to win the World Series this year."

The Cubs were awful, as expected, early on, and were seven games out of their division by April 20. They started May by going a respectable 7–5, but that's when the wheels fell off.

On May 8, Wood pitched his sixth game of the season, giving up three runs in one inning and taking his second loss of the season in a 3–1 defeat to Atlanta. Wood threw his hat and glove into the stands and after the game, in the cramped home clubhouse, he took umbrage at longtime beat writer Paul Sullivan's questioning.

"Irrelevant, dude," Wood snapped. (That quickly became a press box mantra.)

Wood pitched four more times in the next 10 days and then hung up his spikes for good after getting one last out on May 18 during a White Sox–Cubs game at Wrigley Field. His oldest son ran onto the field to hug him as he bathed in the applause.

Wood's addition to the team was an ownership request. After serving as the closer to the 2008 team, he went on to Cleveland where he saved 20 games in 2009. The next season he was traded to New York. He returned to the Cubs in 2011, where he threw 51 innings of relief.

He was still unsigned going into the 2012 Cubs Convention, where the Cubs staged a made-for-rubes announcement, announcing his signing during the opening ceremonies. Aside from Wood, the biggest star that evening was Theo Epstein.

"If [the GM] ever becomes the show, you probably don't have a very good product to begin with," Epstein said that night.

Those were prescient words. And given that the 2011 recap video that played that night included Tony Campana and Brad Snyder highlights, they were apt.

Wood's retirement game came in the middle of a 12-game losing streak from May 15 through May 27.

"Sometimes, when you rip the scab off, there's some pain until we grow some new skin," Epstein told reporters at the time. "We're going places. This is a tough road."

Before a May 28 home game, both Epstein and Hoyer called the losing streak "torture," even though it was precisely what they signed up for. That day, the Cubs beat the Padres 11–7 to start a three-game sweep to end the month with an 18–32 record and a 10-game deficit.

That success wouldn't last, but that was also the time of Epstein's first draft as Cubs president. While Jim Hendry was loath to take credit for any good draft decisions—as a former minor league guru, he left that to his minor league guys, like Tim Wilken—Epstein worked with Jason McLeod on scouting top prospects.

That June 4, the Cubs picked Albert Almora Jr., a high school outfielder from south Florida, with the sixth pick of the draft.

With the Cubs' compensatory picks in the first round, Nos. 43 and 56, they picked pitchers Pierce Johnson and Paul Blackburn. The next day, they drafted pitcher Duane Underwood Jr. and the day after that, infielder David Bote in the 18th round.

(Addison Russell, the Cubs' future shortstop, went 11th in the draft to Oakland. Carlos Correa was the top pick that year for Houston.)

Johnson, Blackburn, and Underwood were part of the plan to restock the pitching in the farm system, but their individual failures epitomized the Cubs' organizational failures at developing pitching, something that would cost the Cubs prospects in the coming years as they built a perennial playoff contender. "This is the year of Cubs pitching," became an annual exercise in self-promotion by the Cubs, and, eventually, a joke among the writers.

While Epstein raved about the teenage Almora's character and skill set, he didn't rocket through the system. It took him 3½ years to make his debut in 2016.

Almora would come up big in the 2016 World Series when he pinch-ran for Kyle Schwarber in the 10th inning. Almora tagged up on a fly ball and raced to second. He then scored the go-ahead run on Ben Zobrist's historic double.

Almora saw himself coming through in that moment. At his pre-draft meeting with the Cubs, he oozed confidence, particularly for a 17-year-old kid. He said he got interested in baseball history after seeing *61**, the HBO movie on the Roger Maris–Mickey Mantle home run race. He was nine when the Marlins beat the Cubs in 2003, and all he cared about was seeing a parade in his hometown. But he knew about the Cubs' history by the time he was a hot prospect.

So he told Epstein he wanted to be the guy that helps the Cubs win the World Series. That impressed them.

"Absolutely I knew what that would be in regards to the fan base," he said. "Because growing up you knew about the Cubs, the lovable losers, that they had great talent, but the curse. Whatever the case may be, I knew. I knew. I was a baseball rat. I knew everything about baseball in regards to the history and stuff. I loved to learn about it. I knew what was at stake, the fanbase, all that good stuff. That's why I said that. I want to be on that team to break that curse."

Almora was already on the Cubs' radar before Epstein took over. Tim Wilken, who ran the scouting department under Jim Hendry, lives in Florida and was all over him.

"I saw him probably play 10 games before the new crew even came in," Wilken said. "I was extremely strong on him and eventually Theo and the guys came around on him later that spring. If that would've been me making that pick, totally just me, I would've been on him or Carlos Correa, if he had dropped there."

Epstein loved Almora's national team experience on the 18-and-under U.S. team that won the IBAF world championships in 2011. Almora was USA Baseball's player of the year. While the Cubs can have all of the proprietary data in the world, Epstein considers it his job, and his staff's job, to discern the personalities of their prospects. Will these guys be leaders? Can they hack it in a game predicated on failure? All of the Cubs' first-round picks had something in common: confidence.

"I was confident, not a doubt in my mind," Almora said of their initial meeting. "I knew the type of player that I was, that I am, and I've always been a confident person in that regard."

Deeper in the draft, the Cubs took junior college infielder David Bote with the 554th pick in the 18th round. Bote would be an anonymous minor league hand for four more seasons, before becoming a surprise contributor to the 2018 team. Of all the picks in that first draft, those two were the only ones who panned out. The sixth pick and the 554th pick. That, as they say, is baseball.

July was an eventful month, as it usually is for any baseball team trying to win or trying to lose.

At the July 31 deadline, the Cubs traded Ryan Dempster to Texas. This is how ESPN's Rangers writer Richard Durrett led his trade story: "The Texas Rangers acquired veteran starter Ryan Dempster from the Chicago Cubs for two minor leaguers—a position player and a pitcher—just minutes before the trade deadline expired on Tuesday."

Five paragraphs down, he revealed who was leaving the Rangers organization: infielder Christian Villanueva and pitcher Kyle Hendricks.

The Dempster trade was complicated by his 10-and-five rights (10 years in the majors and five consecutive with one team), which allowed him to reject any trade. It was a hard-fought concession won by the players association in its salad days.

"Yeah, it's nice being the hammer and not the nail," Dempster told reporters. He was joking, but there was, as the saying goes, more than a hint of truth there.

He wanted to be traded to the Dodgers, where Ted Lilly was pitching, but the Cubs couldn't work out a deal.

The trade to playoff-bound Texas happened at the last minute, but Dempster was ready. He was hanging out in the office to give his thumbs up or thumbs down to any deal.

"[Epstein] would come in and be like, 'What about St. Louis?'" Dempster said years later. "I'd be like, 'I can't do that.' Can't accept a trade to the Cardinals, midseason, from the Cubs, especially how much I love being a Cub. So he's like, 'Okay.' Finally, it was like literally 12 minutes to go, he's like, 'We really like the package from Texas, can you do that?' I was like, 'I can do that. They're a good team, first place. I'll do that.'"

And that's how the Cubs wound up with Kyle Hendricks.

Dempster wound up making 12 starts for the Rangers, though none in the postseason as the Rangers lost in the Wild Card Game to Baltimore.

He won a World Series the next season, however, pitching for Epstein's old team, the Red Sox, working in relief in the postseason. He retired at 36 and rejoined the Cubs' front office soon after.

Meanwhile, in 2012, Hendricks was a promising 22-year-old Class-A pitcher without the explosive stuff necessary to pop up on prospect lists.

On John Sickels' Minor League Ball top 25 prospect rankings for the Rangers in January 2012, Hendricks was listed in the "others" group. Of that list, the third, fourth, seventh, 10th, and 12th best prospects for the Rangers all wound up playing in the Cubs' organization, but only Hendricks became a mainstay.

Hendricks' growth and success is what's dubbed as an organizational success story, player development alchemy at its finest.

In 2013, while the big league Cubs were starving for starting pitching, Hendricks started 27 games between Double-A and Triple-A and finished with a 2.00 ERA in 166⅓ innings. Twenty-one of those starts were in Double-A Tennessee, where he compiled a 1.85 ERA in 126⅓ innings. He gave up just three homers and walked 26.

Hendricks made his Cubs debut in 2014, with 13 starts. He had a 2.46 ERA and the Cubs went 7–2 in those outings.

Hendricks started 32 games in 2015 and 30 in 2016, where he finished with a sparkling 2.13 ERA. It was in that historic 2016 season where the then-26-year-old made the biggest jump of his career.

In May 2016, Cubs catching coordinator Mike Borzello, a Yoda-like figure among the pitchers and catchers, had been trying to get through to Hendricks that he had become too predictable with his pitch mix. Despite an unassuming demeanor and the Ivy League pedigree, Hendricks was more stubborn than he seemed.

"There were conversations I had with him before many games and how I thought we should go about attacking this particular lineup," Borzello told The Athletic's Sahadev Sharma in 2016. "And he would always 'Yes' me, just say 'Yeah, yeah, okay,' and then not really do any of it. So over about four, five outings consecutively I was starting to get sort of frustrated watching it. I knew that he would have to be too perfect with each pitch to consistently be effective the way he was pitching."

Hendricks was leaning on his two-seam fastball and changeup, but Borzello wanted him to use a four-seam fastball and a curveball more often to keep hitters off balance. Remember, Hendricks' fastball usually doesn't touch 90, so he has to have pinpoint control to throw it for strikes. If he doesn't, his changeup isn't effective. The Cubs showed him data that Hendricks, a Dartmouth graduate with a degree in economics, was able to understand and utilize.

Sharma reported that Borzello and pitching guru Tommy Hottovy, the liaison between the front office, coaches, and the pitchers, showed Hendricks that when he fell behind on right-handed hitters he went to his two-seam fastball 82 percent of the time. This wasn't proprietary information, other teams put this on their scouting report. So he was throwing fastballs in the high 80s to major league hitters who had a bead on them.

It took another start in Milwaukee where the Brewers tagged him for four runs in 5⅓ innings to go full boat in with the coaches. It took a couple starts for Hendricks to really use his four-seamer and curveball, but everything clicked thereafter.

From May 28 through October 2 that season, Hendricks started 22 times (and threw two scoreless innings of relief in a July 7 game) and put up an ERA of 1.75 in 143⅔ innings. He gave up just 28 earned runs, walked 32 and allowed a slugging percentage of .324. Thirteen of the 15 homers he gave up that month were during that span, but only one wasn't a solo shot. (It was a grand slam.)

Most importantly, Hendricks showed up in October. He didn't last long in the divisional round, giving up two runs in 3⅔ innings before getting hit in the forearm by a comebacker from Giants outfielder Angel Pagan. In the old, cursed days, Hendricks getting hit by Pagan, the colorfully named former Cubs prospect, in Game 2 of the NLDS would've been a harbinger of doom. But this time, nothing bad happened. He was fine and he came back to pitch in the NLCS, losing a 1–0 game to the Dodgers in Game 2 and winning the clinching Game 6, pitching 7⅓ scoreless innings in a 5–0 win at Wrigley Field that sent the Cubs to the World Series for the first time since 1945.

He pitched in another 1–0 loss in Game 3 of the World Series, the Cubs' first home game, before starting the critical Game 7 at Cleveland. Hendricks was sharp, unfazed by the moment, giving up one run in 4⅔ innings before Maddon went to his checkmate move, inserting Jon Lester three days after his series-saving start in Game 5.

A year later, Hendricks opened the playoffs for the Cubs, pitching seven scoreless innings in Game 1 of the NLDS in Washington, D.C. Quite a postseason run for a small piece of the Ryan Dempster deal back in 2012.

That trade was the Cubs' only big deal that season. But they also signed Cuban outfielder Jorge Soler to a deal on June 30.

Signing international free agents was a big part of "The Plan," the overarching title we gave to Theo Epstein's bold strategy to win a World Series. The Cubs kicked the tires, in industry parlance, on Darvish and Cespedes in the off-season. Given the new rules about free agent compensation in the just-signed collective bargaining agreement, the shortage of prime-year free agents, and the spending restrictions from ownership, international free agents were good value adds for this regime.

Major League Baseball was instituting spending caps on international free agents that summer, but the Cubs got a deal done with Soler, a power-hitting outfielder, two days before the deadline, signing him to a deal worth $30 million over nine years.

Soler, just 20 at the time, was a physical presence. Manager Dale Sveum compared him to a former teammate, Glenn Braggs, who was 6-foot-3, 210 pounds. Soler was about an inch taller and 20 pounds heavier.

"I think you'll be really impressed when you see him physically: a huge, huge person, a very big man," Hoyer told reporters when the signing was official. "He has huge power and it's hard to find power in today's game and that's a big part of why we're willing to make that kind of commitment is that it is hard to find power. He's just a huge guy with bat speed and has always generated a lot of power."

Soler was billed as part of the core of the Cubs' youth movement, while Báez, a Hendry pick, was more of a wild card. But Soler never developed like Báez did over the ensuing years.

In 2015 and 2016, Soler played 187 total games and hit 22 homers, adding two homers in the Cubs' groundbreaking 2015 NLDS win over the Cardinals and another in their NLCS loss to the Mets. In 2016, he was an afterthought. He had just 13 at-bats in the postseason and collected just two hits, both in the World Series. He started all but one of the seven playoff games he played in 2015 and just four of eight in 2016, finishing none of them.

In three seasons with the Cubs, Soler slugged just .434. That's why it was easy for the Cubs to not only move him, but move him for a one-year closer rental before the 2017 season.

Was he a miss? Not really, the Cubs say. But his performance was on the low end of their expectations.

After 2012, the Cubs signed catcher Dioner Navarro and released Bryan LaHair, the team's All-Star representative who was banished to the outfield when Rizzo came up. Their biggest move was picking reliever Héctor Rondón in the Rule 5 draft at the winter meetings.

Possibly their funniest free agent signing came when they signed pitcher Chang-Yong Lim. During their meeting, Lim, who is from South Korea, told the Cubs, through his interpreter, that he threw a "serpent fastball." Daisuke Matsuzaka, the Red Sox's Japanese pitcher, had his gyroball and apparently Lim had his serpent fastball. Lim pitched five innings in six games for the Cubs in the 2013 season, walking seven and giving up three runs. As a Cubs executive joked years later, that fastball didn't slither too much.

The 2013 draft was what would define the Cubs. It came down to one pick, the second overall selection of the draft. Houston had the first choice and had its mind made up.

Three years later, Bryant was in Houston in September and there was a lot of interest in his story. I waited by his locker to get some quotes for a playoff preview. But the Houston media was there too. By this point, the Astros' eventual No. 1 pick that year, Mark Appel, had already been traded to Philadelphia for bullpen help.

But any reporter that wanted some juicy anecdotes about how the Astros blew a chance to draft Bryant and Carlos Correa in back-to-back years left disappointed. Houston just wasn't into him.

"Thinking back, I don't remember having many conversations, or as many conversations, with the Astros as I had with the Cubs and Rockies," Bryant said. "[Houston] kind of had the luxury, picking first, knowing who you're going to choose for awhile and I think that's how it went. Looking back on it, I wouldn't change a thing."

Appel was drafted eighth overall by the Pirates after his junior year, but chose not to sign. He returned to Stanford for his senior year, a rarity for big-time college baseball players because you lose negotiating leverage for your signing bonus. Appel bet on himself and won, going No. 1 in 2013.

But the Cubs were sitting pretty at No. 2, the payoff for 101 losses in Epstein's first season. (Their last two losses of the season came at the hands of the visiting Astros.)

Alex Lontayo was the scout in San Diego and he lived close enough to the University of San Diego campus that he could scout somewhere else and make it back in time for Bryant's final at-bat, he told The Athletic's Patrick Mooney. Lontayo estimated he filmed 16 of Bryant's 31 homers that season. After awhile, his boss, Jaron Madison, said to stop sending him videos of Bryant hitting dingers.

Theo Epstein poses with his 2013 first-round pick, Kris Bryant.
(AP Photo/Charles Rex Arbogast)

"He used to tell me that if I sent him another video of a home run with Kris, he was going to fire me, because I had other players I needed to see," Lontayo told Mooney. "It was just fun to watch."

Epstein and his staff try to put a lot of focus on character—at least in the players they draft—and so scouts are expected to do their detective work. Lontayo hit the phones talking to anyone who knew Bryant: teachers, coaches, gas station attendants, the lady who waited on him at In-N-Out.

"Anybody and everybody that I could get a couple minutes with that had any kind of interaction with him, I reached out," Lontayo said. "It was consistent. There wasn't a single person that I could talk to that had anything negative to say about him. It was one of those situations where it's like almost too good to be true. You almost want to hope that you find something negative on the guy.

"You got to a point where you're like, this is really who he is. I looked at the reports that I had in there: 'He has that demeanor, he has that personality, and the looks to be a face of an organization.' Just never really doubted the decision-making that he would ever put himself into any situation that would harm that."

Cubs GM Jed Hoyer admitted to me that if the Astros had taken Bryant first, the Cubs probably would've taken Appel. Now, maybe Appel prospers in the Cubs' system, though their lack of success with pitching development casts some doubt on that. But more likely the Cubs don't make the playoffs in 2015 and they don't win the World Series in 2016.

For all the planning and foresight and hard work that went into building the Cubs, Epstein and Hoyer will freely admit that you need some luck as well.

"We were very surprised that Houston didn't take Bryant, knowing what a right-handed power bat could do in their ballpark," Bryant's and Appel's agent Scott Boras told Mooney. "Bryant falling to the Cubs… we knew the curse was eroding."

On July 2, the Cubs signed Gleyber Torres as an international free agent and then executed the best trade of the rebuild, sending pitcher Scott Feldman and catcher Steve Clevenger to the Orioles for Jake Arrieta and Pedro Strop.

There are few trades that turned out as lopsided, certainly not in the Cubs' favor.

On July 22, the Cubs finally dealt Matt Garza, again sending a veteran pitcher to the Texas Rangers and again getting back a power-hitting infielder who didn't pan out and another tall, skinny Class-A pitcher who did.

C.J. Edwards (Carl Edwards Jr.), who was generously listed at 170 pounds on his 6-foot-3 frame, had 122 strikeouts (with only 34 walks) in 18 starts for the Rangers' team in the Sally League.

Edwards was the third player listed in the Cubs' email announcing the trade, following infielder Mike Olt and fellow pitcher Justin Grimm. Olt was the Rangers' minor league player of the year in 2012, after hitting 28 homers for Double-A Frisco. Grimm was already on the Rangers' major league club and was one of the best rookie starting pitchers in the A.L.

Olt was the Cubs' Opening Day starter at third base in 2015, before Bryant knocked him off the major league team.

Grimm was a valuable member of the Cubs bullpen for years, famous for his fun-loving, goofy personality.

But Edwards wound up being a linchpin of the bullpen, a closer-in-waiting. On August 1, the Cubs announced the signing of Eloy Jiménez, the top international prospect in baseball. So, in the span of two months, they added Kris Bryant, Jake Arrieta, Pedro Strop, Carl Edwards Jr., Gleyber Torres (who turned into Aroldis Chapman), and Eloy Jiménez (traded for José Quintana). That's quite a haul.

But while the Cubs didn't lose 100 games in the 2013 season, it was inarguably a worse season for the major league club.

The problems began when things started to go bad between the Cubs and their hand-picked manager, Dale Sveum, who generally got good marks from his bosses for the way he handled the first 100-loss Cubs team since 1966.

Sveum was unusually blunt for a modern-day manager, often dispensing his criticisms without a filter. Reporters loved him for this, but running a rebuilding club in a big-city market takes a careful mix of candor and carefulness. It was clear the losing was getting to Sveum. Who could blame him?

He only had two hitters who were part of the future in Starlin Castro, a holdover from the previous regime, and Anthony Rizzo, the golden child of the fledgling Theo era. But after strong seasons in 2012, both scuffled in 2013.

Rizzo signed a long-term extension in May 2013, giving away free agent years for a guaranteed $41 million over seven years. Given the floor of his performance in his 2011 cameo with San Diego and considering Rizzo's health history, no one could really criticize him over the move, though it ended up being a very, very team-friendly deal years later.

"We get some cost certainty in the deal," Cubs general manager Jed Hoyer said at the time. "We got between one and three years of longer control of Anthony, and he gets a lot of security in the deal. It's a great matchup for both sides."

Rizzo was hitting .280/.352/.538, with nine homers and 28 RBIs before his contract press conference on May 13. Over the ensuing 123 games, he slashed .218/.315/.382. His batting average on balls in play was just .243, and while he still hit 30 doubles and 14 homers over that span, he was a major disappointment at the plate.

Before the extension, Sveum, already bummed out by his team in April, hinted that Castro and Rizzo weren't immune to a demotion to Triple-A if they didn't have their act together.

"The bottom line is you've got to perform," Sveum said, according to an April 21, 2013, *Chicago Tribune* story by Paul Sullivan. "Whether they need more development or you decide all those kind of things… there's still that accountability. Many, many people throughout the history of the game [have been demoted]. It's a performance-laden occupation. That's what makes the world go 'round. That's what makes this country what it is."

Needless to say, Sveum wouldn't make that decision on his lonesome. His bosses didn't agree.

After the All-Star Game, Epstein and his staff had a meeting with Sveum.

"A long meeting, a brutally honest meeting," Epstein later told reporters.

The Cubs president, who had a relationship with Sveum going back to their Boston days, felt like he delivered an ultimatum for changes. Sveum felt like it was just a discussion. In mid-September, during another meeting, Epstein said he told Sveum he wouldn't sugar coat anything he told reporters. But Sveum was still dumbfounded by his firing.

"Two weeks ago, I never would have imagined this was going to happen," he said.

As the Cubs stumbled to a 66–96 record, frustrations abounded. Castro and Rizzo were foundering and the one big free agent signing, pitcher Edwin Jackson, was a disaster.

Epstein went full tilt into the rebuild strategy, openly talking about the strategy without officially saying they were trying to lose. Like a paycheck-to-paycheck average joe, Epstein had a little money burning a hole in his pocket before the 2013 season and he was aiming to spend it.

That's why he signed Jackson to a $52 million deal. Jackson did his job in taking the ball every five days, but he finished with a 4.98 ERA in 31 starts with a strikeout-to-walk ratio of 2.29. In 2014, he started 27 of his 28 games and had a 6.33 ERA, the worst—by an entire run—of any MLB starter that year who pitched at least his 139⅔ innings. Well-liked as a teammate, Jackson's deal seemed like a misfire and, while the overall cost wasn't extravagant, it brought to mind Epstein's late Red Sox misses in free agency. (Jackson, who pitched for the Cubs into the 2015 season, lost 34 games in 58 starts, 82 overall games.)

Attendance had taken a noticeable hit in the first two years of the rebuild. While Cubs fans trusted Epstein, the market for tickets nose-dived. Wrigley Field was still able to draw tourists, but high prices and a low quality of baseball had driven away actual fans and torpedoed prices on the secondary market.

In 2013, the Cubs had their worst attendance since 1998, drawing just over 2.64 million. The Cubs had drawn more than 3 million fans each season from 2004 through 2011.

Even the beer vendors were suffering. I wrote a story for *ESPN* in mid-summer 2013 about how vendors' sales numbers were down that season. One vendor who sold beer in the 200 level showed me numbers that had him down around 15 percent compared to 2012, with annual declines. The Cubs' concessionaire, Levy Restaurants, did boost commissions around that time (about $19 for a load of beers that sold for $186) and extended last-call pickup times.

"There used to be a floor," Nicolas Zimmerman, a part-time vendor told me at the time. "No matter how bad the Cubs were, you'd sell a certain volume of beer, and that floor just dropped."

Beer sales were the lifeblood of Wrigley, more than the team would have liked to admit in public. In private, however, an MLB marketing executive said that was all the Cubs executives would talk about. According to a list of concession numbers around baseball, the Cubs were tops on the list for beer sales and only Boston was close.

After I wrote the story, quoting several vendors by name, a Levy representative told the group they weren't allowed to talk to reporters anymore.

But it wasn't just the vendors who were suffering. The tertiary economy around Wrigley was foundering. TV and radio ratings were cratering, local businesses were seeing less traffic during games. The rebuild was a bummer, at least at the major league level.

By 2014, the Cubs felt Sveum's dour nature was creating a negative environment, so they fired him two years into a three-year contract.

"There has to be tough love, but there has to be love before there's tough love," Epstein said. "You have to be patient with them. There has to be a clear, unified message. You can't be getting different signals from different directions. And collectively—myself included—we failed to provide that."

While some old-school types welcomed Sveum's approach— no-nonsense mixed with a healthy dose of teaching and hitting wisdom—the Cubs had grown tired of it.

"We're at a critical point in our building process where our very best prospects are going to be young big league players," Epstein said. "And it's absolutely imperative that we create the best environment possible for young players to continue to learn, to continue to develop and to thrive at the big league level. And to win, ultimately. That's not an easy thing to do."

As reporters waited outside Wrigley that day for the "puff of white smoke" to signify a change in managers, what we didn't know was Epstein had already delivered the news the night before at Newport Lounge, a popular dive bar in the Southport neighborhood.

We caught up with Sveum in the players' parking lot, and as he later said, by the time he walked to his Lakeview condo, he already had a job as a coach on his friend Ned Yost's staff in Kansas City. He wound up getting a World Series ring one year before the Cubs.

In Epstein's press conference that day, he was annoyed at the reporters who focused on the bad records and the newly fired manager.

"Around baseball," he said, "the story is the Cubs are coming fast and the Cubs are coming strong."

It would take another year, but Epstein's bravado would soon be realized.

Unlike in 2011, the Cubs' managerial search in the winter of 2013 went a lot quieter. There would be no public interviews and little drama. While the buzz around Sveum built off the arrival of Theo Epstein and the staggered hires of Jed Hoyer and Jason McLeod, this hire felt a little, well, pointless.

Rick Renteria, a name that had been bandied about before the Sveum hire, was an early favorite, despite the loud calls for Joe Girardi (mostly from local broadcaster David Kaplan, who shared an agent and friendship with the Yankees manager). The Cubs quietly hired Renteria without much fuss.

Renteria had a reputation throughout baseball as a good teacher, but given that he worked as a coach in San Diego, he was practically invisible to most fans and writers. Renteria didn't have a big press conference like Sveum did in the Cubs' premium club off Sheffield and Waveland. He didn't even come to Chicago, as he was in California rehabbing from hip surgery.

The conference call introducing him reflected the awkwardness that would ensue in his lone season in charge. Reporters peppered him with questions about his hopeless situation and Renteria seemed almost confused. Wasn't it a good thing to get a major league managing gig? There are only 30 of these jobs.

At one point, he prefaced an answer to a question by saying, "Like I said, I know everybody thinks I'm nuts...."

After 197 losses in two seasons, it didn't look like the Cubs were poised for a big leap in 2014 and we let Renteria know it.

"I mean, if I was to come in here and assume we were going to lose, well, what kind of expectations am I laying for the players here?" Renteria said. "The reality is my expectation is we're going to compete and win."

Renteria was finally introduced to the Chicago media months later. As reporters surrounded him for an interview, I asked Cubs general manager Jed Hoyer, who recommended Renteria from their time together in San Diego, why they hired him. I said it cavalierly, and didn't realize Renteria's wife was sitting right in front of us. Hoyer raved about Renteria's communication and teaching skills. It was obvious that in terms of personality, they wanted the opposite of Sveum. That's usually how coaching hires work.

"You can't find a bad word or even a neutral word on Rick Renteria," Epstein said. "We took our time and wanted to be thorough. We had the benefit of doing so. It was clear to us that Rick was the right man for the job."

The job, as Renteria found out, was a temp one.

Renteria, as reporters found out that spring, was an awful quote, seemingly afraid to offer any kind of opinion that should be construed as critical.

As a strategist, he wasn't exactly the next Tony La Russa. When it came to his press conferences, he was no Ozzie Guillen. But his cheery disposition lightened the mood and, most important, he listened to his bosses.

Rizzo and Castro had bounce-back seasons in 2014, both making the All-Star team.

Báez made his debut on August 5 with the Cubs in the thin air of Colorado and he showed off immediately, hitting a solo blast in the 12th inning to give the Cubs a go-ahead run in a 6–5 win. Two games later, he smacked two homers in the sixth and eighth innings, driving in four runs in a 6–2 win. While excitement was high, Báez struck out three times in his debut and strikeouts became the defining stat of his rookie year.

Báez struck out 95 times in 213 at-bats that year. He had five games where he struck out four times and nine where he struck out three times. Those 14 games constituted almost half of his total strikeouts. He only played in six complete games where he struck out zero times. Interestingly enough, four of those games were in his first week of action.

Báez's all-or-nothing approach was concerning, but his swing and his bat speed were seductive. Two years later, hitting coach John Mallee described Báez as having the perfect swing, from a mechanical standpoint. It was the matter of him keeping his head on the pitch, a problem that bedevils coaches from T-ball to the majors.

Soler made his debut that summer as well. It was the first real glimpse of the waves of prospects that were bubbling in the minor leagues. Soler had a monster 2014 season in the minors, hitting 15 homers to go along with 23 doubles in just 200 at-bats. His minor league slash line was .340/.432/.700. While he had fought minor injuries (muscle pulls and the like), he came into the Cubs lineup and immediately got fans salivating.

Soler hit a two-run homer off Mat Latos in the first at-bat of his Major League debut on August 27 and then two days later, hit two homers in a win over the Cardinals. He only hit two more homers in September, but he added eight doubles and a triple and while he struck out 24 times in 89 at-bats, he had nothing on Báez.

The most important performance of 2014, though, was in Double and Triple-A, where Kris Bryant was raking to the tune of .325/.438/.661 in 138 games. Bryant hit 43 homers between the two leagues and drove in 110 runs. Of his 160 hits in 492 at-bats, 78 were for extra bases. He was, obviously, ready for the majors, but the Cubs wanted him to spend an entire season in the minor leagues, a fair demand, but one tinged with labor realities.

Bryant was named the Player of the Year in the minor leagues, matching his College Player of the Year Award from the previous season.

The advent of Twitter made his minor league exploits part of the nightly conversation in Cubs Twitter, a loosely held group of Cubs fans, bloggers, and journalists who became friends or fought for turf to converse about the team. Bloggers like Brett Taylor at Bleacher Nation, Tom Loxas, and the late John Arguello of Cubs Den (he passed in 2017) became household names among fans as they broke and/or disseminated news. The hierarchy of who Cubs fans trusted was altered around this time, as it was for most pro sports teams once blogging became popular. Now, bloggers like Taylor were just as trusted (if not more) than full-time writers like Paul Sullivan of the *Chicago Tribune*. While Taylor wore his heart on his sleeve—his posts were smart, but typically glass-totally-full optimistic—writers like the acerbic Sullivan were thought to have a negative "agenda" by some fans.

Part-time journalists, fans, and minor-league ballwriters built followings online by posting instant videos of Bryant, Báez, and the rest from their minor-league games. Oftentimes, Bryant's exploits in the minors, disseminated by grainy, distant smartphone videos, were more engaging than those of the big-league club. That would soon change.

CHAPTER 6
THE FUTURE IS NOW

A s the 2014 season ended, the Cubs' future still looked bright and Renteria seemed safe for the winter.

"Overall, for the organization, I think 2015 will be a little bit different than the previous three seasons in that we now think we have the talent to compete," Epstein said in his end-of-year address to reporters on September 30, 2014. "And any time you have enough talent to compete you want to set your sights high."

And then, on Tuesday, October 14, Tampa Bay Rays general manager Andrew Friedman took the Dodgers' general manager's job. That move triggered a clause in Joe Maddon's contract that gave him a window to look for a new managing gig.

Friedman, just 37 when he was hired, was thought to be a contender for the Cubs' job in 2011. I, among many others, referred to him in print as a "Theo Epstein type."

The Cubs, of course, got the actual Theo Epstein, but that left Friedman in Tampa Bay and opened the door for the Cubs to acquire Maddon. Just another domino that fell the Cubs' way.

On Friday, October 31, after a week of rumors—Jed Hoyer even flew out to meet with Renteria the previous week to tell him they were pursuing Maddon—the Cubs didn't mince words in their email release announcing Renteria's firing.

The media relations staff didn't use any of the catchphrases or aphorisms in the headline. They used the word "fired." In most cases, these press releases are written by team media relations officials or outside PR agencies. Sometimes they're dictated. In this case, it was clear Epstein, a gifted stylist in his own right, wrote the entire press release. He owned his decision with a 538-word explanation.

"Today we made the difficult decision to replace Rick Renteria as manager of the Chicago Cubs. On behalf of Tom Ricketts and Jed Hoyer, I thank Rick for his dedication and commitment, and for making the Cubs a better organization.

Rick's sterling reputation should only be enhanced by his season as Cubs manager. We challenged Rick to create an environment in which our young players could develop and thrive at the big league level, and he succeeded. Working with the youngest team in the league and an imperfect roster, Rick had the club playing hard and improving throughout the season. His passion, character, optimism, and work ethic showed up every single day.

Rick deserved to come back for another season as Cubs manager, and we said as much when we announced that he would be returning in 2015. We met with Rick two weeks ago for a long end-of-season evaluation and discussed plans for next season. We praised Rick to the media and to our season ticket holders. These actions were made in good faith.

Last Thursday, we learned that Joe Maddon—who may be as well suited as anyone in the industry to manage the challenges that lie ahead of us—had become a free agent. We confirmed the news with Major League Baseball, and it became public knowledge the next day. We saw it as a unique opportunity and faced a clear dilemma: be loyal to Rick or be loyal to the organization. In this business of trying to win a world championship for the first time in 107 years, the organization has priority over any one individual. We decided to pursue Joe.

While there was no clear playbook for how to handle this type of situation, we knew we had to be transparent with Rick before engaging with Joe. Jed flew to San Diego last Friday and told Rick in person of our intention to talk to Joe about the managerial job. Subsequently, Jed and I provided updates to Rick via telephone and today informed him that we will indeed make a change.

We offered Rick a choice of other positions with the Cubs, but he is of course free to leave the organization and pursue opportunities elsewhere. Armed with the experience of a successful season and all the qualities that made him our choice a year ago, Rick will no doubt make an excellent major league manager when given his next chance.

Rick often said he was the beneficiary of the hard work of others who came before him. Now, in the young players he helped, we reap the benefits of his hard work as we move forward. He deserved better and we wish him nothing but the best.

We have clung to two important ideals during our three years in Chicago. The first is to always be loyal to our mission of building the Cubs into a championship organization that can sustain success. The second is to be transparent with our fans. As painful as the last week was at times, we believe we stayed true to these two ideals in handling a sensitive situation. To our fans: we hope you understand, and we appreciate your continued support of the Cubs."

Whew. That was a lot of words for a temp job firing.

How tenuous was Renteria's gig? In my *ESPN* column back on November 7, 2013, my lede was:

"The Chicago Cubs are expected to name Rick Renteria as the 53rd ex-manager in team history Thursday. Congrats, Rick. We hardly knew ye."

Little did I know how prescient I was.

Epstein wrote a similar press release when he fired Sveum, but that one included clear criticism and, if you read into it enough, some lightly coded messages about Sveum's weaknesses that frustrated the Cubs to death:

"Today, we made the very difficult decision to relieve Dale Sveum of his duties as Cubs manager. Dale has been a committed leader for this team the last two seasons, and I want to thank him for all of his dedication and hard work. I have a lot of admiration for Dale personally, and we all learned a lot from the way he has handled the trying circumstances of the last two years, especially the last two weeks, with strength and dignity.

In his own authentic and understated way, Dale always put the team first and never complained about the hand he was dealt. He and his staff helped us excel in game planning and defensive positioning, contributed to the emergence of several players, and helped put us in position to make some important trades. I have no doubt that—much like Terry Francona, whom we hired in Boston after his stint with a losing Phillies club—Dale will go on to great success with his next team. We had hoped Dale would grow with our organization to see it through the building phase to a period of sustained excellence; instead, I believe Dale, who felt the weight of losing perhaps more than any of us, will grow because of this experience and find excellence elsewhere.

Today's decision to pursue a new manager was not made because of wins and losses. Our record is a function of our long-term building plan and the moves we have made—some good, a few we would like back—to further this strategy. Jed and I take full responsibility for that. Today's decision was absolutely not made to provide a scapegoat for our shortcomings or to distract from our biggest issue—a shortage of talent at the major league level. We have been transparent about what we are, and what we are not yet. Today's decision, which was painful for all of us, was made to move us closer to fulfilling our ultimate long-term vision for the Cubs.

Soon, our organization will transition from a phase in which we have been primarily acquiring young talent to a phase in which we will promote many of our best prospects and actually field a very young, very talented club at the major league level. The losing has been hard on all of us, but we now have one of the top farm systems in baseball, some of the very best prospects in the game, and a clear path forward. In order for us to win with this group—and win consistently—we must have the best possible environment for young players to learn, develop, and thrive at the major league level. We must have clear and cohesive communication with our players about the most important parts of the game. And—even while the

organization takes a patient, long view—we must somehow estab-
lish and maintain a galvanized, winning culture around the major
league club.

I believe a dynamic new voice—and the energy, creativity, and
freshness that comes with this type of change—provides us with the
best opportunity to achieve the major league environment we seek.
We will begin our search immediately—a process which will be com-
pleted before the GM meetings in early November and perhaps much
sooner. There are no absolute criteria, but we will prioritize mana-
gerial or other on-field leadership experience and we will prioritize
expertise developing young talent. We have not yet contacted any
candidates or asked permission to speak with any candidates, but
that process will begin tomorrow morning."

Sorry for reprinting press releases, but Epstein's writing is a fasci-
nating glimpse into his thought process.

In the case of Renteria, Maddon was the obvious choice to manage
an up-and-coming team once his agent let everyone know he was a free
agent.

Locally, no one in Chicago was really willing to defend Renteria's
job, given his stilted relationship with most of the media and his brief
tenure. There was no connection between Chicago and Renteria and
anyone with a brain realized he was a stop-gap solution. Renteria didn't
exactly charm the Cubs beat either. He was nice enough, but standoffish
and was unwilling to throw any red meat to the lions in his twice-daily
press conference.

On a national level, typically forward-thinking, plugged-in *USA
Today* baseball writer Bob Nightengale suggested in an ill-considered
column that Maddon should take a year off so as not to make a baseball
team fire their manager for him. It was an odd tack for a professional like
Nightengale, and one that everyone pretty much ignored or mocked:

"The hottest speculation is that the Chicago Cubs now plan to hire
Maddon, and fire Rick Renteria after just one year on the job.

Yet, does anyone else have an ethical problem for the Cubs to even be considering Maddon? Renteria has been on the job for all of one season.

If the Cubs fired all their managers for not reaching the World Series, they'd have 106 new managers since their last title.

Really, there's only one honorable option for Maddon.

Take a year off. Go work for Fox. Or ESPN. Or the MLB Network. Or CNN. Or Good Morning America.

Just pull in a seven-figure salary for talking a few days a week, sit back, and then become the most prized free-agent manager in baseball history come 2016."

Obviously Maddon wasn't worried about the optics. He wanted the Cubs job. (He tried to get in touch with Renteria after it went down, but it took about a year for Renteria to get back to him.)

The Cubs immediately got in contact with Maddon, and as word spread, they had to quickly close the deal. Hoyer flew to San Diego to talk to Renteria in person. Would other organizations take that trip? Some, but certainly not all.

The Cubs met with Maddon in Navarre Beach, Florida, just outside of Pensacola. Maddon and his wife, Jaye, were driving his 43-foot Winnebago, the Cousin Eddie, and Maddon, his agent, and Epstein set up a meeting at an RV park in Florida.

"It was kind of a nice night," Maddon said at his introductory press conference. "It was in the back of the Winnebago. There's a little beach, the sun was setting, it was kind of cool. Theo needed a jacket. Jaye went back in for more beers."

"We'll always have Pensacola," Epstein said.

The deal wasn't difficult to put together. The Cubs were pushing their schedule by a year or so, but opportunity arose and Epstein was prepared. Like the Arrieta trade and the Bryant pick, things just fell into place.

"The fact that it happened now is shocking," Epstein said at the time. "We've always kind of talked about who are the two or three managers we might see being here long-term one day, who the long-term managers are going to be if it doesn't work out. Obviously, Joe was always in that conversation."

Maddon got a pay bump and went from a small-market team that had to be creative to win to a big market team at an iconic stadium that doubles as a tourist attraction.

"As a baseball lifer, to get that kind of opportunity, working for that kind of owner, that kind of management, that group of players, to get that chance—once I processed all of it, I thought I had to do it," he said.

Maddon was 60 years old, but he gave off the vibe of someone much younger. It was part of a his lifelong quest for learning and enjoying himself.

Maddon managed in the minors and coached in the Angels organization for decades. He learned at the feet of executives like Buzzie Bavasi, as well as a famous owner in Gene Autry. Chicago reporters would soon grow familiar with these names.

He didn't get a chance to manage a major league roster until 2006, when the 51-year-old was hired to replace Lou Piniella. The Devil Rays, a 1998 expansion team, were the worst organization in baseball, cursed by bad ownership at its outset (Vince Naimoli), poor location (St. Petersburg, Florida), a lousy stadium, and bad management .

But a new ownership group, led by Wall Street investor Stuart Sternberg, fully took over after the 2005 season, emphasizing advanced analytics in the wake of Epstein's success in Boston. The Rays started making smarter draft picks, signing guys with upside. And they hired Maddon, who had been Mike Scioscia's bench coach for the Angels, winning the World Series together in 2002.

After two bad years, the Rays (they dropped the Devil) were the surprise team of baseball in 2008, winning the AL East with 97 victories. Maddon was the toast of baseball with his freewheeling ways; magicians and zoo animals and new-age thinking.

His lineup was solid, with young players like Evan Longoria and Carl Crawford, along with five starting pitchers between 24 and 26. Maddon, and the Rays, were the future of the game.

Joe Maddon argues with home plate umpire Kerwin Danley during a June 2015 game.
(AP Photo/Nick Wass)

When Maddon was hired by the Cubs, Chicago sports talk radio, not to mention the burgeoning blogosphere, was well-familiar with analytics amd the new baseball order.

But when Epstein was hired, it was a sea change. At his press conference, one veteran reporter tried to get a question out about the Red Sox's computer system, Carmine, but wound up blurting something like, "What's the deal with the computer?" (Another writer clumsily said, "You're so smart and good-looking, what are you doing in baseball?")

Maddon prided himself on his Hazleton roots and the lessons he learned in his minor league years, but his lifelong curiosity for knowledge made him amenable to the new ways of baseball. Gone were the old-fashioned days of Dusty and Lou.

But, Epstein said to me at the time, you couldn't rank Maddon by managerial WAR, a fairly popular idea in some circles.

"Sometimes, I think in today's day and age, we try to quantify too many things instead of just appreciating the essence of them," Epstein said that day. "What does it mean to have a dynamic manager? I think it means you have the potential to have an edge in everything related to the events on the field. Whether it's preparation, decision-making in the game, knowing you can get the most out of your players, trying to ensure the whole is greater than the sum of the parts. All those things... it's really nice to just have complete trust and faith that the person in charge of running that on-field operation is going to put you in the best possible position. It's hard to quantify. How often does it show up? There are some games it never shows up. In other ways, it shows up every single game. It's really a hard thing to quantify."

Because of construction at Wrigley Field, Maddon's introductory press conference was at the Cubby Bear, a famous bar across the street from the stadium. Maddon, Epstein, and Hoyer sat on a podium and took questions. The floor was sticky. The air smelled like stale beer.

Maddon offered to buy everyone a round.

"That's a beer and a shot," he said. "That's the Hazleton way."

Many Cubs managers had caused fans to drink, but few, if any, offered to buy.

Maddon's hiring had changed the calculus for 2015. It was time to go for it.

"Going for it" started in early December.

On December 9, the Cubs traded minor leaguers Jefferson Mejia and Zack Godley to Arizona for catcher Miguel Montero.

On December 12, they signed pitcher Jason Hammel, whom they'd traded to Oakland with Jeff Samardzija at the previous trade deadline, to a free agent deal. On December 23, they signed free agent catcher David Ross, a veteran in his late thirties.

In between, on December 15, they signed Jon Lester to a six-year, $155 million deal. It was the most important free agent signing in Cubs history and one of the two best in Chicago history.

"It's not often you get to win the lottery," Maddon said at the winter meetings.

In 2014, Maddon only had three players making more than $5 million: closer Heath Bell, who made $10 million; franchise-cornerstone Evan Longoria, who made $7.5 million as part of a massive contract "extension" he signed days after making the majors in 2008; and Ben Zobrist, who made $7 million.

Now Maddon was on a team that was pushing its chips to the middle of the table. Maddon helped make this signing possible. His hiring showed Lester the Cubs were serious.

The Lester press conference would not be held in a bar. Instead, the Cubs booked a room usually used for weddings and parties at swank Michigan Avenue restaurant Spiaggia.

The Cubs wooed Lester with familiar faces and a sales pitch. Come chase "the single greatest pursuit left in sports." How desperate was Epstein to land Lester? Epstein told me not only would he have gone hunting with Lester to seal the deal, but he "was ready to soak myself in deer urine."

Wise baseball analysts say don't sign pitchers in their thirties to nine-figure deals. The Cubs, with a dearth of pitching in their minor league system, needed an ace. They didn't yet know what kind of pitcher Jake Arrieta would be in 2015.

As Epstein explained in one of the most in-depth group conversations you'll get from a team president or GM, the Cubs front office knew Lester so well they felt they could project his future.

After all, they drafted him as a teenager out of suburban Washington. They had all of his medicals. Data plus the gut. That's the true Cubs Way.

"There won't be any surprises," Epstein said. "That's the biggest thing for us, with the comfort level. Sooner or later, someone was going to have to put their trust in us, we were going to have to put our trust in someone. To do it with someone you know well, there won't be any surprises off the field, there won't be any surprises in the clubhouse, there won't be surprises on the field. He is who he says he is."

At the press conference, I asked Lester if he was comfortable knowing that his salary, $155 million, would be attached to his name from now on.

"I played in Boston for eight years," he said. "I think I'm pretty prepared for a lot of things. You just have to accept it. I can't change it now. It's obviously next to my name, it'll always be next to my name, whether it's a good start or bad start. It's how I go about my work. I just have to believe I'm going to be prepared for every start, and that's all I can control."

As it turned out, Lester wasn't quite as prepared as he thought he was.

Lester's signing brought with him Ross, his catcher in Boston, and someone he trusted to be his sherpa. While Lester was successful and taciturn, he was also quirky. He had trouble throwing to first base and he was victimized by the Royals baserunners in the AL Wild Card Game during his brief stay with Oakland in 2014. Kansas City stole seven bags

David Ross and Jon Lester talk strategy during the first inning against the Reds.
(AP Photo/Nam Y. Huh)

in the game, putting Lester's provincial problems on national display.
Still the Cubs had no problems making the investment.

"He's left-handed, and left-handed pitchers tend to perform better
throughout their contracts than right-handed pitchers," Epstein said to
one of my questions that day in Spiaggia. "He's got the right kind of
pitch mix that will allow him to age gracefully. He doesn't get hitters
out just one way, especially now that his curveball is back in the mix,
where he's working both sides of the plate. The cutter is a weapon that

ages very well. If you look at Andy Pettitte, he aged extremely well through his thirties. He's a reasonable [comparison]. The second half of Jon Lester's career you want to look like Andy Pettitte."

The Cubs were riding high, and in January they made a trade to shore up the 2015 team.

On January 19, the Cubs traded pitcher Dan Straily and third baseman Luis Valbuena to Houston for outfielder Dexter Fowler, a leadoff man to set the tone.

The deals for Fowler and Montero, two veterans, were important additions, ones that could've gone overlooked had the Cubs not been covered so intensely by local and other media as they vaulted back into a national story once again.

The story on the Cubs had been their rebuild from within, the aggressive stockpiling of prospects and the sea change inside the organization itself. But it was never going to be a team of all prospects, not if the Cubs wanted to win within a certain timeline.

So adding veterans was a crucial part of the plan. In a month's time, the Cubs added two veteran starters in Lester and Hammel, a center-fielder in Fowler, and two catchers in Montero and Ross.

Hammel would probably be the only one not considered a club-house voice or a potential leader. While Fowler wasn't considered a leader, per se, by the brass, he was perfect in terms of attitude. Not only was he generally a happy, funny presence in the clubhouse, he was always playing in a walk year. People familiar with him told the Cubs he's the perfect guy to put on your roster in that situation, because he's going to be playing for a contract. They would get his undivided attention and the full focus of his abilities.

When they got to camp, the Cubs realized Maddon would be different. There were his slogans and his gimmicks, the stuff that makes for viral Twitter fodder. But his light touch was more about setting an atmosphere where the Cubs could focus on the only important things about spring training: getting better and getting in shape. He let longtime strength coach Tim Buss run the morning stretch activities. Bussy, as he was known, was the living embodiment of the Cubs, the person old players came back specifically to see. It was wise for Maddon to align himself with him.

The new vibe at spring training, along with the infusion of talent, made the Cubs a popular team to follow that spring, but no knew quite what to expect in terms of wins and losses. In Las Vegas, Westgate SuperBook set the Cubs win total at 82.5, or one more than the White Sox.

Unfortunately, perhaps the most important Cub of all-time didn't live to see the team return to relevance. Ernie Banks, Mr. Cub himself, died of a heart attack at 83 at the end of January.

Banks was the smiling face of the "lovable losers" long after his Hall of Fame career ended, his trademark line, "It's a beautiful day. Let's play two!" surpassed the Cubs and became a national baseball saying.

He had a warm personality, though he was a little weird in his later years. He lived most of the year in California, but was still a regular fixture at Wrigley Field during the season.

Banks started his career in 1953 as the first black Cub and played until 1971. He hit 512 home runs and his 277 homers as a shortstop remains a National League record. He made 14 All-Star teams and won back-to-back MVP Awards for losing Cubs teams. He was inducted on the first ballot to the Hall of Fame in 1977.

"You don't become Mr. Cub because you play a lot of baseball games or hit a lot of home runs," Tom Ricketts said shortly after his passing. "You become Mr. Cub because you love the team, you love the fans, and you love the ballpark. We all loved Ernie, so we really appreciate this opportunity for people to come by and pay their final respects to the great baseball player and more importantly, just a great person."

Before he passed, the Cubs had removed his statue in front of Wrigley Field, where it served as a popular picture spot and a meeting place before games, because of ongoing construction. That allowed the team to move the statue to Daley Plaza downtown so fans could pay their respects.

There was a Chicago politics backstory to it. In the summer of 1967, there was some dissension in town about the 50-foot abstract Picasso statute the artist made for the city. Was it Chicago enough?

Back in 1967, an alderman from the 47th Ward sponsored a proposal to replace it with a statue of Ernie Banks. It took until 2008 for the Cubs to create a statue to honor him, but there was a sense of poetry that the statue eventually made its way downtown.

With both Santo and Banks gone, Billy Williams and Fergie Jenkins were still around to carry the torch from that generation to the current one.

The Cubs opened at home on April 5, 2015, and the Joe Maddon/Jon Lester era began with a 3–0 loss to the Cardinals. The stadium was still under construction, the first phase of the renovations that would modernize Wrigley Field and the surrounding area, so there were no fans in the bleachers, making for an odd environment for the players. The bleachers are part of the game-day experience for the players as well as the fans. Opposing players can have good or bad relationships with the often-inebriated fans in left and right field and the fans love the energy they bring to the ballpark.

"We miss them, because we're always looking back at them yelling," veteran shortstop Starlin Castro said that night. "Yelling at each other, yelling at left field, yelling at right field."

Construction in the 100-level concourse caused long lines for the bathroom and creative ways to co-opt them, which became a Twitter sensation. The Cubs postponed their second game because of "weather," though many assume it was to fix the problems that cropped up during the game. When the Cubs played next, there were port-a-potties lining the already cramped hallways of the 100 level.

In the opener, the Cubs managed just five hits off starter Adam Wainwright and none off the Cardinals' bullpen. Those hits came from Dexter Fowler, Starlin Castro, Chris Coghlan, David Ross, and Tommy

La Stella. Jorge Soler batted second that game, Castro and Coghlan were the four-five hitters. Mike Olt started at third base and La Stella at second.

No one would remember that was the group that started the season that brought the Cubs not only back to glory, but to new heights.

At 9:33 PM Central Time on April 16, ESPN's Cubs reporter Jesse Rogers tweeted that the Cubs were calling up Kris Bryant for the next day's game.

Bryant had destroyed the minor leagues in 2014, but the Cubs passed on calling him up for an obvious reason—MLB's collectively bargained service-time restrictions. Their excuse, since they didn't want to open themselves up to a labor grievance, was that they wanted him to spend a whole season in the minors. It was sensible, as far as service-time dodges go. When the minor league season ended in September, the Cubs said they wanted Bryant to rest. He had gone from college, where he was a star student as well as the best hitter in the country, straight to the minor leagues in 2013, with just a month between his last game as a collegian and signing his deal with the Cubs. As for the start of the 2015 season? Well, the Cubs tried to say as little as possible. It was a money thing.

The Cubs were 5–3 when Bryant came up. His start was inauspicious to say the least, an 0-for-4 day with three strikeouts in a 5–4 loss to San Diego. But it brought to mind his first professional game with the low Class-A Boise, Idaho, team two years prior, when Bryant struck out five times.

"I'm in the dugout with my phone," then–minor league hitting coordinator Anthony Iapoce told The Athletic in 2018. "After the third [strikeout], Brandon [Hyde] texts me: 'What's the deal?' I think it was the fourth one, Theo [Epstein] texted me and was like: 'How bad is it?' After the fourth one, me and Bill Buckner were in the dugout. Kris just walks by us and he's like, 'Tough start!'"

Brandon Hyde, then the farm director (and Joe Maddon's bench coach before he was hired to be the new manager of the Orioles), was listening to the game online from his house in suburban Evanston.

"And then Theo sends me a text," Hyde told The Athletic. "And then everybody, I think, was listening to this fifth at-bat like: 'Please put the ball in play.'"

Bryant struck out again. Five strikeouts in the opener. Strikeouts would continue to be Bryant's only bugaboo through 2015, when he led the National League with 199 of them, 25 more than Sammy Sosa's Cubs record. Sosa had four of the team's top five strikeout seasons, all from 1997 to 2000, though he also hit 215 homers during that span.

Bryant wound up playing just 18 games for manager Gary Van Tol's team in Boise in 2013. He picked up 23 hits (eight doubles, four homers, and a triple) in 65 at-bats and drove in 16 runs. After his debut, he only struck out 12 more times in the following 17 games. (Three players hit eight homers for that Boise Hawks teams, and two hit six, including a utility player named David Bote, who hit a double in Bryant's debut.)

Bryant played 16 games in the Florida State League that year and collected another 19 hits, including five homers, five doubles, and a triple.

Obviously, Class-A pitching wasn't doing much for Bryant's development.

He started 2014 at Double-A Tennessee, and wound up staying there for 68 games. He had 88 hits in that time, with 22 homers and 20 doubles.

He played 70 games with the Iowa Cubs, hitting 21 homers in 244 at-bats. While he struck out 162 times in 138 games that season, he also hit 43 homers, drove in 110 runs, and put up a .325/.438/.661 slash line.

If the Cubs were competitive in 2014, he would've been up by June. But they weren't, so he spent his summer abusing minor league pitching.

If you remember Bryant becoming an immediate hit in Chicago, you're half-right. After his first game, he had five multi-hit games in his next nine.

But he didn't homer until his 21st game of his career. The Cubs went 10–10 in the first 20 games. Over the next 17 games, the Cubs' fortunes changed only slightly, going 10–7, but Bryant got hot and hit seven homers.

On August 1, Bryant went 0-for-2 in a 4–2 win over the Brewers, giving him a slash line of .244/.352/.436. He had 14 homers and 60 RBIs. Decent numbers, but nothing dramatic.

But Bryant had at least one hit in the next 12 games, just as the Cubs finally started heating up, going 11–1.

It was in this stretch where the Cubs separated themselves from the pack. On August 5, they lost to Wild Card leader and divisional rival Pittsburgh and trailed San Francisco for the second Wild Card by a half a game.

That set up a four-game series at Wrigley Field against those Giants.

The Cubs wound up sweeping the Giants by a 22–13 aggregate to take a commanding 3½ game lead for the second Wild Card.

In the first game, a 5–4 win, Kyle Schwarber hit a three-run homer in the second inning. In the second, a 7–3 victory, Schwarber drove in two runs, Dexter Fowler homered, and Jon Lester pitched seven innings.

In the third game, Bryant hit a two-run homer and Maddon used five relievers after Kyle Hendricks worked into the sixth.

In the closer, a 2–0 win, Jake Arrieta threw 7⅔ scoreless innings— he also tripled and scored a run.

It was during that series that Chicago felt like a Cubs town once again and anything was possible. Epstein and his friends were spotted celebrating hard after that fourth game at a local steakhouse.

It wasn't premature. The Cubs went 19–9 in August and 19–9 in September to finish with 97 wins, the third-most in the National League and the third-most in the NL Central. They finished 13 games ahead of the Giants for the second Wild Card, and just three games back of the Cardinals for the division crown.

Bryant slashed .330/.422/.620 with seven homers in August and then .316/.380/.521 with five homers in September.

But while Bryant's second-half surge got him the Rookie of the Year Award, it was Jake Arrieta who became the breakout star of the last two months.

In his 12 regular-season starts from August 4 through October 2, the Cubs went 12–0 and he went 11–0 in decisions. He threw 88⅓ innings and gave up just four earned runs (seven total). He struck out 89 and walked 14. His ERA was 0.41.

Again, an 11–0 record and an 0.41 ERA in two months of starts. And smack in the middle of that run was his Picasso, a no-hitter at Dodger Stadium on August 30. He struck out 12, walked one, and improved to 17–6 on the season with a 2–0 Cubs win, lowering his ERA to 2.11.

Of those four earned runs, he gave up one each in starts on September 11 and September 16, while giving up two in a 6–3 win over the White Sox on August 15.

What most fans didn't know at that time is the White Sox almost landed Arrieta in 2013 before the Cubs got him. I didn't know it either until Bulls reporter Sam Smith, a White Sox fan and confidante of Bulls owner Jerry Reinsdorf, told me about it years later.

In late July 2016, I told White Sox GM Rick Hahn I had something "fun" to ask him about away from the group. This was after he gave a famous interview that essentially started the Sox rebuild.

"This one's not so much fun," he said. "It was fun from their point of view."

That the Sox almost landed Arrieta wasn't a secret, per se, but no one had really looked into how close it was to happening. Even the Cubs executives didn't know.

The Sox were terrible in 2013 and looking to sell off veterans. Reliever Jesse Crain had an 0.74 ERA. Baltimore, in a playoff race, was interested in him. The Sox had scouts on Arrieta as he worked on things in the minors and those scouts were pushing for the deal.

But something was wrong with Crain, who was complaining of elbow soreness. The teams were talking throughout June, but when the Orioles wanted an answer, Hahn couldn't give them any reassurance.

"It wasn't to the point that any deal was agreed upon or any medicals were exchanged or any specifics were nailed down," Hahn told me. "It was just an ongoing conversation that we had to pull out of for the player's health."

On July 2, the Cubs traded Scott Feldman and Steve Clevenger for Arrieta and Strop. They knew they had competition for Arrieta and, in fact, had to add Clevenger to get the deal done.

"We evaluated Jake as a change of scenery candidate as we were scouting the buyers that year," Cubs GM Jed Hoyer said. "I know from all the phone calls I got afterward that we weren't the only team to see him that way."

Imagine Arrieta in a 2015 rotation with Chris Sale and José Quintana. Hahn said he tried not to.

"You try to avoid those thoughts," he said. "You try to avoid those thoughts. Looking at it from a glass half-full standpoint, it certainly is a reinforcement for our scouts and the guys that recommended we target Arrieta."

Crain never pitched in the majors again. The Orioles finished in third place in the AL East, 6½ games behind Joe Maddon's Tampa Bay Rays for the second Wild Card berth.

After the Cubs traded for him, Arrieta went to the minors to keep working on his cross-body delivery and his routine. Pitching coach Chris Bosio wanted him up in the majors to work on some things and Arrieta made his Cubs debut on July 30 in a doubleheader, throwing six innings of one-run ball. He went back to the minors before returning for good in mid-August. In the first start of the rest of his life, he threw seven scoreless innings in a win over St. Louis. In his next start, he got rocked by the Nationals, giving up six earned runs in four innings. For the rest of the season, he mixed good starts in with the bad, but the Cubs knew they had something in him.

Jake Arrieta is doused after throwing his no-hitter against the Dodgers on Sunday, August 30, 2015, in Los Angeles. (AP Photo/Mark J. Terrill)

In 2014, Arrieta put together one of the best under-the-radar seasons a player pitching for the big-market Cubs could ever have. He finished 2014 with a 2.53 ERA, one that stayed under 3.00 from June 8 until the end of the season.

Arrieta had figured it out by trusting in himself and getting good instruction. The Orioles had screwed with his head by demanding he pitch a certain way—as they did with a number of pitchers—and Arrieta nearly quit the sport.

But the Cubs let Arrieta be unique with his cross-body action. The problem was always replicating it. A cross-body delivery is complicated with a number of "moving parts." Arrieta's fitness routine—heavy on Pilates and walking around in cut-off T-shirts—wasn't just a fun personality angle, it was a necessary component of his pitching style. He needed serious core muscles to keep the motion perfect.

There was no mystery to it, he said after winning the Cy Young Award in 2015. But the work he put in in 2013 and 2014 made way for 2015. While that season wasn't to be duplicated, it was the product of his hard work and belief in himself.

"Honestly, the things I had to change and manipulate, whether it was something mechanical or my pitch selection, something in between starts I needed to change, some of those things were known all along," he said. "It was about how do I apply these, how do I make them even better as I begin to apply them. And that's really the process that I've been on in my time with the Cubs. Once I started to be aware of some of those things on an even greater level, with a stronger understanding of how to apply those, things started to take off naturally. I feel like things that have transpired, especially this season, are a byproduct of finally being able to put those small things in place."

Arrieta had an ace mentality. Before he pitched in the Wild Card Game, he warned Pirates fans what was coming. One fan with the handle @Parrot_McFadden tweeted Arrieta: "Be ready for a sea of black" along with four hashtags: #BlackOut #BUCN #crowdIsGoing-ToEatYoualive #walkTheplank

On October 4, Arrieta quote-tweeted him back: "Whatever helps keep your hope alive, just know, it doesn't matter."

The Cubs players loved it.

That was Arrieta, who grew a thick beard and swaggered around Wrigley Field showing off his muscles. He wasn't a loud pitcher, but he was an intense one.

Before the playoffs, I told Epstein how Arrieta carried himself like he was the best pitcher in the game. He laughed.

"He did before he was," Epstein said. "And now he is, so it's even better."

As the days ticked away in the 2015 regular season, the pressure ratcheted up. The Bears were awful, so more attention was placed on the Cubs, who hadn't been to the postseason since 2008.

"The Plan" was working.

The Cubs clinched their first playoff berth with a loss, not a win. After a Cubs loss to Pittsburgh, reporters stayed late at Wrigley Field waiting for a Giants loss in San Francisco to send our stories. We celebrated our newfound relevance with a beer or two at Yakzies, our designated postgame drinking bar on Clark Street

The Cubs went home and came back the next day, September 27, to booze it up after a Saturday game, another loss to Pittsburgh.

The team was adept at celebrating. One of the things that Maddon's bench coach Davey Martinez brought from Tampa Bay was a postgame dance party. After every win that season, the Cubs danced in their spartan clubhouse. A disco ball and a smoke machine livened up the atmosphere.

"Why not celebrate every time we win?" Martinez told me one day. "You should celebrate every time you win. It's a great feeling, you know? When we get to the big dance, the celebration will be even bigger."

After they danced on this Saturday, the Cubs took to the field to drink, frolic, and share in the moment with the fans. Wrigley Field stayed packed after the final out as the Cubs drank to their own success.

"We're going to enjoy this one," Anthony Rizzo told us. "It's been a long time coming, five, six, seven years now. We've had tough years, but we have a confident group and we're going to have some fun."

Epstein didn't think he would get doused—it was just a Wild Card spot, after all—but the Cubs nailed him with $7 bottles of Cuvee Tradition Blanc de Blancs Brut as he ascended the dugout steps to the field.

The Cubs jumped around in a circle and chanted, "We never quit! What?! We never quit! What?!"

For Rizzo, who came in during the dark days of the rebuild, the payoff was here. Starlin Castro was one of two Cubs, along with reliever James Russell, to have played under Lou Piniella back in 2010.

"This is as good as it gets," Rizzo said. "Starlin and I were talking about how we have to enjoy this. We had some tough times here, obviously, and hopefully this is the switch of a new generation of Cubs fans and Cubs players and the organization, where we can do this every year."

Those words weren't bold. It's exactly what happened.

While the 2015 team made "Go Cubs Go" relevant again, the official song of the 2015 Cubs was "Ando En La Versace" by Omega. It's a Latin song with a hypnotic beat picked out by the team's game-day DJ. When Castro started walking out to it, the Cubs began clapping inside the dugout. TV cameras caught on and so did the fans. By the end of September, Castro, who'd moved to a part-time gig at second base by this point, started hitting again and everyone in the stadium began to clap along to the walk-up song.

"We kind of knew early on in the year, when we were clapping in the dugout, we knew fans were going to get in it at some point," David Ross told us. "It took winning and fans to keep believing in us early. We were doing it in June, I think. Fans gotta believe. You've got to convince people."

But Epstein wasn't sold on what would happen next. Yes, they were confident with Arrieta on the mound against Pittsburgh in a one-game playoff. In five starts that year against Pittsburgh, he had given up just three earned runs in 36 innings. The Cubs won four of those games and in their only loss, they got blanked 3–0.

Arrieta was clicking on all cylinders. But the fan who tweeted Arrieta was correct and so was Jake. The crowd at PNC Park was unlike anything most of the Cubs had ever seen in the majors. Players like Jon Lester and David Ross were used to wild, packed stadiums from their days in Boston. But this was next level. The streets surrounding PNC Park are blocked off before games and fans were imbibing like it was a Steelers tailgate party. Men dressed as Pirates stood on the Roberto Clemente Bridge waving skull-and-crossbones flags.

"I think that was the first time ever I couldn't hear myself talk," Kyle Schwarber told me years later. "It was rattling me."

This was the best team the Pirates had since 1992, when Francisco Cordero and Sid Bream combined to send the Buccos on a two-decade tailspin in Game 7 of the NLCS.

Gerrit Cole was facing Arrieta and he looked capable of matching the Cubs' ace. Cole threw seven innings of one-run ball in a win over the Cubs in the end of the season.

On October 7, Dexter Fowler and Kyle Schwarber, the top two hitters in the Cubs' lineup, went 5-for-7 against him in front of those rowdy fans, each hitting a homer. They drove in and scored all four runs. Cole only gave up one more hit, a single to Miguel Montero. But Schwarber's homer gave the Cubs a 3–0 lead in the third inning, a critically important cushion for a young team playing in a hostile environment.

"It's not a dagger, but you give yourself a lot more cushion there," Schwarber said. "You give yourself that room where you can kind of breathe a little bit, where it's not a 1–0 game all the way. You get three runs up on the board. Dexter had a great day too that day."

Arrieta put his pitches where his mouth was, throwing a four-hit shutout. But he was more hittable than he looked to the naked eye. More hittable than he would admit after the game.

In the sixth inning, the Pirates had their chance. They loaded the bases on a single, a hit batsman, and a fielding error by Addison Russell on a sharply hit ball. PNC Park was as loud as any stadium could be. It felt like a Steelers game turned to 11.

"It was crazy," Schwarber said. "All you could do was look into the fans and see a sea of black. That was exciting, for sure."

After a meeting on the mound, Arrieta got Starling Marte to ground out to get out of the inning. Marte hit a hard ground ball up the middle, but Russell got there just in time to make the out. If the ball were hit a hair to the right or a touch harder, it goes through and scores two runs. At least.

I was in the Pirates clubhouse for ESPN and couldn't help but notice the players were complimentary, but not wowed.

"He gives you some pitches to hit, you just got to hit them," McCutchen said. "We hit some balls hard, some balls we hit right at people and they made some good plays on. He was just taking advantage of that strike zone."

After the game, Sahadev Sharma, then of *Baseball Prospectus*, told Arrieta he wasn't "as crisp" as usual. Arrieta, who had been sucking down a giant bottle of cheap sparkling wine, was perturbed. "I don't know what you were watching," he replied.

But Sahadev's observation went beyond the eye test. Both Arrieta's catcher Miguel Montero and a Cubs executive agreed Arrieta wasn't his usual self. The long season was catching up to him, but even at, say, 75 percent, he was alpha male enough to win.

"He was on that roll," Schwarber said. "And he just wanted to keep the trash talk going and keep the boys fired up…. Some of it was thinking we didn't know any better and the other half was just playing with excitement and enjoying the moment."

The Cubs partied hard, very hard, for a Wild Card Game, but were focused enough that they withstood an opening salvo by St. Louis in the National League Division Series, which started in Missouri.

This was a series, a 100-win team vs. a 97-win one, that tested everything we thought we knew about the Cubs. Before the Wild Card Game, the Cubs hadn't won a playoff game since Game 4 of the 2003 NLCS, when Aramis Ramírez hit two homers and drove in six runs. Matt Clement pitched 7⅔ innings and the Cubs won 8–3 to move to the precipice of history. Where, of course, they fell.

In 2007, the Cubs were swept by Arizona, and the next year, they were swept again by the Dodgers.

How a franchise that spent money could go that long without winning a playoff game spoke to the problems that bedeviled it throughout its history.

Clement, back in 2008, thought the Cubs were headed to the World Series, obviously, but the way he remembered in it 2015, "Realistically, the Marlins just got hot. Josh Beckett got extremely hot."

The Cardinals won the first game 4–0 with Cardinals veteran John Lackey getting the win and his buddy Jon Lester, the loss. Each pitched into the eighth inning, true cowboy-off. The Cubs managed just three hits, all singles, and two walks. Kyle Schwarber was responsible for two of those hits and one of those walks.

It looked like the same ol', same ol' for the Cubs.

The Cubs won Game 2 by a score of 6–3 with only three players getting hits. Dexter Fowler, Jorge Soler, and Starlin Castro had two hits apiece. Soler drove in Fowler with a two-run homer in the Cubs' five-run second inning which tore through the cobwebs and whatever curse was haunting the team.

Travis Wood got the win, pitching 2⅓ innings of relief for Kyle Hendricks.

Jake Arrieta got the win in Game 3, but something was clearly off. He lasted just 5⅔ innings and gave up four runs on five hits. He still struck out nine, but given the standard he'd set, this was a warning sign. But the story of the game wasn't Arrieta, it was the six homers the Cubs hit, a postseason record.

Six different Cubs homered that night. If Game 2 blew away the cobwebs, then Game 3 eliminated the spiders as a species.

Game 4 was the coup de grâce, the first time the Cubs ever celebrated a playoff series win at Wrigley Field, another wild statistic that was buried that season.

Three Cubs homered in Game 4: Javy Báez off his future teammate Lackey in the second, Rizzo in the sixth, and then, most famously, Kyle Schwarber in the seventh. Schwarber's homer landed on top of the right-field videoboard, a "Cubby Occurrence" that became a storyline that lasted throughout the playoffs.

Leaving nothing to chance, Maddon used eight pitchers in Game 4, keeping his short leash on Jason Hammel.

Schwarber's three homers put him one away from tying the team's sorry postseason record for career postseason homers. Aramis Ramírez and Alex Gonzalez each hit four in 2003.

* * *

The Cubs want their scouts to write real reports, to be creative. If that sounds antithetical to what you think their statistics-driven approach is, then you don't know how the front office really works. With every front office on even ground now in terms of access and understanding of advanced analytics, Theo Epstein espouses the human approach. He always has.

So when Midwestern scout Stan Zielinski, a holdover from the Jim Hendry era, saw Kyle Schwarber bat for Indiana University, he wrote this in the team's internal database, Ivy.

"I believed today," Stan Zielinski wrote after an Indiana-Purdue game, according to an NBC Sports Chicago article written by Patrick Mooney. "I will send clip. To preview, squint your eyes and imagine a grainy film of Babe Ruth hitting a ball in the stands at Yankee Stadium. I swear I saw that reenacted today as the ball flew out over the 2nd fence in RF."

In case his bosses weren't sure how much he liked Schwarber, he also referred to him as John Wayne in the same report.

"Stan was probably the best I've ever seen at creating that picture of the person," Jason McLeod told Mooney.

Hendry told Mooney about other Zielinski-isms, like "seat-belt reliever" or "one-pitch carnival thrower."

Zielinski, who'd been with the Cubs since 2001, died in January 2017. He was the scout that was all over Jeff Samardzija at Notre Dame, among other less-famous scores. And Epstein liked him as much as Hendry did. The Cubs now have a scouting award named after him.

Zielinski's championing of Schwarber was equaled by Epstein's enthusiasm for him. Epstein loved Schwarber, in a pre-draft meeting in Arizona, said it pissed him off people thought he couldn't catch. Confidence is an aphrodisiac to Epstein. That they drafted him No. 4 overall was a surprise and some thought it had as much to do with signability as pure talent. The Cubs could pay Schwarber, projected to go lower in the draft, a smaller signing bonus and allocate the savings to other, harder-to-sign picks below him. But the Cubs were sold that his swing would translate to the big leagues.

They weren't wrong, though he's not quite Babe Ruth just yet. He got his first call-up in 2015 to DH for interleague games after just 130 minor-league games. He picked up eight hits in 23 at-bats, including a homer and a triple and had six RBIs. He returned in mid-July when the Cubs needed catching help and never left. In his first week back, he had a three-hit game and a four-hit, two-homer game. In the first week of August, when the Cubs got hot and took over the second Wild Card spot for good, he picked up 10 hits in six games, with three homers and two doubles.

Needless to say, Zielinski probably felt he undersold Schwarber. His playoff heroics certainly cemented the young slugger into Cubs lore.

(That summer, the Cubs also drafted another Midwestern hitter, though Zielinski wasn't the recommending area scout this time. Ian Happ played for a lousy University of Cincinnati team, but he impressed the Cubs with his bat as well. He made it to the big leagues by 2017. That means the Cubs were 4-for-4 in their top first-round picks making the majors from 2012 to '15, with only Almora, the lone high schooler, taking longer than two seasons to do it. Unfortunately the draft and international signings weren't producing scores of major league pitchers. The money the Cubs saved on young controllable position players was spent, and then some, on veteran pitchers.)

* * *

After disposing of the Cardinals, the mood was jubilant in Chicago as an unexpected World Series loomed. How tough would the Mets pitching be, anyway?

The 2015 NLCS proved the Cubs didn't have enough, and looking back at the roster, it's hard to believe they made it that far in the first place. Years later, Epstein and Maddon said it was Joe Maddon's best managing job by far. Not even a comparison.

In the NLCS, Daniel Murphy clobbered Cubs pitching, while the Mets starters held the young Cubs bats at bay.

In Game 1, Matt Harvey pitched 7⅔ innings, striking out nine and giving up two runs, both coming after the Mets had leads.

In Game 2, Noah Syndergaard only lasted 5⅔ innings, but he gave up one run and struck out nine.

In Game 3, Jacob deGrom struck out seven in seven innings, giving up two runs.

In Game 4, Steven Matz was pulled with two outs in the fifth, and Bartolo Colon wound up getting the win in relief to send the Cubs home.

Murphy went 9-for-17 in the four-game sweep, hitting four homers and driving in six runs. Small sample size, but his 1.850 OPS was solid.

Epstein went into the 2015 postseason hoping for the best, but also aware that however the Cubs went out could be a financial boon for his 2016 budget. If the Ricketts family tasted success, they would be even hungrier for more. He was proved correct.

CHAPTER 7
A SEASON
IN THE SUN

"**T**he topic sentence is we would like to add more starting pitching," Epstein said at his 2015 end-of-the-season postmortem with reporters. "I think anyone who's followed the team knows that. We've been open and transparent about it, we're building with a foundation of young position players and we're going to trust ourselves to add pitching along the way and build really effective pitching staffs each year, and over time add impact pitching across the organization. We need more pitching, that's obvious."

It was obvious, but how would the Cubs get it? Would they pay for David Price or Zack Greinke? Jordan Zimmermann?

The Cubs were built, and built quickly, behind young hitting. It was a smart gamble that Epstein won. The thinking was hitters are more reliable and develop faster. With a rebuild on the fly, the margin for error was slim.

He knew he didn't have a decade to build out the farm system in full. In truth, Epstein flipped the franchise like a developer gutting a house and selling it in one swift motion.

Except after the Cubs were flipped, Epstein held onto it.

But for all the talk about pitching, the Cubs only added John Lackey in the winter of 2015. They signed Lester's buddy for $32 million over two years. The deal was done in early December and came after Epstein unsuccessfully lobbied former Cub Jeff Samardzija to come back to the team on a one-year flyer. That negotiation happened at the Newport Lounge in the Southport neighborhood of Chicago, the same spot where Epstein told Dale Sveum he was getting fired. (Sadly, Newport, a well-liked dive bar that had an attached laundromat, has closed. A Capital One bank/coffeehouse is located there now. Too bad the Cubs couldn't get it landmarked.)

The 37-year-old Lackey showed the Cubs he could still deal in the NLDS, but they also thought he could add a little fire to a young, friendly clubhouse. With Lester, Arrieta, Hendricks, and Hammel coming back, the Cubs felt comfortable with what they had in the rotation, knowing they could use their farm system to add a piece if necessary.

But it was in the lineup where they spent more money, signing Ben Zobrist to a solid deal and then Jason Heyward to a wild one.

Heyward was a hot free agent at the time, and he too had a good performance against the Cubs in the NLDS. Heyward collected five hits in 14 at-bats, including a homer, and played his usual excellent defense.

Heyward was billed as a sabermetric dream player that off-season, with his true value overshadowing pedestrian power numbers.

Because Heyward didn't have big homer totals every year, much of his value, both sabermetric and eye test, was linked to his defense (sixth-best in baseball, according to FanGraphs' Defensive Runs Above Average), his baserunning (fifth-best in baseball, according to FanGraphs' BsRmetric), his contact rate (16th in contact percentage in the zone, according to FanGraphs' Z-Contact%), and how the sum of his parts formed him into a very skilled, multi-tool baseball player. In 2015, playing for the Cardinals, he was a 6 WAR player, the 11th best among qualifiers. Heyward's age—he turned 27 in August 2016—made him the rare young free agent to splurge on.

Interestingly enough with the Cubs gaining fame for their wooing of Lester the previous off-season with videos, gifts, and impassioned speeches, Heyward signed a $184 million deal without ever meeting with Epstein.

"I did not have a meeting with them one time," he told me in 2018. "I did not come to Chicago. Obviously my agent talked to them at the winter meetings and stuff. To me, it sold itself. I got to play here in 2015 in the regular season and then in the postseason. So I got to see first-hand what was going on there. For me, it was just kind of doing my own homework, you know?"

Heyward said he didn't even consult Dexter Fowler, his longtime friend from the Atlanta area who had just finished a wildly successful season with the Cubs. For Heyward, it was all about finding a team that would stay together. He knew the Cubs had young talent and that they wouldn't have to trade players when they got too expensive. As a young player who came up in Atlanta, he had experience in that department.

"I honestly didn't talk to too many people," he said of his decision-making process. "I kind of stayed to myself. I knew what I need to look for myself. I firsthand got to see it in Atlanta, with us having a first three years with a great group of guys and that got moved around. That's not to knock anyone who came after, we won the division in the next year in '13, still a great team, but then that team got blown up. I just wanted the opportunity to roll with some guys because that's what I saw with the Giants. I saw them play together and win."

The Cubs didn't need to look into Heyward's eyes to know what he was about. He got rave reviews from anyone who played with him. So how did the Cubs measure Heyward's value? It was more than just adding up all those numbers.

"It's difficult," Cubs GM Jed Hoyer told me at Heyward's signing. "Every weighting system, every stats system, weighs it differently. But I think with Jason, he's such a well-rounded player. I think FanGraphs just did a thing that said he's the most complete player in the game, because he does every part of the game well. That makes a huge difference. Joe, so many times over the year, said this guy does something every night or does so many things every night to help you win. Whether you're running a ball out in the gap or throwing a guy out or stealing a base or going first to third, whatever it might be."

Heyward's signing event was at Spiaggia, just like Lester's was, and there Epstein told a group of us that Heyward might not be a reporter's dream, as far as pithy quotes, but he was beloved in every clubhouse he's been in.

Epstein was wrong and right. Heyward, over the next three seasons, became a go-to quote, even when he was struggling. His relationship with his teammates, stronger than advertised, culminated in the greatest Cubs' meeting of all time.

On his signing day, Heyward wasn't eager to talk about his defensive metrics. I don't think he spent a second thinking about them. He basically said his greatest skill defensively is paying attention. As Cubs fans knew, that wasn't always a given on past teams.

"I never take a pitch off," Heyward said. "I never take a pitch off. On offense, I only get the at-bat. It only comes around so many times a game. On defense, there are 27 outs you need to make and hopefully in a nine-inning ballgame, I'm not asleep for any of those. I try to do what I can to help my team, whether it's cutting the ball off, throwing someone out, making a nice diving play. You can score 10 runs, but if you give up 11 you're not going to win."

Adding Heyward and Zobrist was an admission that the Cubs needed more mature hitters to surround their young core.

"One of the things about our team, why I think he complements us so well, is we had a lot of guys who are sort of three true outcome players last year," Hoyer said to me at the time. "You know, home run, walk, or strikeout. Having guys like [Ben] Zobrist and Heyward, who aren't like that, these guys put the ball in play, they do a lot of things really well all over the field. They help to complement our guys who are more home runs or strikeouts, power-or-strikeout-type guys."

Hoyer compared Heyward to Kawhi Leonard, then the quiet star of the San Antonio Spurs. Would Heyward signal a sea change in how players are evaluated in free agency? As it turned out, no. But in the winter of 2015, who knew?

"I think when you look at the way you evaluate his total contribution to the game, I think he's an exceptional player," Hoyer said. "People have talked a lot about the standard way people get compensated and paid in the game and how that's changing. I do think more and more teams, and baseball fans, are looking at the totality of the player's contribution to the game as opposed to simply the offensive contribution. We had generation after generation that was entirely focused on one part of the game and now, more and more, I think it's better for the sport. There is a lot to the run-prevention side of the game too."

Of course, the Heyward hype was wildly overdone, not an uncommon occurrence in baseball and especially not with the Cubs. But the Cubs' hype going into the 2016 season? For once, it was fitting.

Throughout the spring, Epstein and Hoyer liked to refer to the Cubs as a "defending third-place team" while also taking on all of the questions about the expectations the team was shouldering.

"What are you going to do?" Epstein said to me in Mesa that spring. "Pretend it's not existing? We acknowledge it. Yes, it's great that people are picking us and we project well on paper, but it doesn't mean jack shit. It's really just an off-season and spring training narrative."

But at the same time, Epstein shared their internal projections had the Cubs winning 96 games, one more than FanGraphs had predicted. That doesn't sound like a lot, but understand these were coming from computer simulations that don't factor in luck, hot streaks, and all the inexplicable things that define a season. Epstein said it showed the Cubs winning as many games as any team over the past decade.

In a bit of foreshadowing, Epstein talked to me that spring day about the character of his team, or what he hoped it would be anyway. Zobrist and Heyward were important additions in that department.

"It's a huge factor," Epstein said of character. "You know, everyone's talented up here and what separates is really the mental makeup on an individual basis. And what sets a lot of championship teams apart is really how connected they feel to one another, which allows them to respond to all the adversity that comes up over the course of the year. We analyze the talent down to a very granular level and that's what's most important, packing your roster with as much talent as you can, but what's going to make you win is complementing that with the right team vibe and the right character."

The Cubs weren't done adding character. Dexter Fowler was a free agent after the 2015 season and it wasn't just because of money they let him go. Fowler was a beloved part of the team, but before they traded for him, the scouting report was he's the kind of player who's best on a one-year deal. That's the art, not science, part of player acquisitions and it's not foolproof, of course. But the Cubs acquired Fowler, with the idea he was a rental. Plus, he was the leadoff man for the surprise team in baseball, surely he'd get a big-money offer, right?

Not quite. Heyward was the star of a slow free-agent market for outfielders and Fowler found himself at home in Las Vegas as camps opened. There were reports he signed with Baltimore, but they were premature. It's tough to keep secrets these days, but Epstein managed to do it by keeping in touch with Fowler's agent, Casey Close. Agents, typically, are the leaks in these kinds of situations, at least when they benefit their clients.

"After we made our move with Heyward, I stayed in touch with Casey," Epstein told reporters. "I was really offering encouragement to Dexter, hoping the best for him in free agency and that I'd be willing to get on the phone with other GMs and testify to Dexter's character, makeup and the great he does in the clubhouse and on the field. And also told him that stranger things had happened and there's a possibility that we have more moves in store and to stay in touch if we're able to free up more money. Who knows? We should at least keep each other in mind."

Stranger things did happen, and Epstein had the opportunity to sign Fowler to a two-year deal, which was essentially a one-year agreement with a substantial $5 million buyout in a mutual option, for $13 million. Fowler was offered more money in Baltimore, but not enough to sign with a last-place team. The rub was he signed for less than the $15.8 million qualifying offer he rejected, but no one was focused on dollars. This deal just made sense.

How could the Cubs announce this move? In a very 2016 Cubs way. Maddon was alerted to the news the day of Fowler's February 25 arrival so he could help set up the surprise.

Maddon called for a team meeting in one of the back fields of their Mesa complex. No one knew what was going on when Fowler and Epstein strolled onto the field.

"I had no idea," pitcher Jason Hammel said. "Joe said we were going to have a moment and I thought for sure he was bringing in some sort of circus animal or some type of weird magician doing a trick. And it was Dex, so it beat all those out. It was awesome."

In fact, some teammates thought Fowler was just visiting them on his way to camp in Florida with Baltimore.

"[Maddon] told us not to look and knowing me I had to turn around and look real quick," Schwarber said. "And I thought, 'Man, that really does look like Dexter walking here. I thought he was with the Orioles?'"

"With social media these days, it's hard to keep something quiet," Fowler said. "But I think I owed it to the boys to tell them first. Theo and the organization were awesome to keep it a secret."

Not only did the players go crazy, but so did Chicago. Cubs fans were over the moon.

The season couldn't start fast enough.

At that point, Epstein was still relying on Maddon to set the tone. On the day I sat down with him in Mesa—any conversation with Epstein goes on and off the record and at this time, we talked about baseball, parenting, and the possibility of Donald Trump winning the presidential election—Maddon had a local wildlife preserve bring in two tiny bear cubs to frolic with the players.

"Definitely, my quality of life has increased being around him every day," Epstein said. "Instead of, you know, having to prepare for a professional discussion about something, I just feel like I'm checking in on a buddy. He always has something new and invigorating and refreshing to share."

Epstein was particularly high-minded going into the season. When talking about a loose culture Maddon helped create, Epstein said, "We fill empty spaces with formality and structure and rules and expectations. When really it would be better to fill those empty spaces with, like, authenticity and freedom and allowing folks to just be themselves to get better results and better performance."

Years later, as young Cubs failed to develop, Epstein's thought process changed, but as the 2016 season beckoned, everything was possible. Heyward's ugly swing in spring training? He'll get into the groove. Maddon being Maddon? Exactly what they needed.

The Cubs opened in Anaheim before going back to Arizona, a six-game segue while the revamped Wrigley, complete with a cavernous underground clubhouse lair, was dressed up for the opener.

The Cubs swept the two-game series against the Angels, but in their series opener at Chase Field, bad luck hit baseball's cursed franchise. When Fowler signed, Maddon was presented with one of those "good" problems: how to manage playing time for four outfielders. Six if you included Ben Zobrist and Kris Bryant, who filled in there as well.

He had the highly paid Heyward in right field—Heyward was supposed to play more center field until Fowler returned—Fowler in center and Schwarber in left. Then there's power-hitter Jorge Soler, who was coming off a postseason where he hit three homers and walked six times in 25 plate appearances.

"This makes it even more confusing, in a good way," Maddon told reporters after the Fowler news. "So I'm not going to tell you that I know everything right now. I'm just going to really try to listen and absorb this. We'll make our best guess on a nightly basis. I don't know exactly how this is going to work yet."

Hoyer created a matrix in his office that showed all the different lineups Maddon could use. The Cubs certainly don't go into anything without preparation. This was an exciting time. But as the saying goes, the game has a way of figuring things out.

In the second inning of the Cubs' first game in Arizona, Diamondbacks infielder Jean Segura hit a deep fly ball to left-center field. Schwarber ran full-speed toward the ball. So did Fowler.

At the 413-foot sign where left and center fields converge, Schwarber caught the ball with his outstretched arm. That's when Fowler connected with the former Ohio high school linebacker, sending him toppling to his right. After watching this video years later, I caught something different. When Schwarber first hits the ground, the ball is caroming off the wall. Schwarber reaches to try and stop it. His instincts were to make the play.

He misses and begins writhing around in pain. The Diamondbacks brought out the medical cart. The Cubs won that game 14–6, but no matter. At first Schwarber was simply diagnosed with a bad ankle sprain, but the next day it was revealed he tore the ACL and LCL in his left knee. He was immediately ruled out for the season.

Before the injury, Epstein went over the variables for the season with me.

"Look, every season can play out a thousand different ways on paper," he said. "If we were to replicate the upcoming season a thousand different times, there would be a thousand different outcomes. The extreme bad outcomes are really fucking bad. But it's because we had guys underperform, we had a lot of injuries, we didn't handle them. The extreme great outcomes, everything goes right. You rarely see that. We kind of did see it last year. Almost everything went right for us and we know it's probably going to be somewhere in the middle. You just fall back on the talent and character of the players and the depth that we've built up, which I think is significant."

Depth would save the Cubs.

Schwarber was resilient and he used crutches to be introduced at the home opener days later. Because the Cubs built a state-of-the-art medical facility as part of the massive upgrade to their clubhouse complex, he could rehab at home, rather than at the spring training facility. This turned out to be quite useful.

An injury like this would have crippled previous Cubs teams and would've been proof that a curse existed. *This is why we can't have nice things.*

The 2016 Cubs were, by design, as close to curse-proof as they could be. The Fowler deal was like hanging garlic and crosses on your door in a vampire-filled town. A sign that this team wouldn't be cowed by history.

And they wouldn't have subpar facilities to complain about any longer. The Cubs finished construction of a 30,000-foot underground compound made up of the clubhouse, weight room, assorted offices, and training facilities.

The old clubhouse? It became the batting cage. Check that, half the batting cage.

"When the Ricketts bought the team, I remember calling Tom, getting his number and calling him saying I'd like to go to dinner and say this is what I think we need," Dempster said. "We were behind on everything. No batting cages, our weight room, our nutrition, everything was lacking. The Ricketts family, they've done everything you could possibly imagine to get that back to where it should be. Not even get it back to what it should be, to get it to where it should be. For Theo to lay it out there, we need this, we need this, we need this. And to me, those resources are far more than payroll, that's for player development. And understanding the Cubs Way."

Epstein was so intimately involved in the design of the facilities, he showed up for the media tour to help explain it all to us.

He designed the clubhouse to be circular to espouse a certain kind of baseball *fengshui*, where no one's locker is in a more important place than anyone else's. The room's diameter is 60 feet, 6 inches, the distance from the pitching mound to home plate. It is lit by constantly changing red, blue, and white neon lights, bringing to mind the future, as determined by Epcot Center. There is a giant Cubs logo in the ceiling and a conversation circle in the middle of the room. All in all, it's a nice place to put on baseball pants.

Epstein also designed a players' lounge with pop-a-shot machines and TVs and guitars donated by super-fan Eddie Vedder. The players' kitchen served healthy meals all day—I wrote down the number for delivery, but was too afraid to use it—and the training area is like a recovery Shangri-La, with an underwater treadmill, hot and cold tubs, and a float pod. There is also a separate cryotherapy room. The training room even has a hospital-grade X-ray machine, so players no longer had to go to a nearby hospital. This new set-up presented a problem for the training staff. Early on that first season, players were hanging around so long after games, they would put off their treatment, thus leaving the staff waiting around until late at night.

Equaling the training room and clubhouse in importance was the weight room.

In the old clubhouse, strength and conditioning coach Tim Buss had 400 square feet to work with.

"It was like 20 by 20 at best, 400 square feet," Buss said. "We had an elliptical, a Woodway [treadmill], a couple bikes. Back in the day, the lifting was different, we had a leg press and a leg curl. When I first got here there was a big desk. I was like, we got to take that desk out."

That was in 2001. Eventually, the Cubs moved to a slightly larger room adjacent to the interview room. Buss estimated it was 600 square feet.

But Buss didn't get his desk back until 2016 as the weight room was expanded to 6,800 square feet, not including Jake Arrieta's Pilates studio.

"For years, they would have to make do in a really small space with sub-standard equipment," Epstein said. "That's a horrible feeling from a competitive standpoint, knowing that your guys are at a competitive disadvantage. So we wanted to go all out here and in Mesa with the strength and conditioning because it's such an integral part of the game now. Guys don't stop working when the season starts. Last night after the game I saw four or five guys in here getting postgame workouts in. This morning, I saw some guys getting their morning workouts in on their off day."

The Cubs finally got an indoor hitting facility with the remodel of the old narrow clubhouse, so pinch-hitters no longer had to drop a net down from the ceiling to take a few hacks. That hack was a relatively new addition to the clubhouse. They only added the net in the previous decade. Before that, they used a small apparatus with a net in the back.

"It was [clubhouse manager Tom 'Otis' Hellman's] idea," Cubs pinch-hitter Daryle Ward told me in 2008. "But I was the one who said I needed this, so I could do my job the best I can. That little net was tough sometimes. If you didn't hit it in the circle, the ball would bounce off the net and people would be ducking in the clubhouse. The reason why we had to change is that Cliff Floyd couldn't hit the ball in the circle and he was almost killing everybody."

With the new facilities in Chicago and Mesa, the Cubs eliminated one big roadblock in their path to the World Series: excuses.

"No excuses," Buss said with a laugh. "Especially from me."

None were needed. The Cubs won eight of their first nine games and 15 of their first 20 and 25 of 31. To go 25–6 was more than a dream.

A normal baseball season ensued from there—the Cubs went 28–26 in June and July—but it was that start that not only changed the way people looked at this team, but also set the standard for seasons to come. Unfairly, perhaps.

"The stuff we did was historical," Lester told me in 2017. "You're comparing history to normalcy right now. Really nobody has gotten off to the start we did last year, this year. So you gotta kind of take it for what it is, you know? It's stuff to talk about. It's unrealistic to expect that every year."

"An April can go one of two ways," Lester said. "Either you get off to an unbelievable start like we did [in 2016] and you just fall off the bandwagon. That didn't happen to us. We pretty much played really good baseball the entire year and that's how we won 106 or 103 games or whatever the hell we won."

Arrieta showed no signs of the previous fall's drop-off. He won all five of his April starts, putting together a 1.00 ERA and a WHIP (walks and hits divided by innings pitched) of 0.78. Overall the starters put up a 2.33 ERA in 142⅔ innings. Maddon liked to say "You go, we go" to Fowler, the leadoff man, but like any team, the Cubs could only go as far as the pitching could take them.

Playing under pressure is nothing new for the Cubs. In 2004, '07, '08, '09, even 2010, there was pressure to win. In 2015, the bright lights returned. In 2016, the Cubs were better equipped to handle the noise.

Javy Báez celebrates with David Ross and Jon Lester after scoring on a sacrifice fly in an April 2016 game against the Reds. (AP Photo/John Minchillo)

"They're so low maintenance because they're just locked in on winning," Epstein told me in June that season. "I think they understand the opportunity and want to make the most of it. They're good character guys and they care about each other. They show up ready to play. They're the lowest-maintenance team I've ever been around."

The 2016 Cubs had better players, better ownership, sharper management, and a more well-rounded coaching staff than those that failed Cubs teams in the past. The resources available to them, from infrastructure to money, were incomparable.

Fowler's signing saved them from having to trade for an outfielder, or employing a sub-standard minor leaguer to buy time while Schwarber was out. The infield was stacked with Javy Báez and Ben Zobrist sharing second base and young all-stars everywhere else.

They had four starting pitchers to lean on and a perfectly acceptable No. 5 starter in Jason Hammel.

The bullpen was the only place they needed to add talent. Of course, every playoff team is always looking for some form of help. That's by design. Pitchers who can't hack it as starters (not enough pitches, can't make it through the order twice) typically wind up as relievers.

Any playoff team with a few bucks in the bank wants a lefty specialist, a swing guy, a quirky guy, and, if they're really serious about being the last team standing, a closer.

Héctor Rondón was the Cubs closer, a former Rule 5 pick made good. But he had some arm problems and he wasn't the proven lockdown guy you dream of rolling out in a raucous atmosphere on a cold October evening.

So the Cubs went fishing for a new closer.

The Yankees, out of playoff contention early, had two options: Aroldis Chapman and Andrew Miller.

They traded for Chapman when he was radioactive after a domestic violence accusation in the winter destroyed his trade value for the low-budget Reds, who signed him out of Cuba before the 2010 season.

Chapman was unhittable with a 100-plus mph fastball and a nasty slider. If any team could handle the backlash for such a signing at the time, it was the Yankees, who still lived by Boss Steinbrenner's "win or else" mantra. They could handle the back-page backlash. Major League Baseball's proactive domestic violence policy (collectively bargained with the union) issued a 30-game suspension for Chapman, despite no formal charges being filed.

The Cubs had looked into trading for Chapman in the off-season, but they looked deeper at the charges and said no way.

The laundering of Chapman through the Yankees, though, would make it feasible.

About a month before the trade deadline, I posed the scenario to Epstein, on the record, in a very careful way. You can't ask an executive or manager about acquiring a specific player under contract to another team on the record. It's tampering. Too many reporters clumsily ask these types of questions and it ruins an interview.

For a story titled, "Epstein's moral compass will guide him in trade market—to an extent," I asked Epstein how they think about adding a player who has been in trouble off the field for something serious. He knew exactly who I was talking about.

"It becomes an issue that has to be seriously considered," he said. "And you have to examine both sides. I don't think there are any blanket rules, but we care about representing Chicago the right way. We know our players are representatives of our entire fanbase. That's important to us. At the same time, people do deserve second chances. There are second acts in life. You don't want to necessarily rule people out, but it's a case-by-case basis."

I told Epstein that a lot of fans don't want to root for players they know are "bad guys." This became an issue in later years as well.

"But, examine what you just said," Epstein said. "You said fans don't want to root for guys they know are bad guys. But, yeah there are some things that make someone a bad guy, but we're talking about human beings. We're all a combination of good attributes and bad attributes. We've all done good things and done things we regret. I do believe in the ability for human beings to change and grow and move on and sometimes it's appropriate for this organization to be the environment for a player to have a second chance and sometimes it's not. But I think just sort of blanket statements about people being bad guys because they might have done something in the past is regrettable. That's a dangerous standard to set."

But so is winning at all costs, right?

"Now there are certain things we won't overlook," Epstein said.

He wouldn't go into what those things were, joking accredited media members was one such category.

The Cubs would've loved to have added Miller, who had years left on his deal and no blemishes on his record. But the price was too high. It would have cost them Schwarber plus prospects. As the time ticked off before the deadline, they had to seriously consider Chapman.

As Epstein and owner Tom Ricketts talked with the commissioner and other baseball officials, they fretted over the example they were going to set. They talked to Chapman on the phone, and while he wouldn't say it publicly, Epstein wanted assurance not that Chapman was innocent, that ship had sailed, but that Chapman wouldn't tell the media he was innocent.

The return to the Yankees was considerable in star infield prospect Gleyber Torres. Both Torres and Eloy Jiménez were the team's top bargaining chips in the trade market, as everyone on the major league roster (within reason) was off-limits. The Cubs' highly touted farm system was already decimated by the call-ups, so they were really only going to get a couple opportunities to trade minor leaguers for impact players in this time frame.

The reaction in Chicago was mixed. The #MeToo movement hadn't yet materialized, but athletes weren't getting easy forgiveness for violence against women. Not anymore.

The NFL's mishandling of the Ray Rice case gave way to MLB's domestic violence policy. Many Cubs fans were unhappy the team was even considering Chapman. Others were excited about a lockdown closer. Some were conflicted.

One female Cubs fan came up with a plan that for every save Chapman earned, she would donate to a women's shelter. It caught on.

Chapman's Cubs debut was at U.S. Cellular Field for the Cubs–White Sox series. The buzz wasn't very positive.

I ran into Epstein in the clubhouse before Chapman and he met the media and I congratulated him on the deal. "You were against it, right?" he said. "Yeah," I told him, "but I'm not in charge of a baseball team." It's too far to say he "had to" make this particular move, but as he would explain later, he owed it to the team to give them the best possible chance to win a World Series. Chapman gave them that chance.

Chapman's press conference should've been in the White Sox conference room (which is where the Cubs would hold their Addison Russell domestic violence press conference during the city series two years later), but instead everyone crowded into the visiting clubhouse. The Cubs didn't follow the MLB suggestion to hire a full-time Spanish-speaking interpreter, so they had coach Henry Blanco, a former Cubs catcher, do it.

It didn't go well. Whether it was Blanco's inexperienced translations, Chapman's nervousness, or just a mixture of problems, Chapman came off as dismissive on the seriousness of the allegations against him.

Epstein told reporters he and Tom Ricketts had a serious conversation with Chapman about his past and his future with the Cubs. When Chapman was asked what they talked about, he said, through Blanco: "Nothing. They went over things and welcomed him to Chicago and glad that he was part of this team.... They basically told him what was expected of him and welcome to the club. He's going to be part of this team and hopefully guide us to the World Series."

Follow-up questions weren't getting anywhere, so a Cubs media relations employee had to step in and explain to Blanco what we were asking about.

"It's been a long day, so he's thinking," Blanco said. "He was sleeping when they got in the meeting with him on the phone, so he's trying to remember what they talked about."

More follow-ups ensued and bad answers were given. Chapman's name was attached to a statement that he obviously didn't write. (Most statements from players or executives are, as you might have guessed, crafted by experts. Epstein is the only one I'm sure writes his own.) As a Cubs official joked, "After seeing him write like that, I can't wait to see him pitch."

After the press conference ended, word filtered back to Epstein on how bad it was. He scrambled around the visiting dugout assuring reporters they did have a serious conversation with Chapman and there was some miscommunication. I don't think I had seen Epstein that worried. The Chicago media might annoy Epstein at times, especially during the rebuilding years, but usually he was comfortable and controlled the message. This was messy.

ESPN's Pedro Gomez, through the Cubs, provided us with a transcript and translation of his Spanish interview with Chapman.

"I knew that no matter where I was traded to this would resurface, that the controversy is going to follow me," Chapman told Gomez of his case. "But I'm with my girlfriend. Our family is together. We're working toward making things better in our lives. And really, it's going to be with me.

"I've grown tremendously from that time," he said. "I'm with my girlfriend still, with the family, and I feel that I have absolutely changed as a person. I'm working to be a better person. And now that I remember because they just asked me in the previous press conference what the owners asked me, one of the things they did ask me was about being a better person and being a better neighbor to people. And that's something that I think that I am now, much more so."

Chapman was so angry at the media he refused to talk after a game at Wrigley. Miguel Montero had to act as an intermediary to get it settled.

But it did get settled and Chapman locked in as the Cubs closer. He struck out 46 batters in 28 appearances for the Cubs, earning 16 saves and compiling a 1.01 ERA. He gave up just 12 hits and 10 walks in 26⅔ innings, and three earned runs. He was as good as advertised and worth the risk.

Aside from Schwarber, the Cubs were healthy going into the postseason. All systems were go.

They spent 180 days in first place, from April 11 until October 2, when they ended the season with a 17½ game lead in the NL Central. They clinched the division on September 16 after a loss to Milwaukee and a Cardinals loss in San Francisco. They had more than two weeks to prepare for the postseason.

CHAPTER 8
FALL CLASSICS

It didn't take long for everyone to see how difficult the road to the World Series would be and how clutch the Cubs were.

Jon Lester was the opening starter for the 103-win Cubs in the NLDS. Throughout that second season with the Cubs, he showed how smart they were to invest in him, despite all the worries.

In the opener, he and Johnny Cueto matched each other with seven scoreless innings. Cueto retired the side in order in the first, second, third, sixth, and seventh innings. He gave up a double to Kris Bryant and a single to Javy Báez. No walks, nine strikeouts.

Lester, meanwhile, gave up a bunt single to start the game. Ominous? Not quite. Gorkys Hernandez was picked off stealing second by catcher David Ross in the next at-bat.

Lester didn't have a clean inning until the fifth, but then he did it again in the sixth, seventh, and eighth innings as well. This was a classic, bite-your-nails playoff game right out of the gate.

In the Cubs' half of the eighth, Cueto got Jason Heyward to pop out to first for the first out and then up came Báez.

Báez had a promising season in 2016 as he showed he could cut down on his strikeouts, but the light-tower power that pushed him to the top of the 2011 draft and made him a minor league star was largely absent.

He hit only 14 homers in 450 plate appearances that season.

Earlier that season, I asked Joe Maddon for a swing comp for Báez. I thought I would get the name of some long-forgotten California Leaguer or maybe just Gary Sheffield. But Maddon went to a different sport.

"Um, it's hard to… obviously there's days or maybe a week or 10 days where he shortens up and utilizes the entire field," Maddon said. "But other times, he's pretty much John Daly, you know. That's about as close as you can get."

I thought that was kind of limiting. John Mallee, who was in his second year as the hitting coach, was more complimentary.

"I think technically, he's got one of the best swings in baseball," Mallee told me.

"Sequence-wise, direction-wise, and everything. Sometimes you see it and it looks real big to people because he has such bat speed. And a lot of times he's right in the right position, but when he swings and misses the body has to decelerate the swing at some time and if there's so much force going through it, it's hard to stand there and stay balanced."

Mallee and his assistant hitting coach, Eric Hinske, worked with Báez to refine his swing and they found a willing partner.

"The pre-swing movement, the big leg kick, the big bat tip, the covering a lot of ground during his stride," Mallee said. "Now he's shortened them. He has the same movements, but they're all smaller, which bought him more time so he can make better decisions in the box."

Báez also credited Manny Ramirez, who was a hitting consultant with the team at the time, for helping stabilize his approach and focus on hitting to right-center field.

"It's completely different," Báez told me at his locker one day. "When I came up [in 2014], I was just ready to swing. Now I'm ready to swing, but with a plan."

In the eighth inning, Báez stood in against Cueto with a 3-2 count as Cueto tried to quick-pitch a fastball. The problem was it was right down the middle and Báez connected. He dropped his bat and watched the ball sail as it headed deep in the left-field bleachers. But the wind slowed its ascent and the ball dropped just inside the basket in left, over where left fielder Angel Pagan (a former Cubs prospect) stood.

That drunk-catching basket (Ernie Banks Boulevard as Joe Morgan used to call it) was a cause of consternation for opponents, but it was there for both teams. Báez made his own luck with that swing.

This was where Chapman was worth the PR hit. While he gave up a two-out double to Buster Posey, he got the save by getting a 4–3 ground-out from Hunter Pence.

The Cubs were on their way.

And they went to San Francisco with a 2–0 lead after knocking out ex-Cub Jeff Samardzija in two innings in a weird 5–2 win in Game 2. Why was it weird? Well, Kyle Hendricks drove in two runs off Samardzija on a single to center in the second inning, and reliever Travis Wood hit a solo homer off Chicago-native George Kontos in the fourth. Ben Zobrist and Kris Bryant also drove in runs for good measure.

Wood wasn't a big talker with the media, but he was more expansive with his friends and family. He loved bragging about his hitting prowess.

"We keep telling him he stinks," Lester said to a group of reporters that night. "But he keeps getting chances. He finally ran into one tonight, unfortunately for the pitchers. Great for us, but stinks for us.

"He keeps giving me shit about my hitting, and since I've been here, I think I've out-hit him," Lester continued. "Now he's got a fucking homer. I've got to listen to his shit on the plane tonight. We've already put duct tape over his mouth so he can't talk about it."

In Game 3, the bullpen coughed up a one-run lead in the eighth. It was the kind of inning that gets instantly forgotten about later, but not at the time.

Travis Wood got pulled after putting two on with a single and a walk, making way for Aroldis Chapman to try to pitch a six-inning save. During the season, Chapman told reporters he preferred not to enter games in the eighth, but that attitude has no place in the postseason.

So Chapman came in two hitters into the eighth inning and things didn't go well. He struck out Pence, but then gave up a two-run triple to Conor Gillaspie and a run-scoring single to Brandon Crawford. Crawford then took two bases on a steal and an error. Then Chapman walked Joe Panik and he was taken out for Justin Grimm, who got a pickoff and two groundouts to end the threat.

Down 5–3, the Cubs tied it up in the bottom of the inning on a two-run homer from Bryant.

That was the good news. The bad news was the Cubs had to play five more innings to finally lose 6–5.

Now things were getting serious. In a best-of-five series, things can turn on a game.

John Lackey started Game 4 in San Francisco, which, looking back, was the turning point of the Cubs postseason and likely one of the most important games in Cubs history. That's in hindsight, but also a little in real time.

Because everyone knew what awaited the Cubs in Game 5 at Wrigley Field: Johnny Cueto on full rest. Given the history of the Cubs, that was a fate no one wanted to tempt. So Joe Maddon managed this game like it was the World Series.

"I thought facing Cueto in Game 5 would be the most difficult thing we had to do," Maddon said later. "I thought it was necessary that we won Game 4 in San Francisco to progress as well as we did. I was more focused on that win than anything else."

Lackey fell behind 1–0 in the bottom of the first inning when Denard Span hit a leadoff double and scored on Buster Posey's sac fly. A David Ross homer in the third tied it up. It was his first postseason homer since the 2012 Wild Card Game, a span of 36 plate appearances in which he slugged .281.

(Ross and Lackey were close, but I can imagine what Lackey would've said to himself had Ross meekly popped up to first base.)

Lackey got in trouble in the fourth inning, loading the bases on two singles and a walk with one out. Opposing pitcher Matt Moore drove in one run with a single and Span knocked in another with a groundout.

Ross drove in another run in the fifth on a sac fly, but that was it for Lackey, who was replaced by Justin Grimm to start the fifth. Grimm didn't exactly inspire confidence in Maddon's decision.

After one out, he gave up a single and a double. He was replaced by Travis Wood, who gave up an RBI single and a sac fly.

So now the Cubs are down 5–2 and how do they respond? With one baserunner (two, technically, because of a force out) and four strikeouts over the next three innings against Moore.

You might remember that viral image that appeared on the telecast of Theo Epstein scrunched down in his seat, his face locked in agony. He was meme'd.

"I was just concerned," Epstein said after that win. "I would never get mad at our guys. I was just waiting for us to show up and it happened in a hurry.

"I was trying to think why I was so pissed in the first eight innings of that game and it kind of reminded me of the feeling in Game 4 of the 2004 ALCS, when we were losing," he said. "At that moment it looked like there was a chance we were going to get swept by the Yankees and it was the feeling of tremendous potential not capitalized on. I knew that team was great and I knew we'd win the World Series. All of a sudden it looked like we might get swept by the Yankees and it was a feeling of missed opportunity."

Baseball executives, even those as famous as Epstein, mostly sit in the stands during road playoff games, which is one of baseball's quirks. There should be a dynamic pricing option for seats around where visiting GMs and presidents sit, right? Perhaps for the Cubs' next World Series, should that happen, I'll do some digging and expense my own ticket in that section.

Cameras were focused on Epstein, Jed Hoyer, and Jason McLeod during those last few innings and another meme-able image would come from it.

The Cubs were set up with their best hitters to start the ninth: Kris Bryant, Anthony Rizzo, and Ben Zobrist.

Bryant singled past a diving shortstop, knocking out right-handed reliever Derek Law. In came lefty Javier Lopez to face the left-handed Anthony Rizzo. He walked on six pitches. Sergio Romo entered to face Zobrist and the veteran turned on an 89 mph pitch and laced a line-drive double to right field to drive in one run.

The cameras cut to Epstein, Hoyer, McLeod, and Hoyer's wife sitting in the stands.

Aroldis Chapman began his jog to the open-air bullpen, which, along with the Cubs at the time, was one of two still situated in foul territory.

You remember all of this, perhaps, but what you might not remember is Chris Coghlan coming to the plate. That's because Giants manager Bruce Bochy came out to pull Romo and bring in Hunter Strickland. The Cubs brought back Coghlan and went with Willson Contreras. Contreras then hit a ground ball that ricocheted in front of the pitcher and bounced into center field, scoring two runs and tying the game. Contreras pounded his chest as he ran to first as pandemonium erupted in the Cubs' dugout.

Now it was a tie game with no outs. Jason Heyward, cold as a San Francisco evening, bunted, and the Giants got a force out at second, but a throwing error by shortstop Brandon Crawford for the double play veered right and put Heyward at second.

Another pitching change by San Francisco. (And people wonder why playoff games take so long?)

Up came Báez, who had three hits and a walk in Games 2 and 3.

Hunter Strickland got ahead with an 0-2 count, but it wasn't a classic Javy 0-2 count. Báez took strike one and then fouled off the second pitch. The cameras stayed on Báez's face, which was calm and collected. There was no panic in his eyes. He looked… relaxed?

Strickland threw a fastball, down and away in the zone, and Báez calmly poked it up the middle. The ball had a lot of giddy-up on the way out, looking like it was aimed directly at Heyward, who had taken a small lead off second. It landed in shallow center to give the Cubs a 6–5 lead.

David Ross hit into a double play, but it didn't matter. Chapman was coming in to pitch the ninth.

Three swinging strikeouts later and the Cubs were headed to the NLCS for the second straight season. This set up an NLCS that was a revenge series for Cubs fans who remembered how the Dodgers swept them out of the 2008 playoffs.

The champagne and beer celebration that night was raucous, with Epstein captured chugging beers on TV as he greeted each player who came into the clubhouse.

Before we get there, though, let's backtrack.

After Game 2, Jon Lester was drinking beers at his locker in full entertainer mode as national reporters drifted over. By this point in his career, Lester was an elder statesman in his early thirties, full of baseball wisdom and skilled at turning a phrase, often laden with expletives. (I was nervous the first time I printed what he said in full at The Athletic, but I never got any complaints from him or the Cubs.)

I stuck around talking with him after the likes of Jeff Passan and Bob Nightengale had moved on, and while I have no clue if he knows my name or affiliation, he had been, and is still, a more-than-willing conversationalist with me. I'm not alone, of course. When Lester gets going, it's hard for him to stop. He might say he has five minutes before he has to go work out, but he'll talk for 20.

So, with some Miller Lite fueling him, he started talking with me about the way writers, and athletes, throw around the term "superstar."

"Nowadays, man, I feel like everybody is willing to give the superstar status to everybody, you know," he said. "I don't love that. I don't love that a guy has one good year and you're trying to give him superstar status. When you look at the game, there's only, hell, I can only think of one superstar in this game right now and he's fixing to retire. David Ortiz is the epitome of a superstar and I think everybody is trying to live up to that deal right now.

"There's a lot that goes along with being a superstar," he continued. "David Ortiz comes out on deck and [the fans] don't care what the situation is, they don't care who's up. Manny Ramirez could be up with the bases loaded, two outs, the bottom of the ninth. They don't care about that. They care about David Ortiz on deck. That's a superstar. The show stops when that dude walks on deck. That's how I judge a superstar."

"A superstar is able to come into the clubhouse and answer questions every single day," Lester said. "And do it properly and have his teammates' back and handle that. And also handle the media outside of that. And also handle the commercials."

I never found out if there was a deeper meaning behind these comments. Did Lester think we had anointed Kris Bryant and Anthony Rizzo as superstars too soon? (Lester and Rizzo were close, but Rizzo, in particular, seemed unwilling, at times, to handle the postseason media crush. It was something he improved on by 2018.)

Perhaps it was just Lester being Lester. He liked to bill himself as a simple guy when it came to baseball, a still-youngish pitcher who fancied himself 10 years older. He learned from vets and carried himself like he was older than his friend John Lackey.

(During our conversation, Lackey, no friend to any reporter, told Lester he should be quiet and Lester shot back, "I don't want to be quiet, John.")

Going by Lester's definition, I decided, he was the only thing close to a superstar on the Cubs' roster, so it was a good thing he was starting Game 1 of the NLCS.

Lester appreciated the ceremonial honor of being the Game 1 starter for the most important Cubs series since 2003.

"Obviously for me it's a great honor," Lester said at the time. "Especially with the staff that we have. To get picked again to go number one, that's really a cool honor. Our staff has been really, really good this year, and I think that, really, if you put all of our names in a hat and pulled one out, I don't think you could go wrong."

The Cubs didn't want to pull names out of a hat. They wanted Playoff Jon Lester.

"It's a good feeling," Epstein said before that series began. "You saw what he did against the Giants. He's done it consistently enough now in his career that it becomes part of his well-earned reputation."

The Cubs won Game 1 at Wrigley Field, though Lester didn't get the win. He gave up just one run (on an Andre Ethier homer in the fifth inning) and four hits and a walk. He lasted just 77 pitches before Maddon started one of those bullpen parades that are so prevalent in October.

The Cubs were up 3–1 going into the top of the eighth. Lefty Mike Montgomery lasted one hitter—Andrew Toles, who singled—before Maddon went to the right-handed Strop to face Chase Utley. Utley walked and Justin Turner hit a ground-ball single to load the bases.

Tension comes to Wrigley Field, right? So Maddon went to his nuclear option: Aroldis Chapman. And by nuclear option, I mean, what if, say, President Trump could fire nukes any time he wanted? That kind of everyday, nuclear option.

Chapman, as he is wont to do, struck out the first two hitters he faced before giving up a two-run single to Adrian Gonzalez that tied the game, costing Lester his win. He got out of the inning with a ground out.

If playoff ghosts still inhabited Wrigley Field, making fans nervous for the bottom dropping out at any second, it didn't affect the actual players.

Ben Zobrist opened up the bottom of the inning with a double, followed by an out, an intentional walk, an out, and then another intentional walk, to set up pinch-hitter Miguel Montero.

Up until that point, Montero had just 59 postseason plate appearances over 19 games, going back to the 2007 NLDS (where the Diamondbacks swept the Cubs).

In that span, he had 10 hits (seven walks) and three RBIs with no home runs. His slugging percentage was .231. During the season, Montero hit eight homers in 241 at-bats, bad enough for a .357 slugging percentage, the second-worst of his career in any season. (Montero only played 86 games in 2016, his fewest since 2010.)

Montero wasn't thrilled with Joe Maddon at the time, but he was confident in himself.

So when he hit a grand slam off Joe Blanton, you know he was feeling it. Montero yanked a belt-high, 0-2 fastball into the right-field bleachers, setting off a frenzy at Wrigley. The Dodgers didn't pull Blanton and Dexter Fowler followed with a homer of his own to make it 8–3.

The Cubs even won their first NLCS game since Game 4 of their 2003 series. But this series couldn't be sans drama. The Cubs lost Game

2 at home by a 1–0 score, a not surprising outcome considering Clayton Kershaw was on the mound.

No big deal, getting shut out by Kershaw. On to Los Angeles... where the Cubs got shut out by Rich Hill, who gave up two hits in six innings.

Hill was an ex-Cub pitcher, a homegrown left-hander who looked like he was going to be a keeper.

Perhaps his best-known contribution to Cubs lore was when he commented unfavorably about A.J. Pierzynski's punch-out of Michael Barrett during a classic Cubs-Sox game in 2006. Hill called the White Sox catcher "gutless" and when that got back to Ozzie Guillen, well, it wasn't good.

"Tell that Triple-A [expletive] to shut the [expletive] up," Guillen said. "Tell him to start throwing some strikes or he's going to get Dusty [Baker] fired."

Hill *was* demoted to Triple-A and Baker *was* fired after the season. Hill returned to the majors in 2007 where he made 32 starts and compiled a 3.92 ERA in 195 innings. He battled injuries and ineffectiveness after that, pitching for Baltimore, Boston, Cleveland, the Angels, and the Yankees. He went to the independent Atlantic League before resurfacing with the A's in 2016 and then getting traded to the Dodgers at 36 years old.

He only made six regular-season starts for the Dodgers, but he had a 1.83 ERA.

Hill is a deep thinker and when he was with the Cubs, I got the feeling that was more of a detriment than a boon to his livelihood. His locker was filled with the kind of self-help books that have become de rigeur in sports, but I always got the sense he was looking for something to make him believe in himself.

But at this point in his career, he was a different kind of archetype: the veteran lefty, the eccentric.

"Yeah, yeah," he said after Game 3. "It's the biggest game of my career, and just to—again, it's all about staying in the moment and executing when you're in that moment, and that's all you can think about. And that's all you can control is that pitch. In the second inning, walk a few guys, it's over with, can't control it, and you move on. You execute the next pitch, and you execute the pitch after that. And you continue to execute until the ball gets taken out of your hand.

"But for me, looking back and getting to this point, it's just putting in the work, putting in the time, having a routine, persevere, all those things that you can kind of say to sum up some kind of endurance or resiliency. For me, that's all I've ever known, is just work and just continue to do the work."

During Game 3, something nobody could've noticed happened in the Cubs' dugout, a gesture that paid off in Game 4.

Matt Szczur, the reserve outfielder left off the roster all postseason, gave one of his bats to Anthony Rizzo, who was in a deep slump.

Rizzo liked using Szczur's bats (Szczur didn't have his own signature bat, of course, but rather he used a Kris Bryant model Marucci bat with his own name on it) because of the weight. He got a broken-bat single.

In Rizzo's first two at-bats of Game 4, he struck out. In his third at-bat...

"I saw him walk up with my bat and I just started laughing," Szczur told us later. "And he hits the home run."

Rizzo picked up three hits and drove in three runs as the Cubs won 10–2. Addison Russell borrowed Szczur's shorts to wear under his baseball pants and he hit a two-run homer.

The visiting clubhouse at Dodger Stadium was almost as cramped as the one at Wrigley Field, and it was electric after the game. The Cubs were grousing about our negativity after consecutive shutouts, but after this game, you could feel a lightness set in. The Szczur anecdotes were perfectly timed.

One of Jim Hendry's football players, Szczur was a popular teammate and a bit of a renaissance man. He was a prolific painter on the side and was known for his charitable work. He donated bone marrow to a young girl in the Ukraine while he was a college football player at

Villanova and ESPN had just aired a special about that story on the day of Game 4.

Hendry fell in love with Szczur at a football camp he attended thanks to his friendship with NFL executive Bill Polian. The Cubs had been tracking Szczur, but now Hendry got to see his speed in person. Hendry loved drafting athletes and he considered college football players to have a special competitive edge from playing in front of big crowds with something at stake.

While Szczur didn't have a regular role on the postseason team, he etched himself in Cubs lore by being a good teammate, an intangible Epstein would harp on all season and beyond.

They didn't look back after this game, winning Game 5 in Los Angeles 8–4 behind three RBIs from Javy Báez and then, at home, beating the Dodgers, and Kershaw on full rest, 5–0.

Hendricks got the win, throwing 7⅓ scoreless innings with everything on the line.

The Cubs put up two runs in the first and one in the second to give them an early cushion against Kershaw, while Hendricks gave up one baserunner on an error. Dexter Fowler led off the bottom of the first with a double and Russell did the same in the second. The Cubs scored their runs on a pair of singles and a sac fly.

Then Willson Contreras and Anthony Rizzo homered in the fourth and fifth innings to salt the game away.

Maddon took no chances, bringing in Aroldis Chapman with one out in the eighth inning. He got a double-play to end the eighth and a double-play ball to end the ninth.

And then euphoria.

Near the end of the game, with no deadline keeping me in my seat, I got in line by the Cubs clubhouse to gain field entrance to document the historic moment. But first, I walked across the concourse to the 100-level where I stood among the fans wanting to see how it ended, how the Cubs won their first pennant since 1945.

For so many years, the Cubs had been a punchline, their fans adherents to a blind faith that guided them in good times and bad. Listen, fans of any team are happy when they make it to the World Series. When they win *any* playoff series. But not like this.

I saw tears, I saw release, I saw joy.

And then I went on the field.

Imagine being this Cubs team, which was tasked with the historically impossible and doing it? Well, almost doing it. Making it to the World Series wasn't the goal, but it was an historic step just the same.

Báez and Jon Lester were named co-MVPs of the series. Of Báez's seven hits in the series, four were doubles, and he drove in five runs. Lester gave up just two runs in his 13 innings.

Things I remember from that night. Tommy La Stella hugging ESPN's Jesse Rogers, a reporter who developed a close relationship with the pinch-hitter. Carl Edwards Jr. walking around with a W flag like it was Superman's cape. Asking Travis Wood if he remembered all of his Cubs teammates from those lean years before 2015 and his wife cracking that she could remember more than him. I remember Billy Williams beaming, Theo Epstein shivering from the booze dumped on him.

The clubhouse was insane. Bullpen catcher Chad Noble was wearing nothing but a hot dog speedo. Everyone was wasted. Jason Hammel had Eddie Vedder on his shoulders. John Lackey was spraying beers. Theo was now very drunk.

"I was glad we played so well in our biggest game of the year because that's so fitting for this type of club," Epstein said that night. "You know it's our 110th win of the year. It's not an accident."

"We've reached the pinnacle," Lester told us. "It's us vs. them and we've got to keep going."

I felt for all of the Cubs who wanted this so badly, but couldn't be a part of the party. The Cubs organization did its best to bring in those people who mattered.

"It means more to win here with Billy Williams on the field and [Ron] Santo's family here and Ryne Sandberg in the stands," Epstein

Kyle Hendricks celebrates with fans after Game 6 of the NLCS against the Dodgers.
(AP Photo/Nam Y. Huh)

said. "That stuff makes it resonate more for us, but no one is weighed down by it. It's not a burden. Everyone in the organization is here to be part of this. Our free agents who signed all took less to be here and be part of this. Our young players who signed from the draft or internationally, they wanted to be part of this. They understood, 'I'm going to be part of the team that brings the World Series back to Wrigley.'"

Epstein lives close to Wrigley. He walked to and from work and on that day, he felt a special surge of optimism.

"It was awesome," he said. "The town was ready to explode. I walked here. There was a lot of people stopping their cars and waving, wishing good luck. The whole city is part of this. They all deserve it. The energy is incredible. Probably nowhere else in the planet you could get something like walking through your neighborhood on the way to the ballpark."

But wait, I left something out. Something very important.

Let's backtrack a second. On my flight home from Los Angeles, I didn't pay for the Wi-Fi. In fact, I think the Wi-Fi was broken. Thanks Virgin Airlines. When I landed, I turned on my phone and immediately checked Slack, the messaging app is designed to torture you with connectivity.

We got a tip that Kyle Schwarber was secretly working on a comeback and could possibly play in the World Series. It was the kind of message you have to read twice.

We knew Schwarber was in Arizona and was working out with the Arizona Fall League team. I put out a flyer on Twitter asking if any journalism student in Arizona could cover a Fall League game.

We had to wait to put out the story and when an AFL Twitter account reported Schwarber was in the Mesa Solar Sox lineup and the *Chicago Tribune* put out a quick story about it, without confirming the key detail we had. We published the story. Here was Sahadev Sharma's lede:

The Athletic has learned that Kyle Schwarber will join the Mesa Solar Sox in the Arizona Fall League on Saturday night with the open possibility of returning to the team as a designated hitter if they advance to the World Series.

As Schwarber rehabbed at Wrigley Field, there had been running jokes both online and in real life about an imminent return. We could see Schwarber testing out his surgically repaired knee before games and he was in good spirits at his locker. While Epstein would always brush away our questions about a possible comeback, we noticed sometimes people would leave the door open, just a sliver.

"He's there every day working his butt off," Lester said during the postseason. "You see him coming in from the weight room and he's drenched and we know how hard he's working to try to get back to help us. He doesn't look for attention. You turn around and he's drenched and soaking wet in sweat and just gone through a workout and there's a very slim chance he could be playing for us."

We all caught Lester's "very slim chance." But I figured it was a slip of the tongue.

But during the NLCS, Schwarber had one of his regular doctor visits to Dallas to see Dr. Daniel Cooper, who performed the surgery. Cooper, the team doctor for the Cowboys, had a lot of experience with ACL and LCL tears.

On this trip, Cooper essentially cleared Schwarber. His knee was sound.

"It was Kyle who asked, 'Hey, can I hit?'" Cubs assistant trainer Matt Johnson told The Athletic years later. "Just like a shot in the dark and Cooper [says], 'I'm very comfortable with that, yeah.' And so we're both looking at each other like, 'Okay, so now what?' We made a couple calls to our docs and the front office. I was 100 percent shocked. There was zero [expectation] throughout the whole [process]. It just wasn't an option ever."

Schwarber snuck in a late-night batting practice session after one of the games in L.A. How it remained a secret was beyond me. As Johnson remembered it, David Ross said, "Kyle, you get ready. We'll take care of this."

"When everybody was doubting whether he can or not, I really thought that he could," Joe Maddon told The Athletic. "The conversation began in Los Angeles. He came in the manager's office, I was with Theo, and we started talking about the thought that he would be able to do this if we advanced."

So they sent Schwarber to Mesa to play with the AFL team. At first, he just watched pitches. Literally. He stood in the box and watched a pitch machine fire fastballs.

"He must have seen hours and hours of pitching," said Ian Happ, who was playing for the Mesa Solar Sox. "He would [stand] on the field watching balls come out of the machine. He would just get in his stance and guys would just feed balls. At first he would just watch them. You have to get your eyes back."

(Happ was actually wearing Schwarber's No. 12 for the Mesa team, so Schwarber wore 66.)

"We had to limit his swings, the volume of swings, because you got to ramp him up," Johnson said. "You're trying to recreate spring training and a season in a week. But he was really good about listening to his body. Then after lunch or whatever, he'd track for hours, literally hundreds of pitches—curveballs, breaking balls, fastballs—out of that machine. It was amazing, buckets upon buckets upon day upon day upon day."

Clubhouses are closed before postseason games, but during that fall, you could usually get Epstein or Hoyer on the field before a game. Epstein, of course, had to address Sahadev's story, which had already been confirmed by everyone with a cell phone and a Twitter account.

The uniqueness of the Schwarber story almost seemed to overshadow the Cubs' situation before the final game of the NLCS. They were up 3–2. We expected them to win that game. No one expected Schwarber to return. It was like he returned from the dead.

Schwarber was playing for the Solar Sox during Game 6 of the NLCS and watched them clinch in the dugout at Sloan Park. When he went into the training room, the staff there drenched him in booze and posted the video on Twitter.

Flash forward to the night before the World Series. There I am standing in the parking lot of Cleveland's private airport, tracking Schwarber's flight. It was delayed and when it arrived, well, all I saw was the landing and an SUV whisk him away.

But my tweet of the plane landing got a lot of likes and retweets. And in today's news cycle, that's something, right?

* * *

The 2016 World Series was one curse vs. another. The Cubs had the more famous one, and LeBron James had already ended Cleveland's civic title drought that summer.

But while Cleveland won pennants in 1995 and 1997, it hadn't won a World Series since 1948. Sure, the Cubs had 40 years on their Midwest peers, but Cleveland's all-around sporting misfortune was still lingering, despite the Cavs' title. At least the Cubs had Chicago. Cleveland, despite various improvements downtown and bustling suburbs, was Cleveland.

Beyond the obvious poetic and historic importance, this series was a logistical dream. Wrigley Field and Progressive Field are separated by 351 miles, a 5½-hour drive. Team Athletic drove to Cleveland, getting there just in time for media day.

My angle that day was a feature story on Javy Báez and Francisco Lindor, two stylish infielders from Puerto Rico who went to high school in Florida and were drafted in the same class in 2011.

They had a high school showdown in Orlando that was a big deal in scouting circles. Lindor played for Orlando's Monteverde Academy and Báez for the visiting Arlington Country Day School from Jacksonville.

Because the game was during spring training, every baseball executive in the Grapefruit League was there, Cubs scouting director Tim Wilken remembered.

"It was 150 [scouts] and his whole school was there," Báez said. "It was incredible to be in high school and having so many people watching you."

"I remember his team rolling up, with all the scouts walking as fast as they could," Lindor said. "And him having BP, putting on a show for the scouts. Home runs everywhere. And they beat us. He had a good game and I had a good game. It was cool playing in front of so many people and showing the world we could do it."

Jed Hoyer was the GM of the Padres that draft and he was smitten with Lindor. Wilken was in charge of the Cubs' draft and he loved Báez.

During the World Series workout day in Cleveland, I talked to Hoyer and Cubs minor league boss Jason McLeod about that draft.

"He's like my favorite ever in-person workout and meeting ever," Hoyer said of Lindor. "Jaron Madison [a Cubs front office executive] and I went down and worked him out at his high school. What I remember the most was how much fun he had. He was a great kid, great personality. But he was just having fun. I remember at one point, I was kind of challenging him to do different things and he embraced all of it. 'Hit five balls off the screen' or 'Hit a double the other way.' He did it, but he was having fun doing it. I remember walking out of there and saying we're taking this guy if we have a chance to take him, without a doubt."

Unfortunately for Hoyer and the Padres, they had the 10th pick in the draft. Lindor went eighth to Cleveland, which was a bit of a surprise in the industry.

"I was shocked," Hoyer said. "I was devastated. I had a man-crush on him."

Báez went ninth to the Cubs.

"I knew the Cubs were going to take him based off a conversation I had with Tim Wilken right before the draft," McLeod said. "I asked him actually about Lindor. 'Are you going to take Lindor in front of us?' He said, 'My guy is Báez. If he's there, I'm going to take him.'"

So much for draft subterfuge.

Why didn't the Padres want Báez?

"Javy at that time wasn't going to be in our consideration for 10," McLeod said. "We just had some questions about the swing and miss, about the ultimate position—we had some scouts who thought he could catch. But we loved the tools."

I billed the World Series as a title fight between the two fledgling stars from Puerto Rico because that's what Alex Cora called it. "It's like a boxing match," he said of the mood in Puerto Rico.

I talked to Cora, who was in Puerto Rico, for my story on the phone from my hotel room. He was working for ESPN as a broadcaster during the NLCS and as the general manager for a team in the Puerto Rican winter league.

It was funny, Cora said, because the previous winter, Báez played in that league after the Cubs bowed out of the NLCS and he was terrible.

"I talked to Theo… and we were joking that Javy was the most talented player here and probably was the worst hitter in the league [in 2015]," he said. "To be honest, he was the guy you wanted to face."

Báez hit .245 in 14 games for Santurce in the winter of 2015. The year before he hit .233 in 11 games.

"He was working on a few things," Cora said. "It's not easy to come down and work on your craft, try different things and compete. This is a league where every day here is like Game 7 of the World Series between the fans, the players, and the way you manage."

Báez's work paid off and then some.

Cora, who has since earned two World Series rings as a bench coach for Houston and as a first-year manager for Boston, was a fantastic quote. I kept thinking to myself, "Why isn't this guy a manager yet?"

* * *

Game 1 was freezing. Baseball Reference said it was 50 degrees at first pitch, but it felt like 20 with the wind blowing in. I did local TV outside the stadium before the game and didn't bring my jacket, thinking my suit coat would keep me warm. I was wrong. All I wanted to do was get back to the auxiliary press box (which was the Indians' play place for children near right field, so our press box had a giant slide in it), but as I re-entered Progressive Field, I spotted two large men in Schwarber jerseys. We were in Ohio. They must be related.

So I stopped them and it turned out to be Kyle's dad, Greg, and his uncle Mike (Kyle's infant niece Reese was sleeping over Greg's shoulder).

Greg was the first call Kyle made from the doctor's office.

"I was totally surprised," Greg Schwarber told me in a crowded concourse. "I never would've believed in a million years that he could make it back here. He was on cloud nine. He said, 'He released me!' He said, 'I'm going to start taking swings.' I said, 'What's that mean?' and he said 'I'll let you know when I get to LA.'"

Because Schwarber was a high school middle linebacker in Middletown (a suburb of Cincinnati), I asked Greg, a retired cop, if he had any football stories that were commensurate with this recovery.

Greg immediately thought about a game in Kyle's junior year.

"He was on the field and he got hit in the knee and dislocated his kneecap to the side," Greg said. "And he got up and I could see him limping. The referee looked at him, blew his whistle, and told him to get off the field. Kyle said, 'No, I'm fine.' He said, 'Get off the field,' and threw him off the field.

"I didn't know what happened. A minute later my phone's ringing and it's a number I don't recognize, but it's the doctor's phone. [Kyle is] calling me saying, 'Tell that doctor I'm okay to go back in.' I didn't even know what happened. He subluxed his kneecap and [the doctor] said he needed to get a MRI before he ever played again. He was ready to go back in."

How many games did the young Schwarber miss?

"I think he missed one," Greg said.

Schwarber hit fifth in the Cubs' first World Series game in nearly 70 years, serving as the DH. In his first at-bat against Corey Kluber he struck out on a full-count fastball, but in his second, he just missed a solo homer, ending up with a double. The legend was building. Schwarber knew after his first at-bat that he would be fine. He was comfortable, somehow.

"There wasn't much time to think," Schwarber said years later. "It's just kind of more reactionary, go do it, try to get ready. Then when they say yes, you more don't want to disappoint your teammates than disappoint yourself. At that point it's not about yourself, it's about the collective, the team. I was more worried about… just trying to make sure I was good enough to go. If I wasn't or I was, I had to be honest with myself."

The Cubs had their chances against Kluber and lefty reliever Andrew Miller, but they went 1-for-11 with runners in scoring position and lost 6–0.

Kyle Schwarber works out before Game 3 of the World Series at Wrigley Field.
(AP Photo/Charles Rex Arbogast)

Cleveland got out to a two-run lead in the first inning against Lester. Lindor had three hits and catcher Roberto Pérez drove in four runs, thanks in part to a three-run homer off Héctor Rondón in the eighth.

The next morning I saw my father-in-law's first cousin Chuck in the hotel gym. He was a longtime season ticket holder and this was his dream moment. The Cubs in the World Series! But he was going home.

Game 1's miserable weather and fruitless result had ruined his experience. He sold his ticket and booked a flight. I don't believe he saw the Cubs win a World Series game in person.

That afternoon, Sahadev and I went to our lunch spot, The Greenhouse Tavern in the trendy East 4th Street area. We wound up sitting next to Cubs executives Jared Porter and Scott Harris. Soon after, Cubs GM Jed Hoyer and his wife, Merrill, arrived and sat with them.

"Hey Jon," Jed said. "You want to take your shirt off so Merill feels comfortable?"

There's a backstory here, of course. A couple years earlier, my son and the Hoyers' son Beckett had a parent-child swimming class together. I didn't realize it, until Jed filled in one day. (We actually didn't know each other until that class.) In every class after that, I would jokingly ask Beckett if "Daddy has talked about any trades."

We had class days after the Matt Garza deal in 2013 and I asked if Jed was happy the deal was done. "I'm happy," Merrill said. "I don't have to hear about it anymore."

In a rebuild, no one thinks about the rebuilding executives' partners.

We had a nice lunch and Jed gave us the "scoop" that Jorge Soler would start that day in the outfield. Soler didn't do much, but Cousin Chuck missed a solid (albeit frosty) Cubs win, their World Series victory since, that's right, 1945 (Game 6, to be exact).

The Cubs got to eccentric Cleveland starter Trevor Bauer, who struggled in Game 2 after slicing open his pitching hand three weeks earlier while repairing a drone. Whether it was the rust or the wound, Bauer's breaking stuff was noticeably not sharp.

Schwarber picked up a pair of RBI singles, and he continued to dominate the news going back to Chicago for Wrigley Field's World Series opener. The new angle was: Can he play the field?

He was really only cleared to hit, but there was a slight chance he could move well enough to play in left field. Could the Cubs win without him? He was the spark they needed after completing the Sisyphean task of just making it to the World Series.

Back at Wrigley, Schwarber tried moving around in the outfield in the workout before Game 3, but it wasn't meant to be. He'd have to be available only as a pinch-hitter.

This was my lede for my Game 3 column:

"The first thing you do when you get to Wrigley Field is check the flags to see where the wind is blowing. When the Cubs got there Friday, it was blowing out hard to left field. By the first pitch, that wind was clocked at 14 mph to center."

That is such a Wrigley Field truth, isn't it? It's not the only ballpark where the weather conditions play such a major role, but it is probably the weirdest park to play in. The saying used to go you had to build two kinds of teams for Wrigley Field, one for when the wind is blowing in and one for when it's blowing out.

And there is a thought that dichotomy is why the Cubs had more futility—let alone the World Series drought—than the average team. Of course, it could've just been the chronic mismanagement of the team. That couldn't have helped. But yes, the weather stuff is weird, and no, the Cubs didn't hit any homers against Josh Tomlin that October evening. They lost 1–0 to fall behind in the World Series, 2–1.

"Flyball pitcher and the wind is blowing out, crazy how he we didn't hit fly balls," Rizzo said.

"I think all the things adding up is a negative," Rizzo said. "Guy's a flyball pitcher, the wind's howling out, it's October. So of course, a 1–0 game with a broken bat to win it. That's the way this game is, you've got to roll with it."

Before the game, Epstein reminded reporters a 5–1 win in Game 2 didn't mean a momentum switch.

"Some people take it too far and are treating this World Series like a coronation," he said. "No, it's a contest and we're playing a really good team and we've got to fight our tails off to win these games."

And score some runs. Two shutouts in three games?

Tomlin had middling to bad numbers that season, but 10 of his 36 homers allowed came in the month of August. As I was walking to a pregame press conference that day, I heard a Cleveland player warning a national writer that Tomlin was going to surprise some people.

Tomlin only pitched 4⅔ innings, but he set the tone. Kyle Hendricks also got pulled in the fifth inning, giving up six hits and two walks in 4⅓ innings. Carl Edwards Jr. gave up the only run of the game in the seventh on a single, a sacrifice bunt, a wild pitch, and an RBI single.

Next up was Corey Kluber on three days' rest against Big John Lackey.

Do you remember that game? My headline for my Game 4 column, which I wrote myself, was: "Hey, at least the Cubs are in a World Series, right?"

So yeah, it didn't go well. Cleveland won 7–2 and Kluber, again on three days' rest, gave up one run in six innings, with six strikeouts and just one walk.

"I see a lot of early swings, a lot of 1-2-3 swings," David Ross said after that game. "We've done a pretty good job of putting together lengthy at-bats all year long, but right now I think the moment and the atmosphere of us wanting to do so much for these fans, that's where I think it comes from."

But while Ross was honest with the media, he was also honest with his teammates when he saw their downcast looks in the clubhouse that night.

"It was silent in that clubhouse, let me tell you," Ben Zobrist later recounted at the Cubs rally. "And then the man, the myth, the legend, David Ross, spoke up. He said, 'No! Don't do that. Don't hang your heads.' He said, 'We're the best team. We've won three games in a row a lot this year and we're going to do it.'"

Before Game 5 is when Anthony Rizzo tried to inspire the team, quoting inspirational lines from movies in a state of undress, a feat he would continue throughout the next two games. Was that what loosened the team up? Perhaps. Or maybe it was Jon Lester going into Game 5 at home.

While a naked, *Rocky*-quoting Rizzo was surely amusing, a fully clothed Lester on the mound is probably more relaxing to a team on the brink.

"I actually remember walking to the field, talking to Theo that day and being like, 'How do you feel, dude?'" special assistant Ryan Dempster said. "He was like, 'I feel good, man.' Who says that as the president of the team down 3–1? He's like, 'I feel good. We've got Lester going. We're going to win tonight's game and then we got Arrieta going and then Hendricks.' He's like, 'We're good.'"

Dempster had been in this situation before. Well, not quite. But he pitched in the opener of the 2008 Division Series and he bombed. The pressure of trying to win in front of Cubs fans at Wrigley Field could be claustrophobic if you don't handle it correctly.

"We actually felt like if we could win that game, Game 5, we were playing better in Cleveland than we were at home. It's a heavy feeling when you're a player and you're out there," he said. "You feel the intensity of everyone in the stands as well as the entire city. It was almost like, *Get it back to Cleveland.*"

But Dempster being Dempster, he tried to lighten the mood before the game.

"I remember walking through the clubhouse before Game 5 and being like, 'Hey guys, I left a bunch of money at the casino in Cleveland, can you guys do me a favor and make sure we get back there?' and walking out and going, 'Was I dumb to say that? Was that a dumb thing to say? I hope I didn't jinx something.'"

Again, it didn't matter. Lester was on the mound.

Lester actually fell behind early, giving up a solo homer to José Ramírez in the second inning, but he held Cleveland down aside from that until the sixth. The Cubs gave him a two-run cushion with a three-run fourth inning. Kris Bryant led off the bottom of the inning with a solo shot and the Cubs added four more hits off Trevor Bauer to bring in two more runs on an Addison Russell single and a David Ross sac fly.

Lester made it through the sixth while giving up another run to make it 3–2. Lester had told pitching coach Chris Bosio he was grinding at the end, so he only made it through 90 pitches.

Carl Edwards Jr. replaced him but didn't last long, giving up a single, a passed ball, and a fly ball out. In came Aroldis Chapman. Yes, in the seventh inning. It was an elimination game, after all.

"Joe talked to me this afternoon before the game," Chapman said after the game through an interpreter. "He asked if I could be ready possibly to come into the seventh inning and obviously I told him, 'I'm ready, I'm ready to go.' And whatever he needs me to do or how long he needs me to pitch for, I'm ready for it."

Chapman wound up throwing 2⅔ innings and a whopping 42 pitches. It was only the third time Chapman had ever thrown more than 40 pitches in a major league game and it was just the second time he recorded more than six outs.

With two outs in the eighth, Chapman's spot in the order came up with Jason Heyward on second. Maddon could've pinch-hit Kyle Schwarber, but he didn't and Chapman struck out against Cody Allen. Did Schwarber think he would hit?

"No, he ain't coming out of the game," Schwarber said with a knowing smile. "I came out on the bench and I just sat there and watched. I enjoyed it."

So the Cubs won and the pressure vanished. Maddon and/or the front office then made one of the smarter moves they could make. It was October 30. The next day was Halloween. Instead of leaving for Cleveland that night or early the next morning, the Cubs gave their players time to trick-or-treat with their families. It was a quick flight to eastern Ohio.

Needless to say, the Cubs with kids appreciated it greatly. Considering most of them lived in the neighborhood it made for an easy, relaxing day.

Once I heard the Cubs were doing that, I thought there was no way they were losing now. It was subtle motivational genius. At a time when the pressure could be at its highest, they said, 'Go spend time with your family.' Reporters with kids appreciated it as well.

The weather had turned after a cold start to the World Series. At first pitch in Game 5, it was 50 degrees. In Cleveland for Game 6, it was 71 degrees and clear.

Kris Bryant homered off Josh Tomlin in the first inning of Game 6, staking Jake Arrieta to a three-run lead. Addison Russell added a grand slam in the fourth and the rout was on. Bryant and Rizzo combined for seven hits and Russell had six RBIs in a 9–3 win.

Arrieta, as Epstein prophesied, was a horse, striking out nine in 5⅔ innings. Interestingly enough, Maddon not only went to Chapman again, despite a big lead, he went to him in the seventh inning again, this time with two on and two outs. Chapman got Francisco Lindor to ground out to end the inning, and in the eighth, gave up a single that was erased by a double play. He was pulled after a walk to open the ninth. He only threw 20 pitches, but what sense did it make to bring him out there with a sizable lead and Game 7 looming?

Maddon defended his move after the game, noting the Indians had made big comebacks before against his team and that it was important to clean up that inning. It showed how little he trusted the rest of his bullpen. More than a few people in the organization were perplexed.

"So for me, the game could have been lost right there, and he's by far our most dynamic relief pitcher," Maddon said that night. "I talked to him before the game once again, he was aware of the scenario. So he went out there and he was outstanding again."

At the end of his press conference, Maddon was asked if Jon Lester could pitch in relief in Game 7.

"Definitely he could be used in relief," he said. "Regarding closing, we'll see how the game plays out. But Jon will be available tomorrow."

We caught up with Lester in the postgame clubhouse. He sat at a table nursing a beer and asking rhetorical questions about the college football playoff. But he was down to talk some baseball too. He said he didn't really want to pitch out of the bullpen. He wasn't campaigning for it or anything—he is a creature of habit, of course—but he was ready.

"We've played what, 170-some games and it comes down to this?" he said. "So that's awesome, especially with these two teams. Why wouldn't it come down to Game 7? You've got 100-something years and you've got, what is for them, 70 years? We can't tie. Somebody has to got to win tomorrow."

Kyle Hendricks would be the Game 7 starter, which engendered great confidence in the clubhouse. Hendricks, the nerdy Dartmouth grad, was particularly popular in a room full of outsized personalities. John Lackey, essentially his polar opposite, was a big fan.

As a rookie, Lackey pitched and won Game 7 for the Angels against the San Francisco Giants back in 2002. How did he sleep the night before that game?

"Actually I slept fine," he said. "I was pretty excited about it. It was a cool opportunity and it worked out alright."

That's so Lackey. Did he want to give Hendricks any advice about Game 7?

"He's not going to ask me, trust me," Lackey said. "Kyle doesn't even talk, hardly. He'll be just fine. He's just got to do his thing. You don't got to be better, you don't got to do anything crazy. Just go do what he's been doing all year, he'll be fine."

"He's the perfect guy for this situation," David Ross said.

Writing for an online outlet after World Series game meant late nights. Especially back then, because we didn't have a overnight desk of editors, which meant I was usually writing my column and likely editing it, and then editing my colleague Sahadev.

By the time I got out of Progressive Field, it was around 2:00 AM. I wanted to hit a bar, but what would be open? Downtown Cleveland isn't Chicago. One of my peers tweeted he was at a bar where Chicago celebrities like Bill Murray and Chris Chelios were hanging out with Eddie Vedder. Now I don't care about hobnobbing with Chicago celebs at 2:00 AM. I just wanted a beer and figured wherever they are will serve late. So I found out where to go, and wound up at the Victory Alley bar near the park just in time to see Chelios escort a very drunk Murray into a waiting cab at 2:22 AM. A bartender started playing Ray Parker's *Ghostbusters* theme.

I ran into ESPN's Sarah Spain and her fiancé, Brad Zibung, and they asked me if I was excited about Game 7. Not exactly, I said. Sarah, a Cubs fan, tried to needle me for being that stereotypical reporter who can't admit if something is fun or exciting, but it wasn't that.

The Athletic was still new, with a small subscription base. This was the biggest story in the world. I wanted to write the perfect column. I wanted people to read our site. I was nervous.

But the Cubs weren't nervous. That seemed more important.

"Exactly, this is the ultimate dream," Hendricks said. "You dream of getting to the World Series, winning the World Series. When you're out in your backyard as a kid, playing Little League at the field with your friends, this is the moment you dream about, Game 7, 3-2, two outs, something like that, bottom of the ninth. But it's always Game 7 of the World Series."

Always.

The next day, Sahadev and I again ate lunch at our usual restaurant. We sat near the window and we watched as Jed Hoyer and some friends, who had already finished eating, left. They didn't see us. Through the window, I watched Jed hug his wife for a long time. It was a nervous hug, not an excited one.

Months later, I asked him about it. He remembered that moment.

"It's funny," he said. "I remember before Game 7 of the ALCS against Cleveland in 2007. I remember going on a super-long walk around Boston trying to clear my head. I remember saying to her, it was my third Game 7 of the ALCS that I've been through. They're pretty hectic. They're such a binary thing. You're either celebrating that night and going to the World Series or going home. I remember telling her I don't know how I'm ever going to handle Game 7 of the World Series, if I ever experience that, because just the idea of being world champs or losing and inevitably regretting or thinking about that game over and over for the rest of your life would be unbelievable.

"To be in that spot, you know, we came here five years ago with the intention of breaking this curse and I remember thinking that during the course of the day. By definition, this is our best chance ever to do this and we've got to somehow get this done.

"I went for a run after that lunch and it kind of cleared my head a little bit. I went home and actually took a nap and then I felt a little better going over to the ballpark. But there's no doubt. At different points during the day, there were a lot of nerves. And I think anyone who tells you they're totally calm [in that situation] is lying to you."

Game 7 was warm again, 69 degrees at first pitch. When the World Series began there more than a week before, it felt like winter. But the spring-like weather was a perfect setting for the most important game in Cubs history.

And Dexter Fowler did his best to calm everyone's nerves with a leadoff homer against Corey Kluber, who was starting his third game of the World Series.

While Cleveland tied it up in the bottom of the third, the Cubs quickly retook the lead. Again, no ghosts made the trip to Ohio.

Bryant and Rizzo reached to start the fourth and one out later, Russell and Willson Contreras drove them in with a sac fly and a double, respectively.

After a 1-2-3 inning from Hendricks, Báez led off the fifth with a solo homer off Kluber, who was then pulled for Cleveland's big bullpen addition, Andrew Miller.

This was Miller's fourth appearance of the World Series. He had given up just one run in his previous three appearances, which totaled 5⅓ innings. He had struck out eight, walked two, and given up two other hits. He got the win in Game 3 and a hold in Game 1. Cleveland was 3–0 in his appearances. Miller was confident.

Facing Miller in the fifth inning of Game 7, the Cubs weren't cowering. Rizzo added a two-out RBI single, scoring Bryant, who had walked.

A 5–1 lead midway through Game 7? I buckled down and started writing my "Holy shit! It actually happened" column. Newspaper editors in Chicago got ready for history.

In the bottom of the fifth, Maddon made his aggressive move of the game, bringing in Jon Lester with two outs and a man on first with Jason Kipnis due up. While it was obvious Lester would be used, this was early. And while Maddon had been consistent about shutting down any potential game-changing innings—using a shutdown reliever in the middle innings is a very progressive managerial philosophy—Maddon said he would try not to bring in Lester in with men on base.

"I don't want to put him into a dirty inning," Maddon said before the game. "I don't think it would be appropriate. But being that it's on his regular workout day, he's probably got a solid two in him, I would think."

Given Lester's well-documented problems holding runners and his lack of relief experience, this was dangerous.

And with Lester comes David Ross and that meant taking away Contreras' bat.

My seat in the auxiliary press box was down the right-field line, so I could watch those two trot in from the bullpen in right field. The duo that was brought here for big-game experience entering in an enormous moment.

And suddenly the specters of the past returned.

Kipnis, the Cubs fan who grew up in the same suburb as Steve Bartman (the national reporters couldn't get enough of that angle), hit a dribbler in front of home plate that Ross picked up and wildly threw to second base, advancing Carlos Santana to third and Kipnis to second. Well, at least Lester didn't have to worry about holding Kipnis, who joked with Lester about facing him in the late innings before the game.

Then on an 0–1 pitch, Lester bounced a slider in the dirt and off Ross' mask, knocking him to the ground. Ross fell back to his left while the ball caromed to the right. Two runs would score. Now it was 5–3.

With the bases now clean, Lester struck out Lindor to end the inning.

But as it so often happens, Ross, the guy who got things off-course with his throwing error, then hit a homer with one out off Miller. Yes, David Ross, who hit one home run (and just nine doubles) in 159 at-bats a year ago, homered off Miller. In Game 7 of the World Series.

I was one of those who scoffed at the outsized attention placed on Ross, a continuation on the mythical status of the white backup catcher as some kind of sage. It's not totally without merit, as backup catchers are often older players whose bodies can't handle the rigors of the job on a full-time basis. These tend to be cerebral players—catchers have to know game plans, strengths, and weaknesses of a dozen pitchers, hitters, every defensive scenario. They are truly managers on the field.

But to hit a homer in Game 7 of the World Series, well, that is the stuff of books and movies.

Lester's next two innings were relatively clean, with just a single and a walk allowed.

"Unbelievable," Epstein said later. "I can't even really understand it. It was a combination of Madison Bumgarner and Aroldis Chapman-type thing. I don't even know what he did, coming in a dirty inning like that, giving up two runs on a wild pitch, and then settling down like he did and throwing big pitch after big pitch."

He started the eighth and got two quick outs against Lindor and Mike Napoli, before José Ramírez singled.

That was it for Lester. Maddon called on you-know-who, Aroldis Chapman.

And the ghosts appeared.

Brandon Guyer, the Cubs farmhand traded to Tampa Bay for Matt Garza: RBI double to center field!

Rajai Davis: game-tying homer!

Before that moment, before Davis became a temporary villain of historical proportions in Chicago and a postseason hero, Cleveland's Lake Erie–sized video board showed a picture of LeBron James and the Cavs in their luxury suite at the game.

Cavs Fever was captivating the city. The same day of Game 1 of the World Series, the Cavs got their rings and raised their NBA championship banner. It was, likely, the second-best day in Cleveland sports history. Certainly the busiest. Cleveland's stadium and baseball park are next to each other downtown and connected in the underground.

When the camera panned to LeBron, fans erupted. When J.R. Smith realized he was on the big board, he ripped off his shirt. The fans got even crazier.

When Davis homered, the male fans in the standing-room bar area in right field tore off their shirts and started a mosh pit. It was as loud as any stadium or arena I've ever been in, more raucous than Wrigley when the Cubs clinched the pennant or the 2015 Wild Card Game in Pittsburgh.

Chapman got out of the inning, but the damage, mental and physical, had been done.

What was Epstein, watching in the stands, thinking at that moment?

"I was thinking, 'Why did we just throw 18 straight fastballs?'" he said later that night. "But in the end it only made it sweeter, man."

Amazingly, Chapman went back out for the ninth and got a 1-2-3 inning.

And then the rain came.

It's been a few years, so you might've heard about the Cubs' rain delay meeting a few thousand times. A few hundred thousand times. A million times, perhaps.

It was so perfectly fitting, I felt like it was Theo Epstein baseball fanfic, like something he'd write late at night when he's feeling wistful.

A meeting called by the team's most disappointing, highly paid player? A chance to prove that brotherhood, *esprit de corps*, the Cubs Way, was more powerful than fate and negativity? The rain washing away the sins of the past.

This was the pause the Cubs needed in 2003 when all hell broke loose at Wrigley Field.

Why didn't Dusty Baker go out there and calm Mark Prior down? Why did veteran Moises Alou go so crazy?

The rain didn't come in 2003, but past is prologue and all that. After it arrived in Cleveland, the Cubs got just enough of a break to snap out of their funk. Yes, players were angry at Joe Maddon. In the top of the ninth, Javy Báez, the MVP of the NLCS, was called on to bunt with Heyward on second. Chapman was hurt and sad and angry. Why did Maddon lean so hard on him?

The nerves must've been unbelievable.

When Epstein and Hoyer signed Heyward, they stressed his intangibles. The first thing we found out about Heyward was he gave his road suite (a contractual perk) to Ross for his final season. The two played together in Atlanta, where the veterans on the Braves helped a very young Heyward feel comfortable on his hometown team.

Now those two were leading a meeting that would live forever in Cubs history. It wasn't announced on TV. No one tweeted about it during the game, but when Epstein and Hoyer walked by it—they left their seats to go into the clubhouse area to check on the weather situation—they were instantly confident in what was to come.

"That just came to me that we should get together and talk real quick," Heyward said after the game. "That was the perfect moment for us, the perfect storm, so to speak."

What was his message?

"We're awesome. Don't get down."

Years later, Schwarber would say, "I think it takes a lot of balls to be able to come in and say we're going to have a meeting right after we gave up the lead. For Jason to say that, man, it shows the type of person he is. It was more of us to be on the same page, to get out what we needed to get out. All the emotions."

Several Cubs told closer Aroldis Chapman they had his back. Some started clapping for him.

"It was very humbling," Russell said that night. "It was a humbling experience. We had all the teammates there. A couple of us poured out our hearts. Whenever you see a man so vulnerable, you can't help but pick him up."

When play resumed, Schwarber started the pick-up with a single, pumping his fist. A picture we've used a dozen times in stories.

Albert Almora Jr., the first draft pick of the Epstein era, entered the game to pinch-run for him. Kris Bryant hit a deep fly ball and Almora tagged up and jetted to second. It was as important a base running play as Dave Roberts stealing second in 2004.

"I mean, you think back on it and it's pretty neat," Almora told me two years later. "But in that moment, it's just a baseball play. You get to second and it's 'Alright, I'm safe.' You think, 'What's next?' But it's not until you score and win and you're like, 'It's pretty special.'"

Bryan Shaw intentionally walked Rizzo with first base open, bringing up Zobrist.

Zobrist is a spiritual man, a Christian by denomination, a preacher's son but not a preachy adult. He reads books, real books, and takes his family seriously. His wife, Julianna, a free spirit and another preacher's kid, is a singer. At home games he walks up to her remake of the Elton John classic "Benny and the Jets." Her version is called "Benny and the Jules." And in a 162-game season, plus playoffs, it is, to be a little critical here, tough to hear every day. At one point, a veteran reporter looked at me in the press box and said, "There's only one option. We have to get him traded." But it's also very sweet and incredibly earnest. Zobrist bought a nice house in the Wrigley neighborhood and he would often ride to games in full uniform like a Little Leaguer.

He was a non-prospect as a teenager, not even on the radar of low-level colleges. He was ready to go to a bible college before paying $50 to participate in a college tryout.

He wound up at Olivet Nazarene University, a small school south of Chicago, best known for being the home of the Chicago Bears' training camp. Sure enough, when you walk to the Bears' media room during camp, there's a small plaque honoring him as a 2014 inductee into the school's hall of fame. He played his last year at Dallas Baptist University, a much better baseball program. He wound up being a sixth-round pick of the Astros in 2004 and was traded to the Rays in 2006, where he prospered under an unconventional manager named Joe Maddon, who moved the very athletic Zobrist all over the field, which Zobrist responded to by becoming an All-Star.

By this point, Zobrist was still capable of playing all over the infield and outfield, but he was getting older. He was the veteran piece they thought they needed that off-season. If Heyward was overpaid, Zobrist was the opposite.

But they both defined their Cubs tenure within, what, a half-hour of each other?

Facing Shaw, Zobrist laced a 1-2 breaking pitch past José Ramírez at third and into the left-field corner.

Almora scored the go-ahead run and Rizzo trucked it to third, where he put his hands on his helmet, his breathing labored, and looked toward first base. His look represented how everyone felt at that time.

Did that just happen?

After an intentional walk to Russell, Montero, the grand-slam hero of Game 1 of the NLCS—seemingly a month ago—hit an RBI single to score Rizzo. It was an insurance run that proved extra valuable.

Carl Edwards Jr. came in to pitch the 10th with an 8–6 lead. If fans were still nervous, I couldn't tell. I was too busy scrambling around finishing my first column, emailing with my editor. My only experience with a clinching game of this magnitude was at the NLCS at Wrigley.

I never got the note passed around the main press box that the Cubs wouldn't be allowed to celebrate on the field. So, not knowing that, I raced down to ground level to get in line to go outside. Another reporter—poor guy—followed me because he figured I knew where I was going. I wanted to see the final out before I made it to the line, but unlike Wrigley, which is so confined, there wasn't really a place to stand. I wound up on the concourse next to Jason McLeod, Kevin Youkilis, and some other Cubs execs. I barely saw Mike Montgomery come in with two outs after Edwards gave up a run on a walk and a single.

I couldn't see Kris Bryant scoop up the Michael Martinez grounder and fire to Rizzo for the third out and everyone run and hug in the middle of the field, but I did see McLeod, Youkilis, and a bunch of Cubs employees hugs and celebrate. That would have to do until I finally got into the clubhouse.

Ben Zobrist reacts after hitting the go-ahead RBI double in the 10th inning of Game 7 of the 2016 World Series. (Photo by Ian Johnson/Icon Sportswire). (Icon Sportswire via AP Images)

The clubhouse scene was what you would expect, a bunch of dudes spraying each other with champagne and beer and guzzling whatever was left.

A few reporters got it too, like the *Tribune*'s Paul Sullivan, who got a bottle dumped on his head by a gleeful Jake Arrieta.

Theo was drunk. Like instantly drunk. It was hard to believe someone could get that drunk that fast, but I'm guessing the nerves and the release had something to do with it.

He told us he was going to go on a bender and let Jed take over. When someone mentioned running for President—the election was days away—Epstein laughed.

"In fact, I'm relinquishing my presidential duties," he said. "Jed is in charge. I'm going on a monthlong bender. Wake me up for the winter meetings."

Hoyer, standing right there, said something I couldn't make out.

"Jed's going all Al Haig on me right now," Epstein said. "But I'm too drunk."

Only Epstein would make a reference to Ronald Reagan's Secretary of State, who claimed he was running the country when Reagan was shot, just when he was wasted after winning the World Series.

After he talked to us, Epstein went on the field to do a live TV hit and dropped an F-bomb. It was that kind of night.

"To see it all come to fruition the way it did, it had to be that way," said Dempster, who wanted so badly to be in uniform for this moment. "You're not going to break a curse after 108 years by just sweeping the Cleveland Indians or winning in five. It had to be backs against the wall, down 3–1, going to win Game 7, somehow magically Rajai Davis hits the game-tying home run off Aroldis Chapman. Are you shitting me? That's really what's happening right now and finally something goes our way where it's like a rain delay, just a short one, enough for everybody to get together for J-Hey and Rossy to have that meeting and J-Hey to speak his mind and say what he needed to say. And for them to go out there and do what they did. It was incredible."

Less than 24 hours after I saw him get pushed into a cab at a bar, I ran into Bill Murray again. He was making the rounds in the clubhouse, doing interviews, grabbing a microphone and interviewing Epstein himself. Celebrity Cubs fans can be an annoying bunch at times, but Murray is one of the true-blue fans.

By this point in his life, Murray had become a rolling party, showing up at weddings, bachelor parties, you name it. For a man that has been famous since the 1970s, this was a life accomplishment he never thought he'd have.

"It's wonderful, it's fantastic," Murray said to us. "You believe in something that actually was true and it's beautiful. The dream came true. It's okay. Dreams come true."

For some Cubs, it wasn't even a dream.

"I never envisioned myself pitching in Game 7 of the World Series and for the Chicago Cubs," Edwards told me years later. "I used to see the Cubs on TV when I was younger, but I never thought, like, I would be that person to come in the [10th] inning after 108 years of drought, so it was fun."

Edwards grew up in rural South Carolina, playing sandlot baseball, literally called the bush league, with old men. He wasn't a big prospect by any definition, a 48th round draft pick with a heater and a 28-inch waist. An African American pitcher from the sticks, he's practically an anomaly in today's game. I wanted to know what it was like for him to come in at that moment. Years later, we talked about it at his locker.

"You can feel the energy, but it was like one of those silent things, you know?" he said. "As soon as I went through my wind-up to throw my first pitch, it was silent. And then I delivered the pitch, it was boom, strike one, the crowd erupts. It was pow, yeah, catch the ball, get ready to pitch. It was like one of those tunnel-vision moments."

By 2018, it felt silly to ask about the World Series. Hell, by the start of the 2017 season, it felt unnecessary. So much digital space had been spent on that team, what was left to say? But I wanted to know if Edwards still thought about it. Most athletes live by those clichés of living for the present.

"I play it back in my mind every day," he said. "Yeah, just because that's something we never thought of. We never thought about it, I never thought about it. Every team comes in at the beginning of the year and their goal is to make a playoff push and win the World Series. That's everybody's goal. And then when it actually happens, that you're there and you're doing all this, you're like, 'Wow, this is really happening.' And then you wake up the next morning and its like, 'Wow, I won the World Series.' It's like a video game. It's basically you're playing a video game and you're trying to get to the highest level and you get there and you have to beat whoever you have to beat and then it goes, 'Okay, you win,' they pull the plug and you gotta do it all over again."

Schwarber has a classic jock mentality. He's a next at-bat, next-game type of guy. But yes, he still reminisces about that series, if not his unexpected participation and contributions. He thinks about Addison Russell's grand slam, Rizzo's big hit, Kris Bryant's base-running exploits.

"I would say I think about it a lot, just the fact that it's such an interesting series, just all the details to it were crazy," he said. "Just how the games were played in general. Just thinking about our pitchers, their pitchers, what moments changed the games. Those are all fun things to think about."

During the NLCS, something happened at Wrigley. Something spontaneous. Something wonderful. Someone, or someones, started writing messages in chalk on the exposed brick wall outside the park on Waveland Avenue.

This wasn't guerrilla marketing. No giant noodles were involved. With all the construction and commerce around Wrigley—the monetization of every inch of the neighborhood—this harkened back to the core of what people loved about Wrigley. It was a home in a neighborhood.

Stadiums and arenas are typically fortresses, islands in the middle of concrete parking lots. While teams have been coming back to city centers, gentrifying "bad" neighborhoods, and getting tax breaks, Wrigley was always there, a mainstay in a prosperous, mixed-use neighborhood.

During the World Series, the chalk wall got more and more popular. The Cubs didn't regulate it. They let it be.

Fans were going there to write messages to late relatives, to mark their kids' names, to let it be known they were supporting the Cubs in this magical run. They passed around buckets, chairs, and small ladders to stand on so they could reach the higher bricks once the lower ones were filled up.

The day of Game 7, The Athletic writer Lauren Comitor went to the chalk wall to observe and interview fans.

She talked to Jay Sirois, a Chicago native who lived in Los Angeles. He and a friend were there to write the names of their late fathers, among others, onto the wall.

"I don't exactly know what the point is," Sirois told her. "But it feels good to come here today, make them a part of it."

Another fan told her, "My parents are gone. But they're here."

The World Series ended early Thursday morning eastern time. The parade was called for Friday morning. The turnaround was immediate. There was no time for the party to stop.

Hundreds of thousands of people crowded sidewalks and thorough-fares to watch the Cubs make their way from Wrigley Field to Grant Park. It was a complete clusterfuck.

But a beautiful one, 60 degrees, sunny with a breeze. No, five million people didn't watch the parade, which only lasted six miles. It was one of those goofy estimates that no one really fact checks.

Fun story: In Cleveland, a sports radio host jokingly claimed 1.3 million people watched the 2016 Cavs parade and credited the Cleveland Sports Commission for the number. Except they didn't come up with it. That didn't stop the Cavs from hyping the number up. Even the *New York Times* went with it. Here's the problem. In 2016, the greater Cleveland population was estimated to be around 2 million people. Expand it to

Akron and Canton as well, and that number jumps up to more than 3.5 million.

The Cavs are popular, but 37 percent of the greater metropolitan area at the parade popular? Uh, no.

Chicago's parade was billed as the seventh-largest gathering in modern history, tied with the 1970 funeral of Egyptian president Gamal Abdel Nasser.

With a combined statistical area population of around 10 million (that stretches from Indiana to Wisconsin), the estimate of five million people in and around the parade is, uh, hard to believe.

Chicago was insanely crowded that day, but not one out of every two people from southern Wisconsin to northwest Indiana crowded.

I got to the rally late—again, the crowds and traffic were crazy —and we sweet-talked our way through the police lines that were keeping fans from entering Grant Park. When we got in, there was plenty of space to stand in the back. But thousands and thousands of people were in front of us. The Cubs were awestruck by the sea of people when they got on the stage.

"How about this shit?" Jon Lester said when he got the microphone from Cubs broadcaster Pat Hughes. "Sorry, kids."

How about it, indeed?

The rally was a rousing success, the perfect coda to a perfect season. The sun finally shining on the Cubs.

CHAPTER 9
THE HANGOVER II

On Friday, the Cubs paraded through the city. The following Tuesday was election day.

I was guest-hosting on the radio the first days of the week, doing the mid-day show with Matt Spiegel on The Score, the Cubs' flagship home and Chicago's original sports talk station. It was both the best time to be on the radio and the worst.

The best because who doesn't want to host a sports talk show in the wake of the biggest Chicago sports championship ever? (No offense to MJ, the Blackhawks, or White Sox.)

The worst because the 2016 presidential election was Tuesday, which was also my birthday.

That Tuesday we had Theo Epstein and Joe Maddon coming on the show. There was a lot to talk about and not all was just *Chris Farley Show* reminiscing.

Remember when you guys won the Cubs' first World Series since 1908? That was cool.

For Maddon, in particular, we had to ask about Miguel Montero's post-parade critiques, which came on the ESPN 1000 *Waddle & Silvy Show*. We also had to talk about all of those quizzical decisions he made late in the World Series.

Montero joined the ESPN show for what they expected to be a light-hearted, celebratory call. But Montero, who was known for his outspoken, honest nature, was going to speak his mind. He only had 12 postseason at-bats, but came through in two huge moments.

"It was different for me," Montero said. "It was a different emotion because I didn't get a chance to play. I was a little disappointed, to be honest, because I felt like I did a good job in the regular season but was left out a little bit. It made me feel a little like not important or maybe not as good to be in this lineup.

"I think the toughest part for me is they never communicated with me," he said, according to the ESPN transcription. "I'm a veteran guy. They talk about veteran leadership. I have 11 years in the game and two All-Star [appearances]. I expected to be treated a little better. I expected

Tom Ricketts holds up the World Series final-out ball, given to him by Anthony Rizzo during the rally in Grant Park. (AP Photo/Charles Rex Arbogast)

to get communication. Just let me know. Put me in the loop. That was the toughest part for me because I never understood what my role was going to be."

In talking to us, Maddon disputed that he didn't communicate with Montero, who should've known that Ross was going to start with Lester and Contreras was going to get the bulk of the other starts. He had a better arm and more power. But Maddon seemed to feel a bit for his veteran.

"I didn't realize I hurt his feelings," Maddon said.

(They straightened things out in spring training, or so we thought.)

Montero also pointed out that Chapman was obviously tired in Game 7 thanks to what looked like overuse beforehand.

"Of course he was tired," Montero said. "The guy threw 40 pitches two days ago. You have guys in the bullpen doing the job all year—they should be able to help, too."

That ties into Maddon's decision-making. Spiegel and I hashed out a plan on how we were going to broach it. We didn't want to be the assholes picking apart the Cubs' first World Series–winning manager in 108 years, but Spiegel and his regular co-host Jason Goff did a fine job of doing weekly interviews with Maddon, where they could lob serious questions at him. Maddon, to his credit, was rarely defensive with his answers.

Okay, that's not totally true. He was usually defensive when questioned, but not in a sarcastic or surly way, as is common with his peers. He would just explain why he thought the way he did and why he was right. But it was usually good radio.

So we figured that Spiegel should ask the big questions and I should have follow-ups ready. We went through the decisions Maddon made and they were interesting.

A month later, Ken Rosenthal had a story that exploded about his conversation with Maddon at the Yogi Berra Museum, where the manager again went over his World Series decisions and I'm thinking to myself, 'We did this interview first. Why did I never transcribe the interview? Why didn't the Score website?'

While I believe the website did have something on Maddon's comments on our show, and it was podcasted, the reason was obvious: the presidential election. Perhaps you remember that one.

And given what happened that night, no one was thinking about Maddon overusing Aroldis Chapman on November 9, 2016.

And oh yeah, I had to co-host again doing a live remote from a paint store in my old neighborhood in Chicago.

I'm not going to go on a political tangent, but Donald Trump winning the presidency certainly took away from the Cubs' World Series glow. What do you talk about at 9:00 AM after that happens? Not the Cubs. Not even the Bears.

The Cubs brass were at the GM meetings for the election and Epstein, an avowed liberal, said the election's results certainly were recognized. "It definitely sort of changed the euphoric cloud we were on after the World Series," Epstein said to me that January. "It changed the tone that week at the [general manager] meetings. I'm certainly not going to trivialize it by how it affected our mood. This is real world shit with geopolitical ramifications."

The Ricketts family, who were turning into a major political fund-raising, were mostly anti-Trump Republicans during the primary season. They even helped fund commercials against him, invoking Trump's Twitter ire. On February 22, 2016, Trump tweeted, "I hear the Rickets family, who own the Chicago Cubs, are secretly spending $'s against me. They better be careful, they have a lot to hide!"

But by the time he won the primary, Todd Ricketts, the youngest brother and most politically active (aside from Pete, the eldest who was recently elected governor of Nebraska) had decided to support the GOP ticket and worked on fundraising through public and dark-money groups where major donors could cut big checks without having their names attached to Trump.

Late that September, Politico reported Ricketts "has raised $30 million for a pair of pro-Trump groups and has discussed a $70 million goal before Election Day, according to three Republican fundraisers familiar with the effort." Around that time, Joe Ricketts, the family patriarch, donated $1 million to Trump's campaign, this after donating $5 million to a Super PAC aligned against Trump.

Days after the Politico story, Epstein made an appearance at Hillary Clinton's Chicago rally, just after signing a lucrative contract extension that paid him a reported $10 million per season over five years. (Epstein gave her $2,700, according to a campaign donation website.)

While Epstein was truly bothered by the election's results, he had his own transition to worry about. He had already signed a new deal during the end of the 2016 season, re-upping for five more years along with his trusted lieutenants Jed Hoyer and Jason McLeod. They were paid handsomely for their success. But how could the Cubs repeat?

While Kenny Williams tried to improve the 2006 White Sox's chances by trading Aaron Rowand and minor-league pitching for Jim Thome and signing pitcher Javier Vazquez, the Cubs knew they'd be losing David Ross to retirement and they wouldn't be re-signing Jason Hammel and certainly not Aroldis Chapman, who wound up going back to New York. They also knew the previous off-season was almost a two-for-one scenario, with the money spent on Zobrist, Lackey, and definitely Heyward.

They signed veteran outfielder Jon Jay in late November and in early December traded Jorge Soler, once thought to be a part of the core but now an afterthought, for one year of closer Wade Davis.

To get starting pitching depth on the cheap, they signed Brett Anderson and traded for Eddie Butler and Alec Mills in two respective deals.

Epstein would later describe Butler and Mills as the poor man's Jake Arrieta and Kyle Hendricks, respectively. Very poor, as it turned out.

Looking back on it now, it's interesting Tom Ricketts and Theo Epstein weren't more aggressive coming off the World Series, Ricketts with the budget and Epstein with creative trades. But the Cubs still had prospects in their back pocket with which to deal and, of course, they were still the defending champs.

What was it like to have won a World Series as the architect of it?

"There are days you wake up and it's like any other day," Epstein said. "There are other days you glimpse World Series champions on the marquee and it hits pretty deep. It's emotional. When you meet someone new and hear their story and process that and think about the alternative, to losing and how close we came to losing, you appreciate everything down to your core. It was a transformative event."

By the Cubs Convention, the buzz was about how the Cubs could improve from within, and how they patched up the small holes on the roster with Wade Davis and the other additions. Mostly the convention, which used to be about selling hope, was about basking in the glow of their success.

While I was there, I caught up with assistant trainer Matt Johnson, a college classmate who had been working for the Cubs organization since he finished grad school at Boston University.

Johnson was the one who shepherded Schwarber through his rehab. The Cubs were generous with their World Series shares, giving out 66 full shares to people in the organization. Johnson received one of them, worth almost $369,000, and he shared with me how it was changing his life. That's a side of winning, particularly in baseball, that isn't always known. The people who work around teams, like Johnson, who log long hours and are integral to winning, don't make that much money. In fact, the Cubs, for years, were known for being cheap with their mid-level employees, trading the cachet of working for the Cubs for the comfort of actual money. I normally don't talk money with people, but I was happy to hear about Johnson's good fortune.

While we basked in the reflected glow of the Cubs' greatest success, the country was preparing to say goodbye to another Chicagoan, Barack Obama. The Cubs worked out a trip to the White House to see Chicago's President before he left office. It was a sticky situation.

Obama invited the Cubs after they won, but the Ricketts family (aside from Laura) are staunch Republicans, as are many of the players and coaches. Epstein, who attended Obama's farewell speech in Chicago in January, was careful not to push this trip out of respect to his bosses, but he wanted to do it while Obama was in office, rather than wait until the Cubs were in Washington D.C. next, which is how teams who play in D.C. every season often plan visits.

They figured they could get the players and their families there after the Cubs Convention and almost all the Cubs went. One player who didn't was Jake Arrieta, who sent an odd tweet after the election, when tensions were thicker than his in-season beard. "Time for Hollywood to pony up and head for the border." He offered to help pack as well.

At the Cubs Convention, he explained the tweet and why he couldn't go to the White House (his reason was family-related).

"I was simply calling out people that said they were going to leave the country if Trump was elected," he said before the start of the team's annual winter convention. "It's not a pro-Trump tweet. It's not an anti-Hillary tweet. I don't care who the president is. I want whoever's president to do a good job.

"People view us athletes as being Republican and only caring about lower taxes, which isn't the case," he said. "If paying higher taxes is going to benefit the majority of society, I'm fine with that…. I'll be open and honest. I just want somebody to lead our country and do a good job. Whether it's Obama, whether it's Trump or Hillary, I just want to see somebody do a good job for the benefit of everybody."

Naive as it sounds, I believed him. Jon Lester also had a family conflict, and John Lackey, well, no one really thought Lackey would go anyway. Both the former Red Sox pitchers had made recent trips to the White House.

But most of the team, regardless of their political orientation, were very excited about the trip.

Cody Keenan started writing President Obama's speech soon after the Cubs won, even though he knew there was a chance the speech would never get made. A lifelong Cubs fan, this wasn't his most important speech a presidential speechwriter could craft—Keenan wrote one for the 70ᵗʰ anniversary of D-Day—but it's probably the one he had the most leeway to write on his own. Obama's only warning to him was no jokes disparaging the White Sox, the president's team.

"I started sketching this one the day after Game 7," he told me. "I couldn't sleep that night—I was just consuming every minute of ESPN and every piece I could find on the internet. And I'd been mentally filing away tidbits from stories here and there. But really, it was simple. I just tried to channel all the conversations I'd had over the years with friends, family, and coworkers who live and breathe the Cubs. These remarks were for every Cub fan."

Before the speech, while reporters hung out in the claustrophobic briefing room—it made the Wrigley Field pressbox feel spacious—Keenan hobnobbed with the Cubs and assorted Chicago politicos in the White House.

"The thing about working at the White House is you see foreign leaders, generals, cabinet secretaries, etc., all day long, and you get used to it," he said. "You carry yourself as you should. But when something like this happens, all decorum goes out the window. I was prepared to approach anyone and try to get something out beyond, 'I love you, man.'"

In the days leading up to the visit, I sent Keenan a joke to use: "Clark the Cub couldn't be here today. Turns out we have a no-pants policy in the White House. (Pause) He might have better luck with the next administration."

Alas, he didn't add that to the speech. But even with that oversight, the speech was fantastic. Funny, warm, engaging. It helps, as Keenan has told me before, to have an orator like Obama deliver it.

"I made a lot of promises in 2008," Obama said. "We managed to fulfill a large number of them. But even I was not crazy enough to suggest that during these eight years we would see the Cubs win the

World Series. But I did say that there's never been anything false about hope. The audacity of hope."

While Obama steered clear of any Trump jokes—he congratulated Todd Ricketts for an upcoming job in the administration that he didn't wind up taking—he did knock the Democratic National Committee.

"Theo, as you know, his job is to quench droughts," Obama said. "Eighty-six years in Boston, 108 in Chicago. He takes the reins of an organization that's wandering, he delivers them to the promised land. I've talked to him about being DNC chair, but he's decided wisely to stick to baseball."

Epstein got in a funny dig that cracked up Obama.

"And of course we have great faith in your intelligence, your common sense, your pragmatism, your ability to recognize a good thing when you see one," Epstein said. "So Mr. President, with only a few days remaining in your tremendous presidency, we have taken the liberty today of offering you a midnight pardon for all your indiscretions as a baseball fan."

This was pretty much Obama's last public appearance in office after eight years. Like he said, there's no chance he would've imagined this is how it would end when he took office in 2009. Nor would he have imagined who he was passing the torch to. But all things must end.

Including the Cubs' dominance.

There weren't any warning signs the Cubs would start slow in 2017, but Ben Zobrist warned us what would happen if they did.

The talk at the end of spring training was about staying healthy in the wake of a long season that ended in November. The players were cognizant of it. Joe Maddon, who likes to mix and match players and rest guys as it is, was focused on it, and so were Theo Epstein and his front office. But, Zobrist warned a few of us one day, the Cubs had the difficult job of balancing caution with a must-win attitude.

"This team is poised to have a good long run of success if everyone stays healthy and we stay together," Zobrist said. "This is a very good team. The biggest thing I go into the season with this year is we have to be healthy and we have to make sure we don't relax too much. I think that's the temptation for teams that just won. 'Okay, we're tired because we had a long season last year.' You just kind of assume things are going to go as well as they did. And you can't assume anything. No matter how good this team is, we still have to go out and execute and perform. That's going to determine where we are in the standings."

Zobrist didn't know how prescient he was.

How would the Cubs handle success was another theme going into the season. Could they turn one World Series into several?

After the Red Sox won in 2004, Epstein called Patriots coach Bill Belichick to ask advice about the pressure to repeat. Belichick told him, "You're fucked." This time, Epstein was thinking about Gregg Popovich and San Antonio.

"I read some stuff on the Spurs," Epstein said. "They're a great model because they are conscious of creating a culture where players opt-in for the greater good and sacrifice personal interest in order to win, in order to have the right rapport with each other.

"They value the same things, even after winning, and that can be hard," Epstein told me. "They're open, they talk about winning. Popovich is intentional with everything he does and the players hold each other accountable."

Epstein, already in the spotlight too much for his liking, got some unintended attention in the spring when *Fortune* magazine named him as "the World's Greatest Leader." Not the best executive in baseball or in all of sports, the greatest leader... *in the world.*

He beat out Chinese businessman Jack Ma, the Pope, Melinda Gates, and Jeff Bezos, among others. It was a ridiculous concept, who gives *Fortune* magazine the weight to name the World's Greatest Leader for one thing? For another, a baseball executive? (The entire list was silly. Ohio governor John Kasich was No. 12. Comedian Samantha Bee was No. 19.) But the idea behind it was sound: Epstein would sell magazines and create a buzz.

According to a story by Patrick Mooney, when Anthony Rizzo brought up this award in front of the entire team, Epstein joked, "I only have one thing to say about that. It's about fucking time."

"The pope didn't have as good of a year," manager Joe Maddon told reporters, echoing Babe Ruth's famous line about making more money than the president.

Epstein told me that spring he got "a significant amount" of grief from friends and family about the award.

"The less syllables I devote to it," he said, "the quicker it goes away."

Good leaders trust their followers and Epstein said he trusted his young players and felt better about the possibility for a repeat than he did in 2005, when the Red Sox made the playoffs but got swept out of the divisional round by the eventual champs, the White Sox.

What he was focused on was keeping the players healthy.

"Injury prevention," he told me on the second-floor balcony of the team's spring training facility one day. "I'm not going to prance around like we've got that figured out. That can disappear on you in a second. We do everything we can to find durable guys and guys who are invested in keeping themselves healthy and give them every resource. But it's so arbitrary."

Mostly, he was worried about starting pitch depth. But the Cubs didn't put big money into bolstering it. Instead, they brought in Alec Mills, Brett Anderson, and Eddie Butler, in addition to trading for Mike Montgomery in 2016 with the idea that he could start or relieve.

"The Mike Montgomery trade was made in large part for 2017," he said. "We realize position players probably aren't going to be our problem for a while, it's starting pitching depth. You look at the 2016 deadline, you're obsessed with finding a lockdown closer, but also finding someone who has a chance to be in or protect our 2017 rotation and that's a big part about what the Montgomery trade was about. I put the Montgomery, Mills, and Butler trades all in the same bucket."

As for repeating, Epstein couldn't focus on that and neither could the Cubs. That was talk for late October, not late February or March.

But the conversation was inevitable. For decades, the Cubs were associated with two things: day games and futility. October was always the goal for a team that could barely make it to July without falling apart, but now it was expected. The Cubs, as Belichick once opined, were fucked, and in a way, Epstein knew it, but it was his job to get them unfucked.

"The main reason it's hard [to repeat] is because it's so hard to win one," Epstein told me in spring training, in a bit of reasoning he liked to repeat to ground everyone's expectations. "There's only one team in the position to repeat each year. But also if you won the previous year it means your guys played, and more importantly pitched, for an extra month, so there are more innings, a shorter off-season. Every pitch thrown in October is a high-leverage pitch, a very stressful pitch, and that takes its toll."

The 2005 Red Sox were in a much different situation than the 2017 Cubs, as Epstein said. The Cubs young talent was overflowing, the maturity was evident. While the Cubs enjoyed their success that off-season, it didn't match the never-ending banquet circuit Terry Francona and the gang enjoyed in Boston. David Ross was on *Dancing with the Stars* but the rest of the group was intact and hungry.

"I guess my mindset is that there are going to be the normal ups and downs that occur every season and there's going to be an adjustment period," Epstein said to me. "I think different people are going to freak out when we lose eight of 10 going into the break like we did last year or we have an injury or players start out with bad first halves like it always happens.

"I think sometimes after you win there's this expectation that everything is going to be perfect, everything is going to proceed at a 100-win pace. Baseball is not that way and anytime you think it is, it bites in you the ass. I've always been trying to internally prepare guys for the things that are going to go wrong and we just have to stay the course and not panic and nothing changed because we won the World Series."

April began and the distractions started.

The Cubs started in St. Louis, losing the season opener, but winning four of the next five on the road. Then they returned to Wrigley for all the pageantry. One day for the World Series flags to go up, another for the ring ceremony.

In one of my dumber stories during spring training and to start the season, I asked Cubs which event a diehard fan, if they could only afford a ticket to one event, should be more excited for, the flag-raising or the rings? Talk about first-world problems, right?

I asked some players on my own, but I asked Epstein in a group interview before the season opener in St. Louis and he looked at me like "Who gives a shit?" But he recovered, as he often does.

"That's a good question," he said with a laugh. "I love that question. Please ask that question every year."

Rizzo had a more thoughtful response.

"If I were a fan, I'd probably say the ring ceremony," he told me at the end of spring training. "I don't know. I think hockey and basketball, as a fan, you can see it better because they're raising it to the rafters. Ours they're just raising it onto a flagpole. The reaction when we get our rings will be pretty cool."

"I'm a banner guy," Joe Maddon said. "The ring's a ring. I know it's wonderful, but I've never been that much into jewelry myself. But I do like banners. Especially in a ballpark situation, they're seen on a daily basis by everybody. I like the idea of when kids come in they get to see that and they hear about how they hadn't won in 108 years and all of a sudden there is one."

At it turned out, Rizzo was more right than Maddon, if that's possible for a subjective opinion. From the vantage point of the fans, the flags the Cubs raised looked tiny, particularly next to the enormous scoreboard in center field and the videoboards in left and right field.

After a rain delay—how fitting, right?—the Cubs made a big production of raising four flags—1907 and 1908 World Series ones, an NL pennant from 2016 and the World Series one—having players past and present take turns hoisting them, and when it was done, well, it was a

Kris Bryant with (from left) Crane Kenney, Theo Epstein, Jed Hoyer, and Jason McLeod as the team celebrates during the World Series ring ceremony on April 12, 2017, before a game against the Dodgers. (AP Photo/Matt Marton)

little underwhelming. The video productions and pomp and circumstance, like the Cubs entering the park from the outfield holding up the World Series trophy, was certainly memorable, but as one front office executive texted me during the game, the 2016 World Series flag looked like "a championship pocket square."

The ring ceremony was another chance to bask in the glow of yesteryear. I joined other reporters and photographers on the field to serve as a half-assed paparazzo for the pregame ceremony. The ring is the ultimate symbol of sports success, which is why Rizzo was correct in valuing this ceremony over the banner raising. Watching sports for fulfillment is the ultimate in reflected glory. When the Cubs win, the fans feel like winners too. When the Cubs get World Series rings, the fans have phantom pains from a giant rock on their fingers.

"It's really nice," John Lackey said after that game. "Seriously. I'm fortunate to have a couple more but this is next level. It's pretty sick."

Maddon called the rings "tasty" and "grande."

While the players mostly put their rings away for safe-keeping, plenty of Cubs employees wore their rings around the ballpark on game days. The Cubs, to their credit, gave rings to everyone, from low-level employees to past players to even recently fired employees like Rick Renteria and Jim Hendry. Every full-time employee got one and so did many of the seasonal employees. There were different levels of rings, so a security guard didn't get the same one as, say, Crane Kenney. But everywhere you looked in 2017, someone in a Cubs shirt had a ring on. Broadcasters, mid-level executives, septuagenarian ushers.

And of course, some front-office employees kept track of which of their peers were wearing their ring too much. Ballplayer types would tell young, single baseball operations executives to make sure to flash the ring when they were out on the town.

Steve Bartman even got a ring in a private ceremony in late July. Both he and the Cubs released statements afterward. Bartman wrote he was "deeply moved" and "sincerely grateful" that the Cubs included him in their largesse.

"I am relieved and hopeful that the saga of the 2003 foul ball incident surrounding my family and me is finally over," he wrote.

That didn't stop national writers and bloviators from debating if he should also throw out a first pitch. Which, of course, he should not do.

Because it was the Cubs and these things happen, it got out that the organization had non-players sign an agreement that essentially forbade them from selling their rings. The Cubs looked a little tacky doing this, but even general manager Jed Hoyer told reporters he signed it willingly. Of course, that stipulation wouldn't really affect Hoyer. Why would a millionaire executive sell a ring? A scout's ring, one who was no longer with the organization, did wind up on an auction website, but was eventually pulled off.

David Ross took a break from his busy dance schedule to attend the ring ceremony. Ross was fully invested in his second career of being David Ross. Not only was there *Dancing with the Stars*, he was also calling games for ESPN, he co-wrote a book that was optioned into a movie, he appeared with teammates on *Saturday Night Live*, made it to Ellen DeGeneres' show, and had a cereal commercial. Plus he was employed by the Cubs as one of their ex-player "special assistants."

A managing future seemed to be in his future, perhaps replacing Joe Maddon when his contract expired. But first, he had money to make.

As Johnny Damon and the gang learned in their rise to fame in 2004–05, there is earning power in a World Series ring. Ross' inclusion in *DWTS* got a lot of laughs in the Cubs' clubhouse, and while he ran the risk of overexposure, he also would say that he never got a Jon Lester contract. This was how he was making his living. Being yourself isn't a bad way to go about it.

"I'm so not stressed about anything in life other than dancing," Ross said after the ring ceremony. "That's more stressful than anything."

I asked Ross if he had been to church the day Lester signed with the Cubs, making his signing as Lester's personal catcher inevitable.

"I should've been, right?" he said. "When you're in free agency, I wasn't just trying to follow Jon Lester. I'm taking care of my family at that point. The fact that the Cubs wanted me as well as him is just special. That it worked is obviously the best decision I've ever made. I tell Theo [Epstein] all the time. He's like, 'Aren't you glad you didn't go here or there?' I said, 'I would've won there too, buddy.'"

But seriously, he said, "I feel like I'm the luckiest man ever."

And unlike his teammates, he didn't have to worry about an encore. He went out on top, like George Costanza dreamed.

While the Cubs' World Series celebration seemed to last the entire month of April, the winning did not. The Cubs went 13–11 that month, not awful, but a far cry from the previous season when they went 17–5 in April and were 25–6 through May 10.

On May 1, I asked Jon Lester about the team's slow start.

"Are we still in first place?" Lester said to me.

Yes, they were. Barely. The Cubs lost on May 1 and went into a tie for first with Milwaukee. By May 7, they were trailing the Brewers. By the end of the month, they were in third place, down 2½ games, after going 12–16 in May.

The Hangover, as we came to call it, was in effect and no amount of Pedialyte and greasy food could alleviate the symptoms.

One Cub who really couldn't duplicate his October magic was Kyle Schwarber.

On a Sunday afternoon in early June, I approached Schwarber at his locker and asked how he slept the night before.

"Luckily," he said, "I sleep well no matter what."

The previous day he had hit a grand slam, the first of his career, to give the Cubs a 5–3 win. It was his eighth of the season, which would put him on pace for 30. The problem was it was also just his 30th hit of the season. On the day we were speaking, Schwarber was slashing .166/.284/.354. He had struck out 63 times in 181 at-bats. "It's early" was morphing into "Is it too early to send him to Triple-A?"

To answer the latter question, it was. By about three weeks.

Schwarber didn't get into a hole by being too comfortable. In fact, the opposite was the problem. He would get to Wrigley Field at 1:00 PM for a 7:05 PM game. The work ethic that allowed his 1 percent chance of a comeback in 2016 to come true might not have been helping.

"We all know ourselves as players," he told me. "We know what helps and what doesn't help. There's going to be days where you think you need to go hit and there's going to be days where you're just like, I need to go relax a little bit."

Schwarber knew the whispers were out there about him getting demoted weeks before it happened. It would've been hard to ignore.

As it was going on, Schwarber was caught in the middle of trying too hard and being conscious not to overdo it, as the Cubs struggled around him. He could draw back on his 2016 experience, but he still needed to produce.

"What I went through last year, I think it does kind of help you realize you can get through anything," he said. "It's just time. I'm going to go out there and keep battling and I know this thing's going to change. I've got all the confidence in myself. I know that I'm a good baseball player and I can make adjustments."

Schwarber was finally sent down on June 22. He spent 11 days in Iowa, where he worked on his swing. He righted himself, hitting four homers and walking eight times in 44 plate appearances.

He was back by the first week of July and through his last 65 games of the season, he put up a .255/.338/.565 slash line. He hit 18 homers in those 200 at-bats and the Cubs went 40–25 in that span.

Schwarber's season was probably the epitome of Theo Epstein's well-worn line about "development isn't linear." We expected Schwarber to keep up his ascent from his rookie year based on how insanely successful his World Series return was. But baseball doesn't work like that.

Schwarber wasn't the only young hitter struggling in 2017. Addison Russell didn't make the statistical leap many expected from him, and then in early June, his wife, Melisa, announced on social media that he had cheated on her and she was leaving him. They shared a young son and she helped him when he had visitation from another child of his. In the comments section of her Instagram post about the relationship, her friend accused Russell of "mentally & physically abusing" Melisa and doing so in front of the children.

Major League Baseball began investigating the case, but as Melisa Reidy-Russell would tell reporters a year later, she put off cooperation until their divorce was final. This story faded away in 2017 but would come back in a major way the following season.

While some of the young players struggled to live up to their hype in 2017, one veteran outlived his usefulness. Or talked his way out of town, depending on how you look at it.

Miguel Montero was a popular player among reporters. He was honest, funny, and sharp-edged without being a dick. But Montero was at an interesting point in his career. As he showed after the World Series parade, he wasn't quite ready to ease into the life of a veteran backup catcher, which is essentially a part-time player, part-time coach.

While he was extremely helpful to Willson Contreras when his countryman was promoted, Montero still wanted to play. And while Ross got a lot of credit for his leadership, Montero was a leader as well, someone also unafraid to challenge his teammates.

Montero was the guy who coined the #WeAreGood hashtag in 2015. He was a spark. In late June, he told The Athletic's Sahadev Sharma that he felt like the Cubs were playing their way back to form.

"Early, I felt like we were going through the motions," Montero told Sharma. "'We got a great team again, we're going to win again regardless, it's gonna happen.' No. 'All we need to do is show up.' No. We need to play. It was not a secret. Yeah, we have a good team, but we were not playing like a good team. I may offend someone, but I don't care, because we're a team and we were all not playing good. I mean all of us. I didn't feel like we were 100 percent there on the field and I was concerned about that. I didn't like that. Doesn't matter who we play, we gotta bring our 'A' game. Because if we don't, doesn't matter if it's an A-ball team, they're going to beat us."

The Cubs were a couple games over .500 when he said that, but they were also a team at or near the bottom in several situational offensive categories. Still, he believed. On June 21, after the Cubs lost a game to the Padres, he tweeted: "Now I can say #weareback so here we come, put your seat belt on @cubs are about to take off." Why did he choose that time?

"I saw a lot of positive things," he told Sharma. "I saw a lot of guys being more excited, the body language was just different than early on. That's why I'm pretty confident in what I said when I said, 'We are back.' Because I believe it. It's just a different attitude now than it was early on. You can see it. I can see it, at least."

Six days after he sent that tweet and five days after he talked to Sharma in Miami, the Cubs lost to the Nationals 6–1 in Washington, D.C. The Nationals stole seven bases—Trea Turner bagged four of them—off Jake Arrieta and Montero. By this point, Montero's arm was regularly being called in question and he was a perfect 0-for-31 throwing out baserunners that season.

With his career seemingly nearing its end and his pride threatened, Montero didn't like the insinuation that Nationals' base-stealing frenzy was on him. He was mostly right about Arrieta, but the way he went about communicating that message set off his bosses.

"It really sucked because the stolen bases go to me," Montero said after the game. "And when you really look at it, the pitcher doesn't give me any time. So, it's just like, 'Yeah, okay, Miggy can't throw nobody out.' Yeah, but my pitchers don't hold anybody on. It's tough because it doesn't matter how much work I put on footwork and throwing and everything, because if I don't get a chance to throw—that's the reason they were running left and right today, because they know he was slow to the plate. Simple as that. Yeah, it's a shame, it's my fault I didn't throw anybody out."

Anthony Rizzo didn't hold back on his regular ESPN 1000 radio appearance with David Kaplan the next day.

"This is his second time barking in the media and not just going to his teammates," Rizzo said. "So, it's something that as a veteran like he is, you would think he'd make smart decisions about it.

"Listen, we win as a team, we lose as a team," Rizzo said. "If you start pointing fingers I think that just labels you as a selfish player, and I disagree. I disagree with that. I think we have another catcher that throws out everyone who steals, so… and he has Jon Lester, who doesn't pick over, you know, it's no secret. I think going to the media with things like that is just, I don't think it's very professional. We win as 25, we lose as 25, like I said, and to call your teammates out via the press is, I mean, what's the point?"

Montero didn't back down. He went on a different ESPN 1000 show and fired back.

"That's who I am," Montero said. "I'm made that way, and some people can't handle the truth. If you can't handle the truth, don't ask me then."

When one of the hosts asked if the team missed Ross' leadership, Montero said, "Nah, I don't think so," before adding, "But I don't know, maybe Rizzo misses him."

Sick. Burn.

And those were basically his final words as a Cub.

Theo Epstein was on a minor-league visit when Jed Hoyer alerted him to the initial postgame quotes. He said it took him about 10 seconds before he told Hoyer they might have to release Montero.

"I basically made my decision [Tuesday] night and wanted to sleep on it," Epstein told reporters after it was done. "I reached out to a number of people, including players, to make sure I was seeing the situation the right way."

This was a chance for Epstein and Hoyer to send a message to their .500 team. They released one of the heroes of their World Series run, a guy who helped change the narrative around the team in 2015. People who paint Epstein as some kind of technocrat wonk were wrong. He liked to preach about character, about selflessness. While Epstein is caustic and sarcastic at his core, he's also a bit of a romantic when it comes to sports.

"I just reminded Miggy that when something goes wrong on the field, we expect our players to take the blame," Epstein said. "To step up and proactively assume the blame for it, even if it's not their fault. That's the way to be a good teammate, to lighten someone else's load and assume that responsibility for yourself. And he completely agreed when I was pointing that out to him and he apologized and he realized that he had, in his words, messed up."

Arrieta is hardly a sensitive type. Who knows what he told Epstein in private, but publicly he stood up for his ex-catcher.

"I love Miggy," Arrieta said. "As you guys know, he'll say some things from the heart, the way he feels. He's open and honest. And that's the way Miggy is. I think that he regretted what he said, he felt bad about it. I told him that I'm not upset or mad at him, I didn't even really see the comments and I don't care what they were. I know what it was about and there was a lot of honesty there. I didn't do him any favors, slow to the plate and [Trea] Turner is one of the fastest guys in baseball."

On the same day, the Cubs visited Donald Trump in the White House, at the behest of the Ricketts family. Give credit to Todd Ricketts for making what turned out to be an accurate prediction:

"We're going to run into [the Nationals] in the playoffs and you're going to see them crumble," he said.

"Probably will," Trump replied.

(An amusing part of looking at the pictures that day was seeing how far GM Jed Hoyer was from Trump.)

Montero wound up getting claimed by the Blue Jays, but if Epstein and Hoyer were hoping for a shake-up with the move, it didn't do much.

From June 7 through July 26, the Cubs trailed in the NL Central. They went into the All-Star break not just with a 5½ game deficit, but a 43–45 record thanks to two home losses to Pittsburgh to end the first half. The Cubs were a losing team? That was a quick descent. Shouldn't a hangover be cured by the end of July?

After shining as the faces of the game the previous season, none of the Cubs who were on the World Series team made the NL All-Star team, a first for a World Series champion. Closer Wade Davis was their sole representative. While the rules had changed so Maddon, the NL manager, couldn't load his team with his own players, as Ozzie Guillen did in 2006, it was interesting that Cubs fans didn't vote a single player into the starting lineup.

Perhaps it was for the best. The Cubs were worn out and no one was complaining about missing the festivities.

But a very important moment in the Cubs season happened at the All-Star Game, just not on the field.

Let's flash back for a second. Back in late November as he assessed the Chris Sale trade market, ESPN's Buster Olney wrote that the White Sox wouldn't discuss a Sale trade with the Cubs because of their civic rivalry. Immediately, fans of both teams flipped out and it was a fairly big story in Chicago until Sale was traded to Boston. The Sox denied that angle, of course. But Cubs GM Jed Hoyer fanned the flames a little.

"Listen, I think both Theo and I have very good and very long relationships with Kenny and Rick," Hoyer told reporters. "We actually talk to them on a fairly regular basis. I guess I would just say that I wouldn't expect a deal to get done between the two teams. I think that they would always listen to a deal and think through the merits of it. But I don't think I'm saying anything that's unexpected."

After the season, I asked White Sox GM Rick Hahn if it would've been hard to trade Sale to the North Side.

"I want to say no because my job is to be objective and take the best deal and not be overly attached to a guy's name or his personality," he said. "If it were the first trade of this entire process and it was to move our most marquee name to the Cubs, on the other side of town, that might've been a bridge too far initially."

But in mid-July with José Quintana, it was a different story. After trading Sale to Boston for a package centered on fireballing pitcher Michael Kopech and Cuban infielder Yoán Moncada, followed immediately by trading Adam Eaton to the Nationals for three highly rated pitchers, the Sox didn't make another big trade for months.

But, along with signing Cuban free agent Luis Robert, trades were on their mind as they executed a Cubs-like teardown of a perennially disappointing team. The key difference between the 2012–14 Cubs and the 2017 Sox is the Sox had more high-end talent to immediately trade. It's not often Chris Sale– and José Quintana–type talents are on the market. The Sox's inability to build around their talents was a reason many owners would've cleaned house on the baseball operations side, but Jerry Reinsdorf is loyal to his employees and Kenny Williams and Rick Hahn took slightly different roles, with Hahn taking the lead on day-to-day duties and making deals.

So with the summer in full swing, and his team appropriately awful, Hahn got in touch with Epstein, who needed starting pitching—Brett Anderson and Eddie Butler weren't working out—and a shot in the collective arm of his team.

The conversation began with a demand from Hahn: Any deal begins with Eloy Jiménez and Dylan Cease. Epstein expected as much, those were his two best prospects, though he would've liked to have kept one of them.

"The deal had zero percent of chance happening without Eloy and Cease in it," Epstein would say later. "We were able to keep some other players out of the deal as additional pieces, as third pieces. We confirmed with Rick after the fact, there was just no way to make this deal happen without those guys."

But Quintana's almost insanely team-friendly deal was Hahn's figurative ace up his sleeve. Quintana was making just $6 million in 2017 and was set to make $8.35 million in 2018. His deal had two club option years for 2019–20 for a total of $21 million. Later, Epstein would say the contract itself was like an extra asset because it allowed them to pick up an elite pitcher at a low cost, which would then allow them to pay big bucks for another one.

Hahn's first sent text message about the deal came just after Epstein watched Jon Lester give up 10 runs to the Pirates. So his timing wasn't bad.

"I was actually sitting at my older son's baseball game the morning I wound up reaching out to Theo," Hahn said. "A buddy, a dad of one of his teammates, walks by me. I was sitting by myself over the left-field wall sitting on the bench. Parents had to walk by me to get to their seats. One of the dads, as he walked by, said, 'If there is anything I can add to the package to get Q to go to Milwaukee instead of the Cubs, let me know.'

"So, we laughed it off. Little did he know I had spent the last hour half-watching this game—I think my kid's team was getting no-hit—and half going through scouting reports on the Cubs.

"As we zeroed on a deal elsewhere and went through every club in baseball, it was, 'Here's the line, who can get over this line?' If the Cubs were willing to start something with Eloy and Dylan Cease, that put them above the line. We at least wanted to have the conversation."

So did Epstein, who needed something to mount a serious charge at a World Series repeat not just in 2017, but through the next few seasons as well.

As they dithered over the final details of the deal, Hahn was down in Miami at the All-Star Game with his son Charlie, hiding behind hotel plants talking to Theo and texting about players during the actual game. They settled on two minor leaguers (Matt Rose and Bryant Flete) and the deal was settled.

Some reporters, including at The Athletic, got wind of the possibility early (we had two stories ready), the deal itself stayed very quiet. In fact, the news was officially broken on July 13 via press release from both teams, sending the city's baseball into a state of shock and excitement.

A Cubs-Sox trade of the Sox's best starting pitcher and the Cubs' best hitting prospect? It was like two longtime listeners of The Score or ESPN 1000 got to be GMs for a day.

"This is the type of deal we've been looking to make for a long time," Epstein told reporters in a conference call after the deal was announced. "It ended up being a surprising dance partner for us. But I think it's a great baseball trade all-around."

The news was unofficially broken on Reddit, where two users named Wetbutt23 and KatyPerrysBootyHole discussed the deal on a White Sox subreddit (a discussion forum).

In the subreddit, KatyPerrysBootyHole posted: "Hey, take this with a grain of salt, but I heard from a friend who's brothers [sic] friend works for the cubs (sounds like bulls**t I know), that Q is going to the cubs in exchange for 4 players. Has anyone heard anything similar?" WetButt23 confirmed: "4 prospects. No pros. Players were meeting with doctors and will be official tonight or tomorrow."

Everyone had a good chuckle about it, though both teams front offices wondered who the leaker was. (When the Cubs opened the second half in Baltimore, Epstein was asked if they had another deal cooking and he cracked, "Ask WetButt.")

As for the Cubs-Sox angle, Hahn admitted it was a part of the internal conversation, but the return was too great to worry about it.

"People at least raised it," Hahn told me. "Were people going to be upset by it? What was going to be their reaction? It was the same thing with the rebuild. It didn't necessarily change anything we were going to do, but what would peoples' reactions were going to be. The sense we got, or the conversation we had, was people should be more upset if on that Sunday morning we see something better than what was on the table and we don't make a phone call because it's the Cubs. We don't travel down the path because of non-baseball-related issues or rivalries or ego or any nonsense that gets in the way.

"After the deal got done. That was on a Sunday and I think it was announced on Thursday. On Wednesday night after ownership signed off and we got the medicals, Theo and I were talking and he was actually the one who raised, he goes, 'I think both organizations should take a great deal of pride of not letting any of the BS get in the way of a good baseball deal that makes sense for both teams.' They've obviously felt it as well. They have had similar conversations as well."

Sox fans weren't bummed about Quintana. They were excited about Jiménez, especially when he started playing. While Epstein has compared Eloy to former Sox slugger Carlos Lee, Jiménez looked like a special talent.

In 29 games with the White Sox's high-Class A team in 2017, Jiménez put up a .345/.410/.682 line with eight homers in 110 at-bats. He didn't disappoint in 2018, eclipsing even optimistic projections with a .337/.385/.557 line and 22 homers in 108 games with the Sox's Double-A and Triple-A clubs. It was clear Jiménez was the best prospect in the system, eclipsing Moncada and the new pitchers.

And Cease looks like he'll be an impact pitcher in the majors after a very successful 2018 season in which the fireballer struck out 160 in 124 innings between two levels. He posted a 1.72 ERA in 10 starts with the Sox's Double-A team. With Michael Kopech shelved for the 2019 season following Tommy John surgery, Cease went into the season as the organization's top pitching prospect.

But what about Quintana?

While he didn't have the new prospect glow of those two players, he made a quick splash. In his first start in Baltimore, he showed a glimpse of why the Cubs valued him so highly.

Quintana didn't have a great start to the season on the South Side and it looked like it might jeopardize his trade value. He had a 5.22 ERA in April and that ballooned to 5.60 after giving up 15 runs in consecutive starts to end May.

But Quintana cleaned up his mechanics in June and the first two starts of July, with the Sox winning six of his seven starts and him putting up a 2.70 ERA in 40 innings. His timing was impeccable. One last gift to the organization that rescued his career.

"We had spent enough time going back to the winter meetings having conversations about Quintana with other clubs and internally about what is his appropriate value here," Hahn told me. "Then he gets off to a difficult start and bounces back and that shifts it a little bit. You've got less time on the contract, so that naturally changes the value and then you get a little closer to the deadline and teams get a little more aggressive, so the value changes again."

While they knew Quintana had to go for the sake of the rebuild, and Quintana was asked about being traded every single time he talked to reporters from SoxFest until his final start, it didn't make the conversation any easier for Hahn. Quintana was the kind of player that organizations dream about. He was a minor-league free agent they signed for nothing and he developed into an All-Star. He was low-maintenance, talented, and valuable. On top of that, he signed an extension for chump change.

"Literally when I'm on the phone with Q, I got text messages from a couple members of the Chicago media," Hahn said of his trade call. "One of them was like, 'Q to the Cubs?' One of them was, 'Eloy?' From two different people. I knew once I hung up with him, we're announcing this thing. So I had to cut the conversation short a little bit, which sucked, but I caught up with him next week when we played him. He was so gracious and so appreciative about everything we've done for him and how much he was going to miss. He was going on and I had to go."

The Cubs began the second half with two wins in Baltimore, with the offense putting up 19 runs. That set up Quintana on getaway day and all he did was throw seven scoreless innings, striking out 12 and walking none as the Cubs put up eight more runs. This set up an unrealistic expectation for the rest of his season, but the Cubs were rolling again. Theo's gambit worked. The Cubs swept their first two series out of the break and within two weeks were leading the NL Central for good. They won 13 of 16 to finish July. August wasn't as successful, but the Cubs managed to run off a five-game winning streak in the middle and a six-game one to go into September.

While they didn't cruise into the playoffs, they won seven in a row at one point in September and clinched their division on September 27 with four games left.

In 14 Quintana starts, the Cubs went 10–4 (he personally went 7–3), and he put up a 3.74 ERA with 98 strikeouts and 21 walks in 84⅓ innings.

The Cubs didn't add much after Quintana. They picked up reliever Manny Parra, backup catcher Rene Rivera, and outfielder Leonys Martin down the stretch. They would go into the playoffs as a 92-win team and the underdog in the NLDS.

Could they repeat? Sure. But it wasn't looking likely. While they went 49–25 after the All-Star break, there was no feeling of inevitability. Houston loomed large in the AL. But it did feel possible to make it back to the World Series.

First up were Dusty Baker's Nationals, a perennially disappointing franchise hoping for an October breakthrough before its star Bryce Harper left for free agency following the 2018 season.

Do you remember anything about that series except how it ended? I didn't before going back to write about it. The only thing I vividly recall is eating a bad meal before Game 3 at Wrigley Field and then driving over to Soldier Field after, a Cubs win to go up 2–1 in the five-game series, to catch the second half of Mitch Trubisky's first Bears start. I felt sick during the Bears game but attributed it to being tired and over-worked. But after the Monday Night game ended, so too did that fantasy. I was ill, and Soldier Field is about 30 miles south of my house in the suburbs.

I wondered how I would make it. I got all the way to the junction separating the Kennedy and the Edens before I had to pull over. Somehow I made it the rest of the way.

But my illness wasn't a subplot in this series. Stephen Strasburg's was. That's what you might remember, right?

On October 10, the day they were supposed play Game 4, Baker talked to the media after it was decided they would push the game back a day because of rain in Chicago. He said Tanner Roark would start Game 4 rather than Strasburg, who started Game 1.

Why? Because he was sick. Why was he sick?

"A lot of my team is under the weather with the change of weather and the air conditioning in the hotel and the air conditioning here," Baker said. "It's just this time of the year for mold around Chicago—I think it's mold. I mean, I have it, too."

Now, Baker wasn't wrong, per se, but it was probably too much information. A major league manager isn't supposed to talk about mold in hotel rooms when he's down 2–1 in a playoff series.

Needless to say, everyone was confused and a lot of people were making fun of Baker, a talented baseball man who took a lot of heat for how things ended in Chicago. And then, the next day, it turned out Strasburg would start, mold be damned.

"Well, he seemed, you know, more focused than normal," Baker said the following afternoon. "He just said, 'I'm feeling a whole lot better,' and, 'I want the ball.' That was kind of the gist of the conversation."

Strasburg was infamously shut down for the postseason in 2012 thanks to an innings limit that made sense in theory but was completely mishandled in practice. That team won 98 games and lost to St. Louis in the NLDS.

So this mold talk—Strasburg had a cold?—was a bad look for him and for Baker, who sometimes talked himself into the news.

What happened next? Well, Strasburg went out and shut down the Cubs for seven innings, striking out 12, and giving up no runs on three hits, and the Nationals got the series back to D.C. for a do-or-die Game 5.

Washington GM Mike Rizzo confirmed Strasburg was really sick and getting IVs and antibiotics the day before. With the season on the line, you had to imagine he was getting a lot of pressure to pitch, right? No, both he and Baker said. He just felt better.

"Woke up this morning, and you know, I wouldn't say I felt like great but, you know, I felt like I was better than what I was the day before," Strasburg said after that game. "And so games like this, you have to go out there and give it everything you have, whatever it is. So I called Mad Dog [pitching coach Mike Maddux] in the morning and said, 'Just give me the ball.' That's what he did."

The Cubs pulled Jake Arrieta with no outs after the fourth inning in Game 4. He had only given up one unearned run on two hits, but he had walked five and thrown 90 pitches. Jon Lester replaced him and threw 3⅔ innings of one-run relief. It was only 1–0 when Arrieta came out, so Lester was used because it was still a clinching scenario.

"Why not use Jon Lester right there?" Maddon said after the game. "He's done it before, he's one of the best pitchers in all of baseball, and I could tell before the game he was ready to do it.

"How? If he walked up to you the way he walked up to me before the game and the look in his face—he never comes up and gives me a fist pump before the game, never. Jonny's different tonight. I thought that's the feel part of it.

"The science part of it, his matching up against his team is a good thing. Also thought that he was going to bat third the next inning; not bad, not bad. Because even if somebody got on, he could bunt him over.

"So to me it was a good gamble. If it was 3–0, 4–0 against us, Jon would not have pitched it. Would have been [Mike] Montgomery and a cast of thousands. But the fact it was 1–0, I thought that's tantamount to 0–0, why not use Jonny right now? That's what he was there for, and that's what we had talked about. That's the thought process."

But Maddon also used Carl Edwards Jr. in the eighth. He lasted two batters, both of whom he walked. Then came Wade Davis, the closer. He gave up two hits and walked one without getting an out. One of those hits was a grand slam to Michael Taylor.

Brian Duensing and Justin Wilson had to finish it off. Aside from Lester, none of the other four relievers threw very many pitches, but it was still additional work in a short series.

Then again, who knew what was in store for Game 5? No one could've pre-written that game. And with the travel day erased because of the rainout, neither team were fresh for it.

The day for me started at O'Hare. I knew my friend Jesse Rogers was on my afternoon flight to D.C. But little did I know, so was celebrity fan Laurence Leavy, aka Marlins Man, the guy in the orange jersey at every sporting event. I can confirm he's the kind of guy who has loud, personal conversations on his phone as he waits to board a plane. I guess when you spend that much time at games, in spots where you're on TV constantly, you make time where you can.

When we reached the plane, I realized he was sitting next to Cubs owner Tom Ricketts in first class. Was that a good omen for the Cubs or just bad luck for Ricketts?

I was amused that Rogers, a frequent traveler, was also in first class. Meanwhile, I was sitting in a middle seat near the back of coach.

I got on the plane around 12:45 PM. About 12 hours later, I was in the maelstrom of a visiting clubhouse, plastic on the lockers, booze flowing everywhere. If you want to know what catharsis for baseball players feels and smells like, it was that room.

The first person I saw was GM Jed Hoyer, dressed in a T-shirt, shorts, and sandals to avoid ruining his work clothes.

"What the fuck just happened with this game?" I asked him.

He laughed.

"Hey," he said. "That game was an absolute mess."

Tell me about it. The Cubs won 9–8 in a game that took more than 4½ hours to finish. Thirty-eight total players were used and none of them could really explain what the heck just happened.

"We got by on pure guts, it was incredible," Theo Epstein told me. "It was not pretty. It was very, very gutsy."

"I've been a part of some weird ones," Lester said. "But as far as the score goes, yeah."

"At the end of the day," Jason Heyward said, "no one is going to say how it happened, just who won."

The Cubs trailed 4–1 in the second when Michael Taylor—yes, Taylor again—hit a three-run homer off Kyle Hendricks. Daniel Murphy had led off that inning with a solo shot. While Hendricks was the metronome of this team, doubt creeped in their minds.

"We thought early on, it was over," Lester said.

Hendricks managed two scoreless innings and the Cubs scored a pair of runs in the third inning to cut the deficit to one. Then came the fifth inning.

"The fifth inning was the single-weirdest inning I've ever seen in my life," Hoyer told me. "Without a doubt. I've never seen anything like it."

With a one-run lead, Baker brought in Max Scherzer, the ultimate flex. Scherzer would go on to win the Cy Young over Kershaw.

But, in typical Nats postseason fashion, things went awry. With two outs, Willson Contreras beat out a single, Zobrist followed with a base hit and Addison Russell hit a hard grounder between third baseman Anthony Rendon and the bag to drive them both in and give the Cubs a 5–4 lead. That quieted the park.

Okay, that part wasn't crazy.

But what happened next was.

The Nationals intentionally walked Heyward and Javy Báez reached on a passed ball strike three. It was a borderline call that could've been disputed, but wasn't.

Washington catcher Matt Wieters grabbed the ball and made a throwing error to first base on the play, which allowed Russell to score to make it 6–4.

Then pinch-hitter Tommy La Stella reached on catcher's interference and Jon Jay brought in another run when Scherzer hit him on the leg with the bases loaded. Now, the Cubs were up three.

"It was a series of bad events," Baker said later.

The Cubs added to their lead, but the Nationals got back into it with two runs in the sixth. The teams traded runs in the seventh and Washington got another one in the eighth when Taylor hit an RBI single off Wade Davis, who was the sixth pitcher Maddon had used since pulling Hendricks after the fourth.

José Lobatón followed with a hit, putting two on. With Trea Turner batting, Contreras threw to Anthony Rizzo on a pickoff move and the call on the field was safe. To us, it looked like Lobatón got back to the bag in time. But the Cubs coordinator for video scouting, Nate Halm, saw something and the call was overturned.

"Nate Halm, the video guy, deserves a ton of credit because with the naked eye it looked like he was clearly safe," Hoyer said. "But he picked up on that [Lobatón's foot] came off the bag and that was really honestly, probably the pivotal moment of the game. First and second, if they get a hit there, they tie it up and it's a different ballgame."

"We were trying to find a way to get to the finish line," Epstein said. "I didn't even think we were going to challenge it, but Nate saw something on the replay, his foot coming off the base, and that was a huge moment in the game to get an out without having to throw more pitches."

At this point, the only pitchers left were the almost unusable Justin Wilson and John Lackey. Quintana was already used in relief and Lester went the day before.

So it was Davis' game to finish and that's what he did. The game ended with Davis, on his 44th pitch of the night, striking out Harper for the Cubs' win.

How did Epstein feel watching this game, I wanted to know.

"Nervous as fuck and bemused," he said.

The next series wouldn't do much for nervousness or bemusement.

The Cubs flew straight to Los Angeles after the game, but the series never really got going for them. There was a feeling in the air of that Washington, D.C. clubhouse that night. The Cubs knew they were lucky and they knew their pitching staff was taxed. With that rainout screwing up the schedule, the Cubs would need some kind of infusion of energy. Kyle Schwarber wasn't coming out of the cornstalks like the second coming of Shoeless Joe this time.

The Cubs' best hope was the Dodgers pitching screwing up. And early in Game 1, that looked like a possibility.

The Cubs took a two-run lead in Game 1 when Albert Almora Jr. homered off Clayton Kershaw, a sentence no one really thought they'd write. But the Dodgers scored five unanswered runs off three Cubs pitchers—José Quintana, Héctor Rondón, and Mike Montgomery. John Lackey wound up pitching 1⅔ innings of mop-up work.

Game 2 didn't go much better for the Cubs hitters. Jon Lester didn't go long, getting pulled with two outs in the fifth and a whopping

103 pitches, but it was the hitters who were flummoxed by Rich Hill. The ex-Cub struck out eight in five innings and four Dodgers relievers combined to give up zero hits and zero walks.

(John Lackey, again, pitched the ninth and gave up two runs.)

Coming back to Wrigley with a 2–0 deficit, this felt more like the 2015 NLCS. The Cubs took an early lead when Kyle Schwarber homered off Yu Darvish, but the Dodgers chipped away with runs in four of the next five innings en route to a 6–1 win.

The Cubs hitters were M.I.A., an absence that would help cost hitting coach John Mallee his job. In the first three games, against very good Dodgers pitching, the Cubs managed 15 hits and just four walks. Not that Cubs hitters had a lot of opportunities to drive in runs, but when they did, they also failed, going 0-for-11 with runners in scoring position. Báez was 0-for-20, going back to the NLDS, and Rizzo, well, I glossed over the Rizzo moment in the NLDS.

In the eighth inning of Game 3, the Cubs were tied at 1–1 when Rizzo came up with a man on second, two outs, and first base open. Dusty Baker brought in veteran lefty Óliver Pérez and instead of walking Rizzo, Pérez pitched to him. Rizzo came through with a bloop single to center, scoring pinch-runner Leonys Martin. Rizzo, who was thrown out trying to take second on the hit, responded by yelling "Respect me!" on his way back to the dugout.

"I don't care," Baker said about that slight. "I'd have screamed, too."

But maybe crossing Dusty was bad juju because Rizzo went 1-for-25 over the next seven games.

The Cubs didn't quit after going down 3–0, holding a pregame meeting with the entire team. After their 3–2 win, some hitters held a postgame meeting. Jake Arrieta survived five walks and a homer to throw 6⅔ innings in his final start with the Cubs.

The Cubs felt Jake Arrieta's career had an expiration date and it was sooner rather than later. At a lower price, they would've likely rolled the dice on the known, but with Scott Boras at his side, Arrieta had resisted any overtures to sign an extension. In a way, I think the Cubs were relieved.

But whatever doubts they had about his future, no one could criticize what he had done for the Cubs, particularly in October.

In his nine postseason starts, beginning with that Wild Card Game, the Cubs won five times. His ERA was 3.08. He made two starts in the World Series and the Cubs won both times. He gave the Cubs their edge.

The Cubs could've used his bat, though. They only collected five hits in that Game 4 win. They could've used like 50 in Game 5, an 11–1 loss that ended any residual dreams of a Cubs repeat.

But the mood in the clubhouse was celebratory, if you can believe it. The season was over. The Cubs won 92 games and made it back to the NLCS. John Lackey was retiring. What was there to cry about?

"I mean obviously nobody likes to lose," Lester said. "We've been to the NLCS three years in a row. It's the first time in my career I got to do it. You know how special that is. I know obviously everybody goes back to the first half of the season and likes to nitpick. But we won the division, we made the playoffs, won the division [series] again and made it to the NLCS. You're not always going to be in the World Series."

Kris Bryant looked exhausted as he talked to us. Physically spent. Lester was drunk, as was Lackey.

"It caught up to me at last," Bryant said. "I feel pretty drained. But it's always a good thing to be one of the teams playing at the end of the year."

Quintana made it easy on everyone but himself, giving up six runs in two innings. The players were satisfied, but the front office was not. That's how it should be.

"It's hard to win 100 games in a year and we've done it," Lester told us that night. "It's hard to make it to the NLCS, or the CS period on either side, three years in a row and we've done it. So you know what, it's one of those Catch-22s. You look at it as it's a disappointing season because we didn't make it to the World Series, but you've got to look at the positives too. You've got to go home and whenever you get on the plane or get in your car and go home, you have to look at the positives. We gave ourselves a chance, it just didn't happen this year. We got beat by a better team."

CHAPTER 10

BIG BUSINESS AT WRIGLEY FIELD

By 2012, Tom Ricketts thought he had a deal with mayor Rahm Emanuel, the pro-business, pro-growth heir to longtime "Da Mare" Richard M. Daley, to help fund the renovations of Wrigley Field. They had moved past the idea of the amusement tax fund and into a more straightforward deal where the city gives the Cubs money.

Crain's Chicago reported at the time Emanuel was looking to give the Cubs at least $100 million to help finance the renovations, which would completely transform the Wrigley Field campus and the area around it, which the Ricketts family was gobbling up.

In 2011, the Ricketts family's real estate subsidiary paid $20 million for land on the northwest corner of Clark and Addison that contained a McDonald's and a large parking lot. A fight with the owners of the rooftops around the park would soon begin, going from ward meetings to federal court.

The long process of rebuilding and monetizing Wrigley Field would soon begin.

And then, the *New York Times* dropped a bombshell story.

On May 17, 2012, the *Times* released a story with the headline: "G.O.P. 'Super PAC' Weighs Hard-Line Attack on Obama."

The Super PAC in question was funded by Joe Ricketts, the founder of TD Ameritrade and the father of Tom Ricketts. While Joe knew almost nothing about baseball and went to fewer Cubs games than the average White Sox fan, it was, essentially, his money that paid for the team.

Beyond the obvious crassness of the idea—John McCain refused to link Obama and Rev. Jeremiah Wright Jr. in their 2008 election fight—what was the big deal? Everyone knew Joe was a big conservative donor. Pete Ricketts had used his chunk of family money to run, unsuccessfully, for a Nebraska Senate seat in 2008. Todd Ricketts was involved in Republican politics, while Laura Ricketts was the family's lone Democrat, and she was a big Obama supporter and a fairly prominent fundraiser.

Chicago is a Democrat's town, but it's not like the previous owners of the Cubs, the Chicago Tribune, were liberal. Daley, the Democratic machine mayor, took every chance he could to stick it to the Trib, his regular critics. The city gave Wrigley Field landmark status in 2004, which wound up costing the Tribune, and later the Ricketts family, time and money when it came to making changes on the protected parts of the park.

Emanuel, while being known as an across-the-aisle dealmaker in his days in Washington, D.C., was also running President Obama's 2012 re-election campaign. As the former chief of staff for the first African American president of the United States, he was not pleased when he found out the Ricketts family was asking him for money with one hand and paying to possibly run a divisive campaign to link Obama to his former pastor, Wright Jr., with the other.

In his historic win in 2008, Obama had to fight back criticisms of his relationship with Wright, whose more incendiary words on race and nationalism, cut and spliced into cable-friendly sound bites, were prime fodder for campaign stories.

Now, as Obama prepared to run again, Ricketts was spending big to defeat him. According to reports, both Pete and Todd Ricketts were there for the presentation that called for commercials linking Obama and Wright. The plan was titled "The Defeat of Barack Hussein Obama: The Ricketts Plan to End His Spending for Good." The group who created it even noted that it would have to combat assertions the campaign was racist and suggested hiring an "'extremely literate conservative African American' who can argue that Mr. Obama misled the nation by presenting himself as what the proposal calls a 'metrosexual, black Abe Lincoln.'"

In an awkward twist, months before this came out, the Cubs had hired Julian Green to be their vice president of communications and community affairs. Green, who is black, worked for both Obama and Richard M. Daley. It was believed Green's ties to Emanuel were a major factor in his hiring.

When the story came out, Emanuel refused to talk to Ricketts, making him grovel publicly, while leaking stories to local news outlets about how angry he was at the team.

Tom Ricketts immediately released a statement disavowing the ad campaign, which was never agreed upon, and reiterated the team's independence from his father's politics, despite two board members, his brothers, being very involved.

A week later, he told WLS 890, a talk radio station in Chicago: "The key for us is to make sure that people that know us and know the Ricketts family know that we weren't trying to do anything that was insensitive in any way and that the people that don't know us don't jump to any conclusions.

"The mayor has got a lot on his plate. Whenever we get around to talking about that, that's fine with me. I'm cool with whatever timing works. It's just a matter of we've just got to kind of get through this and get it behind us."

At a press conference, a reporter asked Emanuel why he hadn't returned Ricketts' calls and Emanuel just smiled and walked out of the room.

Emanuel wasn't someone to piss off. A mayoral source told the news stations Emanuel was "livid" at the Ricketts' "blatant hypocrisy."

But after Obama's win over Mitt Romney, Emanuel held a press conference on January 23, 2013, where he sounded amenable to making a deal to get construction started at Wrigley Field, if the Rickett's family were footing the bill.

"When I first started this discussion, the Cubs wanted $200 million in taxpayer dollars. I said no," the mayor said, according to a *Chicago Tribune* article. "Then they said we'd like $150 million, and I said no. Then they asked whether they could have $100 million in taxpayer subsidies, and I said no. Then they asked about $55 million in taxpayer subsidies. I said no. The good news is, after 15 months they heard the word 'No.'"

This press conference infuriated at least one Ricketts family member, Todd.

"I think we should contemplate moving, or at least recognize that we are maybe not the right organization to own the Cubs," he wrote in an email to his father and siblings that day. Splinter News published the email in December 2018 as part of a series called "The Billionaire's Inbox," which consisted of a trove of Joe Ricketts emails, that got him in hot water.

Todd later replied, "I just hate the thought of Tom having to grovel to this guy to put money into a building we already own."

Joe Ricketts responded, "Yes, Todd, it makes me sad, it hurts my feelings to see Tom treated this way. He is way superior to the Mayor in every way. I have been brought up to deplore the type of value system adopted by the Mayor of Chicago. This is stating it mildly."

After Joe Ricketts' racist and Islamophobic emails were released, Emanuel put out a biting statement agreeing with Ricketts about their different values.

By March 2013, the Cubs floated a threat—or at least tacitly encouraged—to move to the team to Rosemont, the business-centric village that is home to convention centers, hotels, office buildings, and O'Hare International Airport. The land for the stadium would be adjacent to a runway.

David Kaplan, the colorful, bombastic multimedia king of Chicago sports, is the one who created the story. He reported that the mayor of Rosemont wanted to give the Cubs free land to build a new stadium free from Chicago meddling. It was a cynical, foolish idea—the Cubs would leave a cash cow in the middle of a bustling city to build a park directly next to one of the busiest airports in America?—which meant it got a lot of play in Chicago.

Considering the Cubs cultivated a fan base of drunk 20-somethings, Chicago-based adults, and rich North Shore adults, the Rosemont plan was an obvious bluff, but enough journalists in town took it seriously to make a running story, including the editorial page of the *Chicago*

Tribune, the most pro-business editorial section left of the *Wall Street Journal.*

Other teams in town, particularly the Bears and White Sox, had threatened to leave for the suburbs when they were fighting for city, county, or state money. So this wasn't a new plan, just a nonsensical one. In the end, cooler heads prevailed.

On April 15, 2013, the Cubs and the city unveiled plans for a $500 million (up from $300 million) renovation of Wrigley Field and the surrounding area, anchored by a hotel in the McDonald's property and a giant office building where the Cubs' parking lot sat on Clark Street. The latter building had been discussed for years and a previous deal the Cubs made with the city over renovating the bleachers included a provision for them to build a so-called "Triangle Building" in that space.

Ricketts' new plan included more night games, advertising signage, and, most importantly, at least one giant videoboard. That addition would trigger a drawn-out fight with the rooftop owners, one that was settled in federal court, and require city approval because of the ballpark's landmark status, which protected the "sweep and contour" of the outfield. Wrigley Field's alderman Tom Tunney wasn't laying down for the Cubs and became their nemesis in their fight to modernize and monetize the park.

The team had a 20-year contract with the rooftop owners, signed in 2004, to give them views of the park in exchange for a healthy cut (17 percent) of their gross revenue, which they got for charging fans an arm and a leg to sit on a rooftop and drink beer.

As you might recall, Tom Ricketts pitched his father on buying the Cubs at a rooftop party.

On July 12, 2013, the Cubs got an approval from the city's landmark commission for most of what they asked for, including the installation of a very large videoboard (commonly known as a jumbotron) in left field, along with other signage in right field (which became another videoboard) but the Cubs refused to start the process until they could get the rooftop owners, who had banded together, to promise not to sue them.

That the landmark commission approved the Cubs' wishes without the support of their alderman, breaking typical Chicago procedures, showed that Emanuel, despite his bluster, was backing the Cubs.

A year later, with nothing started, the commission approved a beefed-up proposal that was moving closer to $600 million. The rooftop owners tried to negotiate, but were mostly rebuffed.

I was at some of the city council meetings during this period as a reporter for ESPN. Perhaps my favorite public comment came from a man named David Duggan, who asked for the state department to possibly look into the new LED lights that were going to be put in the ballpark because they might interfere with the Migratory Bird Treaty Act of 1918. Duggan told the audience the lights would harm migratory bird behavior along the Mississippi Flyway in mid-October, if the Cubs were playing, that is.

"I'm here to speak for the birds," Duggan said.

In late May 2014, the Cubs decided to go through with their plans, even with a lawsuit pending. The construction would begin in July on the former parking lot abutting Clark and Waveland, with underground construction on the new clubhouse compound.

The project was now being ticketed for $575 million and included a second videoboard in right field. This was a new addition to the plan, which was growing more aggressive.

A week before the Cubs announced that change, Tom Ricketts filmed a video declaring the team was done waiting for the rooftop owners and that their previous 20-year deal with the group allowed expansion with governmental approval to Wrigley Field's landmark status.

In August, the rooftop owners sued the city, not the Cubs, for not following the 2004 landmark rules and for denying them property rights, as the Cubs could now strong-arm them out of business. They later sued the Cubs as well, but lost both court battles.

With the value of certain rooftops supposedly declining, especially with the unknown views going forward, the Cubs wound up buying several buildings for themselves and cultivating working relationships with other ones. Despite the cries from rooftop owners, their business still does fairly well, with fans clamoring for the ever-changing, but still enjoyable Wrigley Field experience. The left-field videoboard doesn't block any views, while the right-field one abuts the foul pole. It was made famous when Kyle Schwarber hit a homer on top of it during the 2015 NLDS.

Crane Kenney, the team's president of business operations, was often the heavy in the news. But for whatever faults he had—he tended to get himself into trouble when speaking to the media or negotiating with rooftop owners—Kenney worked hard on the Wrigley renovation.

While some fans rightfully worried about how the Cubs would modernize the park, Kenney said they were thoughtful about it the entire time and the results prove him correct.

"We are going to be incredibly authentic, almost religious about what makes Wrigley Field special," he said of his thinking at the time. "We were harvesting lots of photos from the '30s, which is when we felt the ballpark had its prime appearance before the Wrigley family took down the wrought iron and terra cotta before adding chain-link fences."

Kenney said he went to Tim Samuelson, the city's cultural historian, for a personal architecture tour of the city. The thinking was, "What would Zachary Taylor Davis, the architect of Wrigley Field, do today?"

Obviously add enormous videoboards. But besides that.

Kenney also used his fact-finding mission to make trips to Augusta National, Keeneland Racecourse, Fenway Park, the Rose Bowl, Lambeau Field, Madison Square Garden, any famous venue that had undergone renovations in recent years.

But even the Cubs' research had some ulterior motive. They were going to use the renovations to get a tax break for taking care of a historical landmark. The devotion to history was part of the pitch.

A view of the back center-field entrance of Wrigley Field on March 18, 2015, as construction crews and equipment can be seen as part of the 1060 Project.
(AP Photo/Scott Boehm)

Once the Cubs got all the green lights from the city, the 1060 Project began. Kenney used to work in a cramped office space inside Wrigley Field. When we spoke on the phone in late November 2018, he was overlooking ice skaters at a rink in the park below the looming office tower.

The Cubs' changes have certainly altered the tenor of the neighborhood and the area bars and Cubs-related stores were right to be nervous. Through the end of 2018, at least, the changes, though, seemed largely successful. The best addition is probably that park that adjoins Clark Street, the Cubs' new office tower, and Wrigley Field.

While the team fought with alderman Tom Tunney over restrictions to the park—namely that only ticket holders can access it during game time and the lead-up to it—those rules might actually be beneficial to the fans that use it, if not the Cubs' beer sales.

No matter how much money the Cubs put into Wrigley Field, it's always going to be a little cramped. This park, which contains seating, a small green space, and vendors for food and drink, allows fans to hang out and enjoy the weather, while watching the game on a massive videoboard attached to the office building. For fans with children, it's been particularly popular.

The Hotel Zachary opened along with the 2018 season and it contains several middle-to-higher-end restaurants, along with a spot for a brand-new McDonald's and the Chicago-famous Mexican restaurant Big Star. After the season ended, the infamous Taco Bell on Addison was torn down.

By 2018, the Cubs' office building housed two bars, a large team store, a Starbucks, and an ice cream shop.

Construction was ongoing over the winter of 2018 alongside Sheffield and Addison, where the team was adding a new bar and renovating the visitors clubhouse.

One of the biggest changes for 2019 is that three new clubs are opening. In 2018, the Cubs opened the 1914 Club, a 700-ticket private club for the priciest of ticket holders, those in the first few rows between the dugouts. The tickets for those seats were increased by a significant amount, with new prices in 2018 ranging from $400 to $695, for the all-you-can-eat-and—with the exception of the really expensive booze—drink options.

The 1914 Club is the realization of the Cubs' dream to separate wealthy fans from their money with the promise of exclusivity and what passes for opulence on the North Side of Chicago. Unlike the private clubs at Yankee Stadium and Dodger Stadium, this one is a touch more understated.

While Yankee Stadium's pricey club offers a table of seafood fit for a king, the 1914 Club is more of a slider and pizza type of affair.

I wrangled a ticket to it through a relative and went to an early-season game. I didn't tell the Cubs I was coming, preferring to act like one of those restaurant reviewers who never publish their face.

Unfortunately, the Cubs do know my face and I was spotted within five minutes. The advantage of losing my anonymity was that I could sic my father-in-law's first cousin Chuck on the Cubs executives. Chuck, mentioned in the World Series chapter, is around 70, very successful, and opinionated. It was, I must say, a treat to watch him tell Kenney that they need to put out some fish or something on a regular basis. (On that day, there was a giant pig on a spit.)

For years, the Cubs only had the Audi Club (a private dining room), the Assurance Club (a relatively new suite in left field), the Dell EMC Legends Suite, the center-field Fannie May Bleacher Sweet, and, of course, luxury suites.

But, starting in 2019, they added the Maker's Mark Barrel Room and W Club, located on the first- and third-base sides of the lower level. Each of those clubs are attached to 250 seats. The 400-ticket Catalina Club replaces the concession stand and patio underneath the press box behind home plate in the upper deck. Tickets range from $235 (Catalina Club) to $495 (Maker's Mark Club).

One positive for the masses was an expansion of concession options in the upper deck, which had been completely ignored in the first few renovation cycles.

Still, though, the Cubs remain unsatisfied with what they got from the city. The Ricketts family reportedly backed a political-action committee to challenge Tunney, the ward's alderman. At the Cubs Convention, they devoted part of a panel to ripping Tunney to the fans.

While the construction was almost done, the Cubs hadn't yet reaped immense profits. Their current TV deal expires after the 2019 season, and in February 2019 they announced the creation of Marquee Sports Network, a joint project with Sinclair Broadcasting Group. The ongoing construction was expensive. But the neighborhood was changing and modernizing, for better or for worse.

CHAPTER 11
ENIGMATIC '18

The Cubs' 2017 season ended on October 19 at Wrigley Field. On October 21, pitching coach Chris Bosio's contract option wasn't picked up.

Five days after that, Cubs hitting coach John Mallee was let go, as was third-base coach Gary Jones.

All three coaches were in place before Maddon was hired, with Mallee getting the gig in his hometown shortly before the Cubs parted ways with Rick Renteria in 2014.

And thus began the off-season from hell.

Bosio was replaced by Maddon's old pitching coach in Tampa Bay, Jim Hickey. Mallee by Boston's hitting coach, Chili Davis, and Jones by Boston's third-base coach, Brian Butterfield.

Prior to Game 4 of the NLCS, Maddon was asked if he wanted his coaches to return.

"Yes, of course," Maddon said. "The staff's done a great job. Our staff's been awesome. And they're tight. It's a tightly knit group. There's a lot of synergy involved, nobody knows everything. Everybody helps everybody, there's a lot of cross-pollination. Nobody's on their own little island. I like that."

After the season ended, Epstein was asked about the coaches as well. His response was much different.

"We're actually not yet at a point where we've extended any formal invitations," Epstein said. "We started the process of having exit meetings today with the coaches and players. So I don't want to comment on the makeup of the coaching staff until I know what it is exactly. It's a two-way street also. There are invitations, but there are other factors, coaches having opportunities elsewhere. But rest assured, Joe will have every coach back that he wants back. On the whole, it's a great group that worked extremely hard to help accomplish the things we've accomplished the last three years."

That phrase, "Joe will have every coach back that he wants back," stuck out. Needless to say, our antennas were up. While Bosio was best described by Epstein as "a force of nature," he was also hard-headed and grating. While he certainly helped his pitchers achieve great things with the Cubs, there was a sense everyone, or almost everyone, was ready for a new voice. There was also talk the Cubs thought about letting him go the previous year, but a World Series win saved some jobs, as it should.

Bosio had some health issues with his diabetes during the year, and took a little time off to visit his father before he passed away during the season, but those personal matters didn't factor into the Cubs' decision to not pick up his contract option.

But something as quotidian as the bullpen's high walk rate could've had something to do with it. The Cubs were last in bullpen walk rate during the season and the only team in baseball with an unintentional walk rate over 10 percent.

"We have to figure out a way to help develop those guys and get them more consistent," Epstein said at that time. "And throw more strikes across the board in the bullpen. That's partly a player personnel thing but I think it goes beyond that a little bit because if you look at—and we have—virtually every reliever we have walked more guys this year on a rate basis, unintentional walk rate, on average through their career. So it was common. It could be a fluke or it could be there were certain situations we tried to be too fine, or certain situations we didn't prioritize getting a strike at the risk of some hard contact. We're going to look at it."

Epstein was quick to deflect some credit from Bosio for his most famous pupil, Jake Arrieta, who went from Baltimore castoff to Cy Young winner in two years. Arrieta, after all, is the one who did the work.

"It was definitely an organizational success, but I don't want to answer that in a way that takes anything away from Jake," Epstein said. "It was his success, first and foremost. This guy wanted it so badly and was so eager to improve and learn and looked at his whole life, every different facet of his life—nutrition, exercise, personal habits, mental skills, mindset, and everything else. He looked at all of that as an opportunity to get better."

But, it should be said Bosio was the most important coaching hire Epstein made before Maddon came aboard. Bosio came on with his friend and ex-teammate Dale Sveum, who, despite his early exit from the Cubs, made his impact with the rebuild simply with that move.

While Epstein and his staff knew how to set up a pitching infrastructure, Bosio helped set up a foundation. He didn't have much to work with at first, but Epstein started to get him some talent and the relationship blossomed.

Bosio wound up going to Detroit to work with manager Ron Gardenhire, but a reported racist comment in the coaches' locker room got him fired midway through the 2018 season. Mallee ended up in Philadelphia and Jones became a minor-league manager.

A Cubs source said they would've probably kept Mallee, or at least offered him a chance to stay, but they would've required him to change some of his hitting methods to de-emphasize launch angle and work on an all-fields approach that Joe Maddon wanted to see from some of his hitters. That would've been tough.

Mallee and Jones were, to use a phrase that was popular around Wrigley Field, "Renteria'd." Which is to say, they weren't fired for poor performance, but because someone better came along.

Epstein and Maddon were both very high on Davis, who played in the Angels system during Maddon's heyday there and worked under Epstein in Boston. Chili Davis was a very popular and successful hitter in his time and he had a good rapport with hitters in Boston. The Cubs promoted minor league hitting coordinator Andy Haines to replace Eric Hinske, who moved on to a new job with the Angels.

"I think what Chili brings as a hitting coach that's different from John, to a certain extent, this is a guy that had an incredible career, almost a 20-year career as a switch-hitter in the big leagues," Hoyer told me that spring. "His gravitas is remarkable. His connections with hitters is remarkable. His ability to talk through an at-bat or a game from a strategic standpoint—'Here's how to compete with this pitcher. Here's what we need to do in this situation.'—I think is probably unrivaled.

Our guys have developed the physical skills both before they got to the big leagues and then working with John Mallee. They've developed these things, but I think the next gear for us, the next step, is that complete team offense. That ability as a young veteran to think through your at-bats and learn from what happened before, I think Chili is going to bring that maturity that he had as a hitter. I think he'll help instill that in our guys."

Butterfield was an energetic coach who specialized in base running and infield defense. The Cubs were an excellent base-running team under Maddon, and their infield defense wasn't so shabby either with Kris Bryant, Addison Russell, Javy Báez, and Anthony Rizzo.

But it could always be better, right?

"A lot of it is just based on availability," Maddon told reporters in a conference call after the moves happened. "I've known Butter for a long time. He's an excellent third-base coach and beyond that he's a really outstanding base-running coach too. We wanted to add that skill set to our group. I've known [Chili] for a long time also. I worked with him with the Angels. He's really good in regards to getting our hitters to the next level situationally.

"Two out of the last three playoffs we've really been bogged down [offensively] in the playoffs," Maddon said after the Davis hire. "Two outstanding [pitching] staffs, so it's hard to argue against that. We're just looking for a slightly different voice with a little bit different approach that we feel can augment our hitters moving forward. That's it. If I start saying anything else, I'm just making it up. That's pretty much what it comes down to and the fact that Chili was available."

As for Hickey, the Cubs felt, in unison, a different voice was needed.

"It's among all of us," Maddon said after the move was made. "It's myself, it's Theo, it's Jed. It's a conversation. You can never make a unilateral decision like that, I don't believe. I don't feel comfortable doing that. It has to be a group deal, we have to agree."

So, three new coaches, a good start, right? Nope. Two of the three would be gone by the following Thanksgiving.

After a strong postseason, Jake Arrieta walked as a free agent, looking for a nine-figure deal. Lackey didn't officially retire right away, but the Cubs weren't going to bring him back. While they wanted his attitude before the 2016 season, some thought he was a bad influence on Lester with his grumpiness. The Cubs also lost Alex Avila, Wade Davis, and Jon Jay, all good veteran influences.

Davis, especially, was a guy they wished they could keep, a one-year rental who wound up being a mentor to pretty much every reliever in the Cubs bullpen.

"Not only have I learned a lot about pitching, but being the right kind of guy off the field," former Cub Justin Grimm told me in 2017. "Whether it's how you treat people, sometimes the way you're speaking to your wife. Everything, man. He's been great to have around."

Grimm, a renowned free spirit, told me he wanted to live every day like Davis, who was serious but funny, and more importantly, someone in control of his life. He never seemed to be distracted.

"I have this joke, 'Do Wade,'" Grimm said. "Every morning I wake up and I say, 'Do Wade.' He gets mad. He doesn't like that. He'll look at you and say, 'I don't know, man. I don't know what I'm talking about, but here's what I think.'"

Maddon, who had Davis as a starter in Tampa Bay, described Davis as more than a reliever.

"Wade is a pitcher," Maddon said. "You say he's a closer, but a lot of closers are pretty much just animals and they throw. He knows how to pitch out there."

And his success paid off. Davis signed a three-year, $52 million deal with the Rockies on December 30. Three weeks before that, the Cubs paid a little less money for what they thought was a lot more pitching.

On December 7, the Cubs signed their first new player and it was kind of a big deal. The winter free agent marketplace hadn't got going yet, and the winter meetings were days away. But in the Cubs' swank new office building, they held a small press conference for new pitcher Tyler Chatwood, who signed a three-year, $38 million deal. The Cubs felt lucky to get him, despite middling numbers, thanks, in part, to pitching his home games at Coors Field.

Around this time, the Cubs were still in on Shohei Ohtani, the two-way star from Japan. While Epstein couldn't say much about that doomed pursuit, he was happy to praise his new pitcher.

"Uber-talented right-hander moving into his prime," Epstein said that evening. "He has great make-up. We think his best days are ahead of him. We're getting him into an environment where we think he can gain consistency with all of his pitches and play to his strengths a little bit more."

In his Chatwood story that night, The Athletic's Sahadev Sharma wrote what turned into a chilling warning of what was to come: "Chatwood has walked 10.7 percent of the batters he faced at home compared to 11.9 percent on the road. Command is a major issue for Chatwood. One that the Cubs struggled with as a staff last season (mostly out of the bullpen) and one that is only exacerbated when you're allowing home runs at the clip he did last summer. But the walks seem to be the only issue that really lingers once Chatwood leaves Coors."

A week later at the winter meetings in Disney World, the Cubs continued to add pitching, signing relievers Brandon Morrow and Drew Smyly.

Morrow, who pitched against the Cubs in the 2017 NLCS, was signed to close in place of Davis, while Smyly was recovering from surgery and thought to be a possible bullpen arm at the end of the season and maybe an option for the rotation in the future. Morrow had injury problems of his own, but he signed a two-year, $21 million deal with a team option for 2020.

And then, when the Cubs reported to spring training in February, they made their big move, signing pitcher Yu Darvish to a massive six-year, $126 million deal that was marketed as a bargain because he originally wanted like $150–175 million, before the free agent market froze over.

Yu Darvish signs autographs at 2018 spring training in Mesa, Arizona.
(AP Photo/Carlos Osorio)

So, let's run through the 2018 performances of those big off-season additions again with a year-plus of hindsight.

Jim Hickey: one year, resigned for personal reasons.

Chili Davis: one year, fired because the players didn't jibe with him.

Chatwood: in his first year, he walked 8.25 batters per nine innings and was summarily benched.

Darvish: he made eight starts and compiled a 4.95 ERA and, despite a long rehab process, made his last major league start on May 20.

Morrow: he had 22 saves, but last pitched on July 15 before going down with an injury.

Off-season from hell. (In the Cubs' defense, reliever Steve Cishek's two-year, $13 million deal immediately paid dividends.)

The Cubs also said goodbye to bench coach Dave Martinez, Maddon's longtime right-hand man. Martinez surprisingly was the beneficiary of the Nationals firing Dusty Baker, getting that long-awaited managing gig most thought was past his reach.

The Cubs replaced him with organizational stalwart Brandon Hyde and they not-so-secretly hoped his new role would spark Maddon to be a more focused manager in 2018. They replaced Hyde at first base with former player Will Venable, who was also helping the Cubs with base stealing.

The Cubs, Dodgers, Texas Rangers, New York Yankees, Minnesota Twins, and Milwaukee Brewers were all interested in Darvish's services and the Cubs won out with money and a strong presentation that appealed to him and his wife.

"The Cubs—they know how to recruit a player," his agent, Joel Wolfe, told The Athletic's Patrick Mooney. "It's like the University of Alabama. They go the extra mile."

Darvish's quirky personality came out through the drawn-out process.

According to Mooney's story, Darvish sent Epstein a photo of Darvish as a young boy in a Cubs shirt. When Epstein half-jokingly accused Darvish of only waiting on the Dodgers to sign with the Cubs, Yu texted the same picture back to him.

Darvish spoke without an interpreter to Epstein and Hoyer, preferring to communicate in his own words. The Cubs didn't just BS him either.

"It wasn't just telling him what he wanted to hear," Wolfe told Mooney. "It was legitimate. He showed up, he asked a lot of questions. They asked him a lot of direct, blunt questions. He's a very honest guy. When he starts speaking in English with you, you'll see. He really felt it."

While Heyward didn't feel the need for a face-to-face meeting two years prior, the Cubs won Darvish over by meeting him.

"We like to meet in person," Epstein said at the time, "just to understand where a player is coming from, what motivates him, where he is in his development, off the field as well as on the field, what they're looking for out of a destination.

"He had put a lot of thought into things that had gone right in his career, things that he wanted to continue to improve, and what his goals were for the rest of his career.

"We were able to engage and have a pretty in-depth baseball conversation about ways that he could maximize his deep arsenal of pitches and fit in with our approach to trying to get guys out. Without that meeting, we probably don't end up here with Yu."

It was a big deal. Here's a pitcher with pure stuff, signed at a relative discount, to join three All-Star-caliber pitchers in Jon Lester, Kyle Hendricks, and José Quintana. Seemingly everyone agreed that if Chatwood is your fifth starter, you're doing well.

Darvish was years removed from Tommy John surgery and his velocity was there. Unlike the Cubs' other big starters, he was a strikeout guy. They were missing that from the rotation.

While he pitched well against the Cubs in the NLCS in 2017, he faltered quite publicly in the World Series. Some Astros hitters suggested he was tipping pitches, which is easily fixable. Others wondered about his mental makeup, an always tricky tightrope to walk.

"I think there were a lot of reasons for what happened in the World Series," Epstein said at Darvish's introductory press conference. "From the possibility of tipping pitches, the difficulty with the baseballs, and then the Astros were red-hot. They won the World Series for a reason. They were swinging the bat great against everybody.

"But I don't think we'd be doing our jobs if we evaluated based on a two-game sample. He's been over here for six years. He's proven himself as an elite pitcher, a top-of-the-rotation guy who can make adjustments, too, when things go wrong, like they do for everybody in this game."

"If anything, I think getting close to a championship and not getting all the way there has only increased his motivation and his focus on winning a World Series. And that's what we're here to do as well."

Regardless of any concerns, the Cubs were hungry to improve and with a young core of hitters returning, the rotation was the place to do it on a major scale.

The slow free-agent market was a major storyline as spring training began and many high-end players were still without jobs. Agents like Scott Boras were excoriating the owners. The players and their union were upset. Words like "collusion" were being thrown around and not without reason.

The Cubs could at least claim to be one of the more active teams by filling pitching openings. The state of the market turned out to be beneficial for them, as Darvish's initial asking price dropped to a manageable level for them.

When word got out the Cubs were signing Darvish, it cemented them as contenders to return to the World Series. Did they have the best rotation in baseball? Maybe.

On February 13, the media staked out the parking lot of Sloan Park waiting for Darvish to arrive for his press conference.

Reporters, armed with their smartphones, snapped picture after picture of nothing, tweeting their work to the world and letting everyone know they were on the scene.

What's that old saying: a picture of Darvish walking through the back door of the Cubs' facility is worth a thousand tweets?

His press conference was held in the small Cubs' media room in their spring training facility, with reporters filling up every inch of space, including on the floor.

"He was atop our wish list, but early in the off-season we didn't think it was very realistic," Epstein said. "We knew we had to add a lot of quality and depth to our pitching staff and that would require some volume. Like all teams, we have a budget and we needed to figure out a way to add the talent and depth that we needed but also stay on target with our short- and long-term financial planning as well.

"Around the winter meetings we got to a point in assessing the market, the supply-demand atop the starting pitching market, that we might be in a position to end up at least being a contender for Darvish with a contract that we could tolerate. It was a contract we could fit into our short-term plan and our long-term plan. That's when we really engaged in full, made the visit to Dallas and then stayed in great touch with his agents."

And as Epstein presaged the previous summer, the Quintana deal helped grease the wheels for this one to happen.

"When we acquired José Quintana, we made the point then that acquiring him with the great contract that he had may allow us at some point to bring another pitcher with him," Epstein said. "We almost felt like we were acquiring one-and-a-half pitchers in that deal because it would go halfway to acquiring somebody else."

Darvish was a unique kind of pitcher, someone harder to define as a certain "type." In 2017, as a pitcher for Texas and the Dodgers, he threw seven different types of pitches, according to the Brooks Baseball website. While he mostly threw four: four-seam fastball, slider, cutter, and sinker, he also mixed in a curveball, changeup, and split-finger fastball.

Whatever pitches he used, he could strike out hitters. That was the key.

So now the Cubs were set with their roster. All they had to do was play. Easy enough, right?

Spring training was relatively uneventful as the Cubs players got used to new coaches and refocused for a 2018 season in which they would again wear a target on their collective back. But this time, the national media focus wasn't as intense. As in, *60 Minutes* didn't show up.

Once the Darvish business was settled, the Cubs were just another competitive team getting ready for a long season.

Spring training angles were muted ones, like Kyle Schwarber losing weight. Schwarber wasn't too interested in talking about his 2017 failures, especially since he finished strong. I had a long conversation with Jed Hoyer that spring and we talked about Schwarber's trying season.

"In some ways, I think if you can care too much, he cares too much," he said. "I think part of last year, it was the first time in his career he really struggled. And he just tried harder and tried harder, and I think you just dig yourself in a deeper and deeper hole. It's a great attribute as a person. This is the same guy who came back after major knee surgery after six months and was in the World Series.

"He's the kind of person who's going to do anything for the team and anything to win. I do think when things went wrong last year, his way of trying to get out of it was work harder and harder. Sometimes you might have to take a step back and take a deep breath."

He had a point, but one problem the Cubs collectively suffered from in 2017 is that they weren't focused enough. There's a line between working too hard and not hard enough. Different players were caught on each side. In the end, the Cubs wound up in the NLCS, but they weren't mentally and physically in the right shape to win.

"Part of the reason we were exhausted is we didn't have the right focus coming into the season, I don't think," Hoyer said. "We talk about a World Series hangover, but the focus and intensity wasn't there from Day 1. We were two games under .500 at the All-Star break. Give these guys credit, they did a fantastic job in the second half of turning it on, but I think there's a price to be paid for sprinting for two months and having a brutal series against Washington. We got just plain beat by the Dodgers. Part of why we get beat is I don't think we had anything left to give. They were fresh. They had stepped on the gas in the first half. They had the chance to be where we were in 2016, peaking at the right time. We were definitely not peaking at the right time."

During the 2017 season, I talked to former White Sox catcher A.J. Pierzynski about the struggles of a repeat. The 2006 White Sox actually were more proactive than the 2017 Cubs, trading Aaron Rowand for Jim Thome to improve their power and signing Javier Vazquez to start.

Pierzynski watched the Cubs with some interest in 2017. Could they do what the Sox couldn't? In fact, they won just two more games, but the 2006 White Sox finished third in the AL Central with 90 wins and didn't have the benefit of a second Wild Card spot.

"Everyone expected them to run away with it again," Pierzynski said to me. "But it doesn't happen like that. It's so hard to do it again, so hard on so many levels. It's hard to fathom how the Yankees and Braves did it every year. At some point, you run out of energy. You don't get the breaks. People don't realize how hard it is to make the playoffs in baseball."

Epstein had made that point many times, but it was about making the World Series. After covering the 2017 Cubs' fight to make the post-season again, the Braves' and Yankees' longevity impressed me even more. I asked Hoyer about that.

"They did it differently," he said. "The Yankees had an incredible core of players that were in there, year in and year out. [Andy] Pettite and [Mariano] Rivera, [Derek] Jeter, [Jorge] Posada, and Bernie Williams. They had that core of players that continued to get better and better. When we were with the Red Sox, we kept thinking they were eventually going to start to age and it seemed like those guys were timeless. We'll never, in the history of baseball, see a core group of players like that and stay together and have that kind of success."

With that in mind, what of the Cubs' core? Would 2018 be a crossroads kind of year for them?

"I think for me," Hoyer said, "I look at the position playing group and when these guys came up in 2015, that was our farm system coming up to the big leagues. They were all young and competing while learning in the big leagues. Now, even though they're all still young, they're getting toward that prime age. I feel like if you want to talk about a crossroads, there are a lot of players who have another gear in their game, have another level to get to. I think we're getting to that point where a lot of guys have three years in the big leagues, they've had their ups and they've had their downs and part of why guys peak at 26, 27, and 28, it's like that crossroads of experience and physical talent, you know? And I think we're getting to that place. That's what excites me about this team. I think we're getting to that place where this core group of position players are getting into their prime years."

But in his 2017 season-finale press conference, Epstein hinted some of those players weren't secure. Or at least, not all of them could be, if the right deal presented itself.

"I certainly think we have major league talent to move in certain areas, if we're able to find the right deal," Epstein said. "We also have plenty of prospects left available to trade, maybe not headline guys but there are trades to be made without touching our big league team, if we want to. But I think our approach is we're going to pursue all avenues to get better, to make the major league team better and to make our organization better. That's contemplating trades at the big league level, trades with prospects, trades maybe for some buy-low guys that aren't household names, that maybe can become some in the future. Free agency, of course. And then just looking to get better in everything that we do."

Was it time to cut bait with some young hitters?

"It may or may not be," Epstein said. "And those choices, they're not unilateral things. You can't just sit there and say, 'This guy, we're moving him.' Because you don't know what the return might be, you don't know how the different moving parts might fit together.

"So I think going into the off-season prepared to make some tough choices, and execute on them and keep an open mind to anything that's appropriate under the circumstances, where we have some obvious deficits and we have some real surplus with some talented players who are really desirable. We've really benefited from two or three extra—extra in quotes because they're not really extra—starting-caliber players on the roster and that helped us win 97 games in '15, 103 [in 2016], 92 [in

2017]. That's as big of a part of the club as anything, having an Addison Russell go down and move Javy Báez to shortstop. That's an obvious example of it, but those things show up every week for us.

"There's a day where someone can't make the lineup and someone else slides in and you're still starting eight quality guys. That's huge and it helps us win. Sooner or later, you reach a point where you have to strongly consider sacrificing some of that depth to address needs elsewhere on the club. And there's no sort of deadline to do that, but I think we're entering the phase where we have to be really open-minded to that if it makes the overall outlook of the organization and team better."

Epstein's words gave us something to write about. Something to debate. But nothing of that sort happened that off-season, though it was reported that the Cubs looked into trading Russell and possibly Schwarber, but the interest wasn't there in return. So the Cubs went to camp with the same core.

"It was honest," Hoyer said of Epstein's quotes that day. "He was being honest. We have a lot of young position players and we needed to add pitching and we knew teams were coming after our guys. Theo was just being honest. But I hope they're relieved. We want guys to want to be here and I think they do. The way our offense is set up, guys are going to split time more than elsewhere. But I really believe that's for the greater good. They're going to stay rested, they're going to have good matchups, they're going to get plenty of playing time.

"But I think they're going to have to give a little bit more to the team than maybe they would in a different scenario. But I think all of our guys see that as a positive. They'd rather be part of a winning culture or winning organization than necessarily go somewhere else where they know they're going to be in the lineup every single day. I don't envy Joe. I think Joe's got a challenging job this year with the position players, making sure guys stay rested but also making sure guys stay happy and stay focused with the amount of playing time they're getting."

With no ring ceremony or banner raising to distract them, the Cubs got off to a better start in 2018. They went 16–10 after April despite almost no offense from Rizzo, their foundational position player. Rizzo slashed .149/.259/.189 in 18 games from late March through the end of April. Was the end of the postseason the start of a prolonged slump that lasted through the off-season?

Emotionally, Rizzo had to deal with a tragedy in his hometown. His Parkland, Florida, high school, Marjory Stoneman Douglas, was the scene of a grisly school shooting and Rizzo left spring training to pay his respects and speak at a vigil. It surely weighed on him personally.

While Rizzo struggled, Kris Bryant had a hot start, slashing .291/.441/.506 through his first 22 games. He had 15 walks, 11 extra-base hits, and just 14 strikeouts in his first 102 plate appearances through the end of April. Bryant wasn't going into any kind of cross-road type of year, but the Cubs would need him to continue at an MVP-type pace. This was a good sign.

Bryant was the closest thing the Cubs had to a sure thing. Rizzo was still mercurial. Báez still struck out too much. Contreras was still unproven, and plus, a catcher whose body would wear down every season under the strains of the job. No one knew what they were going to get from Kyle Schwarber, Addison Russell, Albert Almora Jr., and Ian Happ. As for Jason Heyward, anything they got from him above his 2016 numbers would be looked at positively.

But Bryant, he was the real deal, going from Rookie of the Year to MVP in his first two seasons. In 2015, while he slugged .488 with 62 extra-base hits in 559 at-bats, he also struck out a league-high 199 times, setting a Cubs single-season record, besting Sammy Sosa's 1997 season by 25 Ks.

The next year, though, he cut his strikeout rate from 30.6 percent to 22 percent. The year after that, it dropped to 19.2 percent. All the while, his isolated power average (FanGraphs' way of measuring power) rose.

Bryant was remarkably consistent during this time, and healthy. He played 151 games in 2015 and '17 and 155 in '16.

But 2018 would be a different season.

On May 19, the Cubs played a doubleheader at Cincinnati. Bryant went 3-for-6 with an RBI in the first game, a 5–4 loss in 11 innings. That gave him 10 hits over his last four games, pushing his slash line to .311/.428/.595. The Cubs were just 20–18 in his first 38 games, but Bryant was, again, pushing the boundaries of his talent. While he "only" had eight homers, everything else was going good. But then he slid headfirst into second base in the 11th inning. No one knew it at the time, but he injured his shoulder on the play.

Bryant played through the injury, but his numbers went down precipitously over his next 28 games. He hit one homer in this span (116 at-bats) and slugged just .336. He walked just 12 times and struck out 38. (Before the injury, he had struck out 28 times and walked 22.)

The Cubs put him on the DL on June 26 after four days off. It was his first trip to the DL in his major league career, and Bryant returned in short order, playing 10 games from July 11 to July 23. He started hot with eight hits, including two homers, in his first six games, before going 2-for-13 over his final three. He re-aggravated his injury on a swing and went back on the DL. This time, it lasted awhile. Bryant didn't return until rosters opened up on September 1. While he was gone, the Cubs went a pedestrian 19–15 and slumped offensively in August, typically their hot month, though they did manage to have their best month of the season, going 18–10 despite a paltry 113 runs scored, making it their worst offensive month of the season.

In August, Cubs hitters had a combined 94 wRC+ with power numbers more comparable to the Reds than the Brewers. I wanted to see what those numbers were in August 2017 and I wasn't surprised to see the Cubs atop the NL with a 122 wRC+ and second with a .197 ISO. In that month, Bryant slashed .343/.457/.588 with 14 extra-base hits, 17 walks, and only 18 strikeouts.

Bryant had nearly injured himself before on headfirst slides. While he was constantly praised for his base-running instincts, being aggressive cost him and the team.

But his injuries did open the door for David Bote.

Bote had already been up twice by June 27, when Bryant went on the DL for the first time. But his third stint with the big league club was his final one. He never left.

Bote was known for his high "exit velocity" in the minor leagues, which is a new-age baseball way to say he hits the ball hard. He was also known as a skilled defensive player, the kind of slick glove man the Cubs would use to demonstrate fielding drills in the early days of spring training.

From June 27 through August 15, Bote started 17 times and appeared in 10 other games and hit the cover off the ball, slashing .355/.453/.581, with 22 hits and 10 walks. He even had his own "game."

The David Bote Game came on August 12 as the Cubs and Nationals played on ESPN's *Sunday Night Baseball*.

The Cubs trailed Washington 1–0 for most of the game, as Max Scherzer pitched seven innings of three-hit ball with 11 strikeouts. The Nationals were 60–57 coming into the game and still on the periphery of a playoff spot.

Things were looking good when ex-Nats pitcher Brandon Kintzler, who was traded by GM Mike Rizzo in July and branded a clubhouse snitch for being an anonymous source for a story ripping the Nats' culture (Kintzler denied it and the article's author, Jeff Passan, also denied talking to Kintzler, even calling Theo Epstein when he was trading for him), loaded the bases on a triple, a walk, and an intentional walk. Ryan Zimmerman scored two on a single to make it 3–0.

But the Nationals had their own bullpen problems. New manager Davey Martinez called on Ryan Madson, who came in with a 4.43 ERA and left with a 5.19 one.

Madson gave up a one-out single to Jason Heyward and hit both Albert Almora Jr. and Willson Contreras. Joe Maddon pinch-hit Bote for pitcher Justin Wilson.

Bote fouled off the first pitch and took a 97 mph high heater for a ball and a low 97 mph fastball for a strike. He got back to even when a 96 mph Madson fastball buried in the dirt failed to fool Bote. That's when ESPN's Jessica Mendoza mentioned Madson has done a good job of getting ahead of Cubs hitters, but didn't have a putaway pitch to finish an at-bat in his favor.

Twelve seconds later, Bote crushed a low 95 mph fastball, just above Madson's previous one, to center field. The ball landed above the shrubbery in Wrigley Field, bouncing off the luxury suite that separates the left- and right-field bleachers.

Bote held his arms aloft like an airplane rounding first as the Cubs rushed to mob him at home plate.

The only other time a major league player hit a walk-off grand slam while down 3–0 was on May 23, 1936. Hopefully Samuel Byrd's relatives got to see or hear his name being mentioned.

"When I got that pitch I was like, 'Just get it in the air,'" Bote said. "That was my entire thing, hit it as hard as I can to center field. That was the approach, get underneath it."

Bote said he had only hit two other grand slams in his life, one in high school and the other in the minor leagues in 2015 as the Cubs were beginning their dramatic August surge toward the playoffs.

Bote's calmness at the plate as he waited for his pitch personified the approach the Cubs preached.

"I mean Tommy [La Stella] is the best in the game at it," Bote said. "And because of that, he's so in control of his emotions, so in control of what he wants to do, you'll see him take pitches and you're like, 'Why didn't he swing at that?' Because he has his approach and he's sticking to it. I think learning from that, learning from him and [Ben Zobrist] just being convicted. I think that's the most important thing, being convicted in your approach and selling out for it."

Bote was 25 when he made his major league debut after a long road through the Cubs system. He was in Theo Epstein's first draft class, an 18th-round selection out of a community college in Chanute, Kansas.

Bote is perhaps the embodiment of "the Cubs Way," the book Epstein and his staff authored to set the standards of the organization under new management. Though don't expect him to quote it.

"Um, I never read it to the tees," he told me one day in Milwaukee. "But they brought it out on certain aspects. It's less about the book and more about the staff that exemplified it. They exemplified what the Cubs Way was and verbalized it. As human beings we love to follow good leadership. Being able to follow good leaders is awesome. And being a leader yourself. If you're a Triple-A or Double-A guy, you're a leader to the incoming draft class. It's a trickle-down effect. I'm going to follow this and I'm going to lead this as well."

While Bote was an unfamiliar name to Cubs fans when he came up in 2018, he was an organizational staple. He played a whopping 355 games at the Class-A levels: 75 games with Kane County, 106 games with Boise, 98 with South Bend, 72 games with Myrtle Beach, and four with Daytona. He played 134 games at Double-A Tennessee. He played 61 of his 77 career games in Triple-A in 2018.

Bote was in the Boise Hawks lineup on July 23, 2013, when newly drafted Kris Bryant made his debut and promptly struck out five times.

"We're just out there playing Eugene," Bote said. "I remember the guy we were facing was throwing fuzz. He was throwing 98 and it's hard to see there. In Eugene you've got the shadows and you've got the sun literally shining on the batters. This guy is throwing 98 and I remember thinking, 'My goodness, it's hard to hit here.' I remember that game. I think Kris hit a homer the next day to right center. I was like, 'This kid's legit.' It's deep to right-center in Eugene."

Bote also played with Albert Almora Jr., who was the top pick of his draft class. He played with Ian Happ. He played with Kyle Schwarber. He played with Willson Contreras. He played with Trevor Gretzky and Giuseppe Papaccio and Rock Shoulders and oh yeah, Gleyber Torres.

"Almost everybody who came through the system, we played together," he said.

Bote even remembers the way things used to be, if only for a little. The Cubs hadn't yet turned over their minor league system to new bosses when Bote signed and started playing, so the class of 2012 had to live by old rules for a little bit.

"We had to wear high socks when I got drafted," he said. "You had to be clean-shaven and wear high socks in the minor leagues. I remember in instructs in 2012, the person said, 'Hey, you guys can wear your pants down and you can wear a beard,' and everybody erupted. It was the littlest thing and we all erupted. It was more of the thing, they want us to be us and they want us to be comfortable with being ourselves and worrying more about playing the game and not being like, 'Oh, I forgot to shave today, I'm going to be in trouble.' Then you're worried about that versus hitting the ball and catching the ball."

Bote praised the quality of instruction he got in the minor leagues, from coaches like Andy Haines, who left the Cubs organization in the winter of 2018 to be the Brewers' new hitting coach, to Derek Johnson, the former Vanderbilt coach the Cubs brought in to run their minor league pitching infrastructure. He's now the pitching coach in Cincinnati.

"The guys they brought in were so quality," Bote told me. "They cared about the player and the person."

While Bote was well-liked in the organization, he wasn't one of the fast-rising prospects. Despite getting drafted in 2012, he spent all of 2015 in Low-A South Bend. In 2016, mostly playing in High-A Myrtle Beach. During that season, he wanted to quit baseball, but his wife talked him out of it.

"I was like, 'I'm done, I'm over it,'" Bote said. "She was like, 'We didn't play in short season for two years and Kane County for three seasons to stop now. If you're going to play every day, let's do it.' She's my biggest supporter. She takes care of the kids when I'm on the road.

People say, 'Could you be further if you weren't married?' I say, 'I wouldn't be here if it weren't for her and the kids.'"

After prospering in Myrtle Beach, Bote prepared for a full 2017 season in Double-A. That's when the Cubs came to him about a swing change. Well, not quite then. They waited until the All-Star break.

"I had one of the highest exit velos in the organization," Bote told The Athletic's Sahadev Sharma. "But with a really low launch angle. So they were saying if we could use that exit velo and get a little bit more launch angle. We worked with numbers and it's not feasible to say, 'I'm at a four [degree launch angle], so now I need to get to a 12,' that doesn't happen. But if we can create path and contact points and repetition and not actually make a swing change, more approach and timing. They didn't want me to buy into the fly-ball, 25-degree launch angle. Just stick to what I do well with line drives. Instead of line drives at four degrees, just get it a little higher."

At that point, who was he to say no?

"They said, 'Hey, I know you worked hard to get to this point,'" Bote told Sharma. "'You're doing well. You're having success with what you're doing. But this is what we see, this is what the numbers show, and this is what you have in your pocket. If you can make this adjustment, you can elevate your game to a level that you didn't think could be there. Do you want to be a great Double-A player or a big leaguer?' They asked that question and whether I wanted to go all in on it. They told me not to be afraid to make the change and left it up to me. I saw what they were saying. The statistics made sense. The science behind it made sense. Everything they showed me was pointing to that direction so I said, 'Let's go for it and see what happens.'"

Bote quickly adjusted to the tinkering, impressing Haines, the coach in charge of this development.

"It wasn't a massive change that was foreign, it was minor thoughts, minor movements," Bote said. "And it was being all-in about it too. If you're going passive or 50 percent, you're not going to see the results, you'll just get frustrated. You can't look at a small sample size. You just have to be all in and trust what they said, what I see, and what I feel. Then you have to live by that. If it doesn't work, then that's what it was. It was my choice and I was 100 percent into it."

Bote finished 2017 with 14 homers in 470 at-bats. In his previous two seasons, he hit 13 in 638 at-bats. He then went to the Arizona Fall League and hit four homers in 19 games. The Cubs put him on the coveted 40-man roster so they wouldn't lose him in the Rule 5 Draft.

Bote's value grew so quickly that I was told he was the most asked-about player on the Cubs roster when it came to the trade season. Other teams coveted his services as a utility infielder with a loud bat. But Theo Epstein denied their advances. Bote wasn't a luxury, he was a necessity with Bryant's ailing shoulder.

Bote's hot streak didn't continue all season. The game after his grand slam, Bote collected another two hits. But after that, his numbers tumbled. From August 16 through September 30, he started 26 of 39 games and managed 17 hits (three homers) while striking out 38 times. Major League pitchers will always adjust. Still, the Cubs are confident in his future with the big league club. He is their organizational example.

Bote's story was a major part of the tale of 2018 for the Cubs, in which unlikely reinforcements helped "save" a season.

But the biggest hero of the season, while not expected, also wasn't a surprise. It was another 25-year-old infielder.

* * *

Javy Báez reported to spring training in 2017 with a giant World Series trophy tattoo on his left arm and a blonde buzzed-down mohawk.

"I was trying to be a little different, so people don't recognize me," he told me one day in Mesa, Arizona. "It didn't really work."

A blonde mohawk to go incognito? That is the epitome of Javy being Javy.

Báez's mix of style and substance had already cemented him as a fan favoirte. He was a holdover of the previous regime, and people wondered if he would be the major leaguer most likely to be traded for veteran pitching. But game after game, he proved his value to the club, culminating in his NLCS co-MVP Award with Jon Lester.

Báez's rise didn't stall in 2017. He played 145 games and got more than 500 at-bats for the first time. He hit 23 homers with his ISO (isolated power average, as calculated by FanGraphs) jumping from .150 to .207. He still wasn't walking much (5.9 percent, which was up from 3.3 percent in 2016) and his strikeouts jumped back up to 28.3 percent, but he was clearly getting better, as a twenty-something should with more opportunities. As for his value, he was almost irreplaceable. He actually wound up starting more games at shortstop than second base because of injuries to Russell.

Going into 2018, there wasn't much discussion about Báez taking any kind of leap. He was already very good, likely great. But no one could predict just how great he would be in 2018.

From 2016 to '17, Báez had an aggregate WAR of 6.1. Does that portray his value? Probably not. Even the Cubs' proprietary numbers can't tell the whole story of Javy.

But in 2018, Báez's WAR was 6.3. Again, WAR, what is it good for? In this case, it probably does show the kind of jump he took as a player in his age-25 season.

No, Báez still wasn't walking much. But no one was complaining about that as he slugged .554 with 34 homers in 160 games. Báez had yet to put up an above-average season in weighted run created plus (wRC+). But in 2018, his 131 wRC+ ranked him fifth in the NL, as did his 5.3 fWAR (FanGraphs' WAR).

Báez led the NL with 111 RBIs and his 34 homers were seventh. He hit .290, sprinkling in more than enough solid base hits to prove his swing has matured. And he played every aspect of the game incredibly well. While he got credit for succeeding on wild base-running plays that would have been derided had he failed, his overall baseball instincts were unimpeachable.

Privately, Cubs executives lamented that more Cubs players didn't approach the game like Báez. While some players carried themselves with a "There's another game tomorrow" attitude, Báez played every game like it was his last. While he wasn't drafted by Epstein's front office, Báez exemplified what they wanted out of their players. While

Javier Báez hops as he watches one of his 34 home runs in 2018 clear the fence, this one in an August game against the Reds. (AP Photo/Jim Young)

Epstein could always bemoan a player's limitations in his more cynical moods during a season, Javy got nothing but plaudits.

"Usually when we talk about Javy, we talk about the big, physical tools, the unbelievable baseball instincts and intellect," Epstein said. "But one thing I know his teammates appreciate being around him every day is just his pure toughness. This guy puts his body on the line every day when he plays, gets beat up quite a bit and always finds a way to stay in the game, always finds a way to get in the lineup next day. Comes back quickly when he does get hurt and just plays with a real edge and aggressiveness, which is great. Not everyone is wired that way, not everyone has to have the same baseball personality on the field, but he brings that and it's a much-needed ingredient.

"And in addition to that, I don't think he gets enough credit for being such a team-first guy," Epstein said. "He cares so much about winning. He cares about his teammates, doing little things to help engage them and make them better. It's awesome. Those intangibles behind the scenes are a big part of what makes him so valuable. As he now settles into this role as a star player—first of all, I think he's handled that really well. I think sometimes when a guy bursts onto the scene, and I'm not talking about anyone in this clubhouse at all, there's a danger of them getting a big head or isolating themselves from their teammates or getting wrapped up in sort of the secondary stuff that comes with being a star player and a known figure. Javy was the opposite, man. He poured that energy back into the team and back out onto the field. It was just really impressive. What a year for that kid."

He would wind up as the runner-up in the NL MVP race to Christian Yelich, the newly acquired star of the Milwaukee Brewers. While you could argue Báez showed more value with his overall versatility, starting 75 games at second base, 52 at shortstop, and 18 at third base, the truth was Báez was the second-best player in the National League. Not too shabby.

* * *

Early on, there were warning signs about the Cubs' new pitchers.

In his first four starts, Darvish gave up 15 earned runs on 21 hits and 11 walks in just 19⅔ innings. He struck out 21, but certainly didn't look like the best strikeout pitcher in baseball.

In his first start, he struck out eight in six innings of one-run ball against the Brewers. Did he take a big step forward? Uh, not quite.

In his next start, at home against the Rockies on May 2, he struck out eight again, but walked three and gave up seven hits and six runs in 4⅓ innings.

He wouldn't pitch again until May 15 and he looked better, but only lasted four innings. On May 20, he gave up one run in six innings, striking out seven in a 6–1 win at the Reds. It would be his final start of the season.

In Tyler Chatwood's first start, a 1–0 Cubs loss, he walked six and struck out four. In his second, he reversed things, he struck out seven and walked one. But in his third start, he walked seven and struck out seven, then five and five in his start after that and four walks and three strikeouts, five and five again, five and six... this was a problem.

In Chatwood's first seven starts, he walked 32 hitters in 37⅔ innings. Opposing batters were only hitting .202 and slugging .287 against him, but their on-base percentage was a whopping .386.

All told as a starter, Chatwood had a baseball-worst (among qualified starters) 19.4 percent walk rate in 19 starts. In 12 of those starts, he gave up as many or more walks than hits. In 13 of those starts, he had as many or more walks than strikeouts. Walking batters, even at that ridiculous rate, doesn't make him an anomaly, but Chatwood was going 3-0 on hitters almost 10 percent of the time, which in 2018, when hitters were striking out with carefree abandon, shows how unusable he was as a starter. Hell, it ranks up there no matter the era.

In retrospect, it's amazing the Cubs kept Chatwood in the rotation through the end of July. But without Darvish, what choice did they have?

Darvish Watch harkened back to the days of Kerry Wood and Mark Prior, when every pregame press conference with the manager had at least one question about where one, or both, were at physically in their never-ending rehab processes.

On June 20, a month after his last start, Darvish pitched his first simulated game as a Cub as he recovered from right triceps inflammation.

"Dominating sim game," Theo Epstein said to me in passing afterward.

The mood was jovial after the outing. Darvish's fastballs were popping, his slider was breaking, and Darvish seemed pleased. He admitted to reporters he was anxious about his health going into the start.

"Definitely the elbow aspect," he said through his interpreter. "The anxiety came from if I could throw with 100 percent condition."

"That was outstanding, actually," Joe Maddon said that day. "Great command, great jump on the fastball, slider was there. I think he threw one or two splitters at the end, but I thought you can't ask for anything more. He looked that good. Delivery was easy, solid. He was smiling, so that meant he probably felt pretty good about it. He'll be evaluated again tomorrow but for right now, that looked really good."

Daily Herald writer Bruce Miles, the designated pitch counter of sim games back in the day, got back into his old groove.

On a hunch, I searched the *Tribune* archives to see if longtime scribe Paul Sullivan had a Prior sim game story on June 20, 2005, and sure enough he did.

Sullivan wrote: "The Cubs are so encouraged by Prior's outing in a four-inning simulated game Friday they believe he'll be ready after one more simulated game Wednesday in Milwaukee. That would put Prior on schedule to return around the same time as Kerry Wood—at the end of June."

Prior did, in fact, return for a June 26 start on the South Side, where he pitched six scoreless innings in a 2–0 win over the White Sox. The rest of the season wasn't as kind, as Prior compiled a 4.07 ERA in 18 starts.

The Cubs might've been happy with those numbers for a Darvish return.

He threw his rehab start five days later in South Bend, Indiana, tossing five innings, but was hesitant to judge it a success. His velocity dipped from 94 mph to 89–90 mph and Darvish didn't know if that meant his triceps was still ailing.

"Not necessarily pain," Darvish said at the time. "But I can't for sure say there's nothing going on in the triceps zone. It's not like anything bad. I feel like everyone who comes off the DL goes through this. So I think it's just part of the process."

The Cubs thought he might be able to start in a home series at the end of the month, but a bullpen session in Los Angeles ended those hopes.

"It didn't go that well," Maddon said. "He was not able to cut it loose, so we're going to re-evaluate once we get back to Chicago and we'll let you know the next step."

Darvish reported pain in his triceps and was shut down again, restarting the entire process. He went to see his doctor in Dallas, who calmed his mind. By this point, Cubs fans, and perhaps some inside the organization, were doubting Darvish's mental toughness. (This was a common theme with Prior as well.) Darvish, through his interpreter, didn't sound too confident in himself either.

Darvish's mental state was such a story, Alex Rodriguez addressed it on *Sunday Night Baseball* in late July, causing a weeklong furor that resulted in a tense meeting with Joe Maddon the next time the ESPN crew was in town two weeks later. It was clear Rodriguez, who essentially called Darvish a bad teammate who was isolated from the team, was getting some kind of information from inside the organization, even if it wasn't completely accurate. It was another headache for the Cubs to deal with.

While Darvish was getting ready to get things going with another sim game and rehab start, the non-waiver trade deadline was looming, which meant the Cubs had to be actively looking for starting pitching help for the second straight season, exactly what they didn't think they'd have to do after signing two starters in the winter.

The Cubs weren't looking to make a long-term investment in a pitcher, just some insurance. They wouldn't need Chatwood in the postseason anyway, and Mike Montgomery was doing an admirable job as the fifth starter. Montgomery would slide back into the bullpen for the playoffs.

Cole Hamels was someone who was interesting to them.

At 34, Hamels was a step down from his ace years, and in four July starts for the Rangers, he had an 11.12 ERA. In 20 starts, he had a 4.72 ERA.

The Cubs got Texas to pick up around $9 million of his $14 million remaining in 2018 and his $6 million buyout on a $20 million option for 2019, in return for some minor-league pitching.

The Cubs and Rangers have been regular trade partners throughout the Epstein era, with Ryan Dempster and Matt Garza going there and Kyle Hendricks and Carl Edwards Jr. going to the Cubs, among numerous other players switching sides. In the fall of 2018, Cubs front office executive Shiraz Rehman, who was shifted from an assistant GM role, went to Texas. Anthony Iapoce went there to be the hitting coach and returned to the Cubs before the 2019 season.

Early in the 2018 season, Hamels noticed his velocity had dipped. In April, he was averaging 91.6 mph on his four-seamer, lower than any month since 2011. He didn't think it was the effects of aging.

"I know I'm not going to be throwing 96–97, but I still know I'm still capable of being a 93–95 guy," Hamels told The Athletic's Sahadev Sharma in August. "I know that and physically I felt as strong as I've been, there should be the results when I have that sort of recognition of the strength I have. I'm not where I feel more tired or just doesn't feel the same. But I do understand as the years go on and the innings keep going up, you're going to lose a tick here and there."

Hamels worked with his Texas coaches to fix his mechanics using the organization's video technology and slow-motion cameras. (The abundance of technology in the game, derided by some purists, has been a boon for this kind of in-season turnaround.)

"A lot of the stuff that we noticed was that I wasn't really engaging—my bottom half and top half weren't syncing together," Hamels told Sharma. "Just the drive that I was using, I was striding out too far and I was striding too open. By the time my top half needed to be utilized, the bottom half was already done. So it wasn't working together."

Hamels shortened his stride and adopted a more crossfire delivery (like Arrieta). That increased his velocity, but hurt his fastball command.

By July, he was throwing 93 mph on his four-seamer, but that fastball was leaving bats even faster. In July, opponents hit .579 off his four-seamer with a .947 slugging percentage.

Hamels, though, knew he was on the right track to fixing himself.

"Then it was, 'Okay, now try to get the shoulders to start to fire more up and down,'" Hamels told Sharma. "It was kind of a combination. It takes a little bit of time and a lot of work to finally get it to be in sync. That's where I started to get to that last start I had with the Rangers. Stuff started to kind of happen a little bit. I was still pulling, but I was starting to get more up and down with the shoulders. Then all of a sudden I got traded, it became a little bit easier."

No kidding.

Hamels started six times for the Cubs in August and compiled a 0.69 ERA. The Cubs went 6–0 in those games, while he earned four of those wins. He threw 39 innings and gave up just four runs (three earned). He struck out 38 and walked just 11. Opposing hitters slugged .227 against him. By the end of the month, I was comparing his August numbers to Jake Arrieta's August 2015 ones. It was close. Arrieta went 6–0 in six starts with a 0.43 ERA in 42⅓ innings. He stuck out 43 and walked 10, giving up four runs runs (two earned).

But each pitcher helped carry his team. Arrieta led the Cubs to an August surge that lasted until October. Hamels helped keep the Cubs afloat in a rocky NL Central.

Hamels wasn't the only thirty-something Epstein had to trade for to save his club of twenty-somethings. He needed an adult in the room, so to speak. In late August, he made another important trade, though this one was controversial for two different reasons.

To Cubs fans, Daniel Murphy's middle name began with an "F" and ended with an "ing."

In the 2015 NLCS, Murphy went 9-for-17 with four homers, a double, and six RBIs in the Mets' four-game sweep. Small sample size, but a 1.850 OPS in a playoff series is pretty good, right?

The infamous goat, as you might've heard, was also named Murphy. That factoid (along with the longtime Wrigleyville bar Murphy's Bleachers being an easy joke) bred about 10,000 tweets with every Murphy homer that series.

Murphy was less successful in the 2017 NLDS as a member of the Nationals, but he did hit a solo homer and an RBI double in Game 5. In between, Murphy had a 1.142 OPS at Wrigley Field.

"I've seen Daniel carry a team," Rizzo said. "It's going to take me a little while to get over seeing him [do that] every day. The nightmares I've had…."

Murphy's addition to the team was a different kind of nightmare to a certain subsection of Cubs fans.

Before the 2015 postseason, before anyone really knew who Murphy was on a national level, he talked to a reporter after a spring training appearance by Billy Bean, the gay former Major Leaguer who was working for MLB as its inclusivity ambassador.

What most people remember from Murphy's interview was that he said he disagreed with Bean's lifestyle. This set off a good many Cubs fans—some gay, some not —because while it's not virulently homophobic, it is anti-gay in that being gay isn't a lifestyle and shouldn't be reduced as such.

But here are Murphy's full quotes, given to Mike Vorkunov, then a reporter from NJ.com who now covers the Knicks for The Athletic:

"I disagree with his lifestyle," Murphy told Vorkunov. "I do disagree with the fact that Billy is a homosexual. That doesn't mean I can't still invest in him and get to know him. I don't think the fact that someone is a homosexual should completely shut the door on investing in them in a relational aspect. Getting to know him. That, I would say, you can still accept them but I do disagree with the lifestyle, 100 percent.

"Maybe, as a Christian, that we haven't been as articulate enough in describing what our actual stance is on homosexuality," he said. "We love the people. We disagree with the lifestyle. That's the way I would describe it for me. It's the same way that there are aspects of my life that I'm trying to surrender to Christ in my own life. There's a great deal of many things, like my pride. I just think that as a believer trying to articulate it in a way that says just because I disagree with the lifestyle doesn't mean I'm just never going to speak to Billy Bean every time he walks through the door. That's not love. That's not love at all."

Now, those quotes don't make him the frothing homophobe that he's been billed as being. But at the same time, the money quote is the money quote: "I do disagree with the fact that Billy is a homosexual." To many fans, it was unacceptable.

No one asked Murphy about the comments when he joined the team on the road, but when he came to Wrigley, the Cubs knew these questions would be asked. (So much so that the Cubs admitted they talked to Billy Bean about Murphy—the two struck up a friendship of sorts after his 2015 comments made news.)

Murphy was asked, "Do you have a message for gay fans that may have said, 'Okay, I'm not going to root for the Cubs now that you're here?'" He seemed taken aback by that question.

"Oh dear," he said. "I would hope that you would root for the Cubs."

Some say his answer as a smirking response. I wasn't as sure.

Given that the Cubs were hosting an "Out at Wrigley Day" event that weekend, his arrival seemed ill-timed at the very least.

"I hope that anyone that comes to Wrigley Field feels welcome," Murphy said. "That's my hope. That's the hope of Major League Baseball. Speaking with Billy Bean, that's what he's trying to do. That's what we're trying to do as an industry. We want people to feel welcome, whatever walk of life it may be."

Addison Russell went to the DL with a sore shoulder to make room for Murphy, who would play second base for the Cubs, costing them a significant amount of defensive versatility compared to Javy Báez. But Murphy quickly proved he could hit. He was exactly what the offensively changed Cubs needed at the time.

(Russell returned off the DL when rosters expanded on September 1 and went 6-for-38 with no extra-base hits in his last 18 games, 11 of which were starts.)

In his first week with the Cubs, Murphy went 11-for-29 with two doubles and two homers. In a related story, the Cubs won all six games. They won two more games to make it eight in a row. The Cubs went 12–4 in his first fortnight with the team.

On September 6, the Cubs won their 12th game in that run while in Washington, D.C., to start a series with the Nationals. With the win, the Cubs moved to a 4½-game lead over Milwaukee in the NL Central.

The race was over, right?

Not at all. The Cubs had serious weather problems in D.C., forcing a doubleheader and a rescheduled game a week later.

They also had problems winning regularly scheduled games, losing four of five before the makeup game on September 13 in D.C., which was threatened by a hurricane battering the East Coast.

Two of those losses came to the streaking Brewers at Wrigley Field. After their September 12 loss, that 4½ game lead was down to one game.

The Athletic had a long-planned event on September 13, a Cubs off day, with Ken Rosenthal and Peter Gammons. Neither of our writers were thrilled about traveling into D.C. with the chance of a serious storm and both were expected to speak at the event.

So I had an idea.

I asked Cody Keenan, the Obama speechwriter who got to write his dream speech for the Cubs' White House visit, if he wanted to cover it for us.

I rushed his credential through MLB and our own internal system, but we didn't think the game would get played. Then, the weather patterns changed and it looked like the game was a go—though the city was technically under a state of emergency—much to the Cubs' chagrin. They hadn't had a planned day off since August 20. Their next off-day, their last of the season, would be on September 20, and that came after an overnight flight from Phoenix. Thirty games in 30 days at the end of a season? The Cubs were furious, but it was Mother Nature screwing them over.

Keenan, still working for Obama while writing a book and doing other things, was thrilled to join the working press for the day. He was nervous, peppering me with questions about where to go and what to say. Little did he know he would get such a newsy game to cover.

Anthony Rizzo was as annoyed as anyone with the team's goofy schedule. But the Cubs were running on fumes and he decided to lighten up the mood, going on the flight to D.C. in full uniform. He posted it to Instagram, thrilling the Rizzo-loving Cubs fanbase.

"Just Rizz being Rizz," Kris Bryant said. "Which is good; I think we all needed that nice little comic relief."

"I mean, we're flying into a state of emergency with rain in the forecast," Rizzo said. "It's kind of a joke. So why not keep joking around about it, and just have fun?"

The Cubs won the game 4–3 in 10 innings, a much-needed victory. But while Pedro Strop got the win, giving up no runs in 1⅔ innings, it was a play involving him that stirred up a lot of talk about Maddon's managing and the future of this team.

Strop replaced Brian Duensing with one out in the eighth inning and the game tied 3–3. He made it through that inning and the ninth with just one hit allowed in 21 pitches.

Then, in the 10th inning, with one out and the bases loaded and the Cubs up a run after a Javy Báez's RBI bunt single, Maddon let Strop hit. He wasn't out of position players. It was only the 10th inning. Strop hit a grounder to third and busted it down the line to beat a double play. He ran so hard he injured his hamstring. This was bad managing—death by overthinking.

"That's so unfortunate," Maddon said. "If we scored, he was going back out. If we don't score, he wasn't. That was it. And we scored. But listen, he hit the ball hard. This guy can swing the bat a little bit; that wasn't a fluke. He tried to beat it out, almost did, and you can never fault an athlete for competing."

Despite his historical success with the Cubs, Maddon had been taking heat, privately and publicly, for decisions like this one. Letting your most reliable reliever hit in the 10th inning of a 30 games in 30 days stretch? That's egregiously bad. (Having pinch-runner Terrance Gore bat in the ninth wasn't great either.)

Strop would miss the rest of the regular season. The Cubs didn't fall into an abyss after that game, like they might have in past decades. But they did finish 10–6, which wasn't good enough.

On September 7, the Brewers trailed the Cubs by four games with 20 games to go. But then the Cubs got swept in that Saturday double-header in Washington. Then they gained a half-game when the Cubs didn't play Sunday. Then they took two out of three at Wrigley Field. On September 23, the Brewers just stopped losing. Milwaukee, down 2½ games, won its last seven in a row, sweeping St. Louis on the road and Detroit at home.

For all the talk about the Cubs' great records in August and September under Maddon, the Cubs wilted in 2018 with a 16–12 September. Again, the schedule was a killer, and maybe that was the best they could do.

All throughout the season, the public talk was about the team's experience and when the Cubs would take off and never look back.

Even in late September, Joe Maddon, the former minor league hitting coach, was left to express optimism about a change in approach, if not results.

"I don't think you'll see anything a whole lot different," Maddon told reporters. "That would be inappropriate to think that. What I'd like to see is the whole-field approach coming back more consistently. Two-strike approach showing up, moving the baseball, making the defense play. That's what I'd like to see. Just to all of a sudden turn on this home run switch—the weather is going to be getting cooler, it's harder to do that."

With several hitters seemingly tuning out hitting coach Chili Davis and struggling to find their niche at the plate, the Cubs couldn't click when it mattered.

The killer losses down the stretch for the Cubs had to be the two home defeats to the Pirates on September 24–25. The Bucs won by an aggregate of 11–1 and the Cubs lost two games off their lead. The Cubs won four of five down the stretch, but of course the Brewers beat Detroit on the last Saturday of the season, while the Cubs lost 2–1 to St. Louis. Despite all of his success in August, Hamels lost his last three starts for the Cubs in September and each one cost the team a game. To be fair, the Cubs scored a total of two runs on those three starts and only one start was truly bad, when he gave up seven runs on nine hits in a 9–0 loss to Arizona on September 19. In the other two, he gave up three earned runs in 13 innings.

While it felt like the Cubs should have comfortably won the division, in truth, they only spent 86 days (including off-days) in sole possession of or tied for first place. The Brewers had or shared the lead for 79 days. The difference down the stretch was Milwaukee won four of six against the Cubs. In the past, the Cubs had an edge over Milwaukee. They felt like they would always beat them in the end.

While no one thought this was a dominant Cubs team at any point in the season, it did look like a team with a very good chance of a fourth straight NLCS appearance, which isn't shabby. It was a division-winning team, for sure.

But Milwaukee caught the Cubs and forced a one-game playoff in Game 163 that Monday. Not only did the Cubs lose another day off, but they could see their mortality. They tried to remain confident.

On their final Sunday of the season, Jon Lester walked in and chose to look on the bright side.

When Lester got into the home clubhouse, he told assistant clubhouse manager Danny Mueller and assistant trainer Matt Johnson to think positively.

"I just got done telling Danny and Matty on the way in here today, Adam Dunn, it took him 15 years just to play a play-in game, you know?" Lester told me before the Cubs beat St. Louis for their 95th win. "So let's look at it that way. Some guys don't even get to play the one-game Wild Card Game. Would it be nice to win today and they lose and win the division? One hundred percent. At the end of the day, we're in."

On one hand, Lester was right. There was no dishonor in winning 95 games and taking a share of the division. The Cubs from 2009 to 2014 could only dream about such a scenario. The 2004 Cubs would've loved a shot to keep their season going.

But on the other hand, when the core of your team is young and just won a World Series two years ago and you led the division by almost five games just weeks before, saying, "Hey, Adam Dunn had it worse than us" is just grasping at straws.

(Dunn actually played 14 years and, to prove Lester's point, he didn't even get a plate appearance in the 2014 Wild Card Game, which Lester started for the Oakland A's.)

Cubbie Exceptionalism, the term I used to describe the attitude that permeated from both the business and baseball sides of the organization at times, couldn't save this team now. The Brewers, the small-market team whose stadium was regularly invaded by Cubs fans during their regular season series, were coming to town with a head of steam and there was nothing the Cubs could do about it. They couldn't even stop Brewers fans from buying good tickets in the lower bowl for the afternoon makeup game that Monday. It was a role reversal in every way.

"Baseball is such a perfect game, in some ways," Maddon said. "It takes 162 games to not decide anything. It's just like it's the first day of the season."

Well, except the Cubs were thinking World Series on the first day of the season. Now, they were just hoping to make the NLDS.

The Cubs started José Quintana and that gave them a dose of much-needed confidence.

In six regular-season games against Quintana this season, the Brewers put up a .177/.246/.323 slash line with 33 strikeouts in 142 plate appearances.

That put Lester in line to start either the Wild Card Game if they lost or the NLDS if they won. Either way, he was good with it.

"When it comes down to it, we're in the playoffs," Lester said that Sunday. "We're in the playoffs. Anything can happen. Kansas City won the World Series winning the Wild Card Game. It's been done, it's gonna be done. I think people around here are ready to jump off bridges about us just getting into the playoffs and not winning the division. So I mean, the playoffs are the playoffs."

Even with World Series expectations?

"I mean, expectations are great," Lester said. "If you don't have expectations, then it's probably going to be a miserable year. That means you're supposed to probably finish last. So I love expectations, but I also feel you have to be realistic about things sometimes and realize a baseball season is a long year and there's a lot of things you can't control. All you can control is showing up and playing. We've done that. I feel like we've played really good baseball and [the Brewers have] played a lot better baseball. That happens, but I feel like we're in this situation but it comes down to us taking care of today."

In case you avoided spoilers until now, the Cubs didn't take care of "today." They lost to the Brewers 3–1 in the play-in game.

Asked to describe the loss, Maddon said, "They got 12 hits, we got three."

"I felt pretty good about the fact we gave up three runs actually," Maddon added.

That the Cubs scored one run was fitting.

The Cubs scored zero or one run 39 times in 2018 and 35 of those games ended in defeat.

In the previous season, which ended with hitting coach John Mallee getting let go, that happened only 28 times.

If you want to compare this to some dark days for the franchise, in 2012, the first year of the rebuild, the Cubs scored zero or one run 40 times. The next season, where the Cubs went 24–45 in the second half, it happened just 31 times.

But Kris Bryant, who missed 60 games because of a lingering shoulder issue, didn't like how the Cubs' hitting misfortunes were being simplified.

"I mean, as a player, baseball is a really hard game sometimes," he said. "You go up there and you see the ball going there and it comes this way and you get jammed. Sometimes it's really tough to square up a pitch. I do think, just seeing some of the at-bats on TV, we did miss some pitches we could've hammered, Rizz being one of the only ones to do damage with a pitch in the middle of the zone. It is a little frustrating."

Rizzo provided the team's only run with a game-tying solo homer in the fifth inning. In the ninth, with two outs and Javy Báez on second, he just missed a game-tying homer off Brewers closer Josh Hader. It fell just short.

The mood was much different now. The Cubs had no momentum. There was no switch to flip. They had to play Tuesday, again with no days off, at home against the Colorado Rockies in the Wild Card Game.

In 2015, everyone loved the Wild Card Game. What fun! Now, it felt like punishment.

"We won 95 games, it just wasn't good enough," Rizzo said. "We won [97] games one year and we were happy we were in the Wild Card. It's just the way it's shifted every year. The expectations have gone up."

After the Cubs lost the Wild Card Game to Colorado by a very familiar 2–1 score in an unfamiliar 13 innings, the clubhouse wasn't morose. No one was crying or throwing things or blowing off reporters. For all the talk about putting it together late, the Cubs knew the end could be nigh.

When reporters walked into the losing clubhouse after midnight, the Theo Epstein–designed room that was meant to foster inclusivity and unity, everyone was hugging each other.

Ex-Cubs turned "special assistants" Ryan Dempster and David Ross hugged Tommy La Stella and Jason Heyward. Albert Almora Jr. hugged Tom "Otis" Hellman, the longtime clubhouse manager. Kyle Schwarber hugged Ian Happ and Willson Contreras. Anthony Rizzo even hugged some beat writers.

Schwarber hugged Contreras for a long time. I watched and it struck me as important. I asked him what he said to Contreras afterward.

"I mean, that guy was the best catcher in the National League," Schwarber said. "What do you say about what this guy did this year? He went out there and he gives his heart every day. I think that's what people should see, because this guy goes out there and he plays his absolute heart out every day. It doesn't matter if we get in at one o'clock and we got a day game tomorrow, he's out there, he's playing his heart out. Just like today, he went out there and he gave it his all. You know what, I'm not going to put words in his mouth, he should be very, very proud of the year he had, personally. For me to see him come up through the minor leagues until now, wow."

After a remarkable ascent through the minor leagues to get to the Cubs in 2016 and take over the starting catching role as a rookie for the World Series champs, Contreras hit a speed bump in 2018, a year in which he made the All-Star team, with a total collapse at the plate in the second half. The Cubs weren't thrilled about his work behind the plate either.

From July 9 to October 1, he started in 54 games (he appeared in seven more) and slashed .195/.293/.282 with just three home runs and eight doubles. He went homer-less in 136 at-bats from August 2 through September 28. He ended the slump in the Cubs' last regularly scheduled game of the season.

Contreras went into the season considered to be one of the Cubs' cornerstones, and perhaps one of four position players they wouldn't consider trading, along with Rizzo, Bryant, and Báez.

But what was his status now?

"I know this from having conversations with him throughout the year," Theo Epstein said at his end-of-year press conference with the media. "This year is going to prove to be a big learning experience for him. He kept saying, 'The game is teaching me. The game is teaching me.' Some of the failure is teaching him too. I think this guy, like Kris Bryant, these guys are going to play 10-plus more years. I think every year is going to be better than what they just did. I think you're not going to see that again out of those guys. But you have to learn from it, you have to work harder and the failure and the game have to teach you, as Willy put it. That's a process and we're here to support him through that. But yeah, it was a disappointing year for Willy, there's no doubt about it. When it happens to your catcher, it's a big deal. We need him back."

One of the few players who didn't try to turn an optimistic angle to the end of the season was Báez, the one Cub who deserved to bask in the spotlight. He finished the year with 111 RBIs, which led the NL, and more importantly, 34 homers, a .290/.326/.554 slash line, and a season's worth of elite defense at three positions. Báez had gotten better every year, which isn't something the rest of the young Cubs hitters could say.

If not for Christian Yelich, he would've been the favorite to win NL MVP.

"I thought we were going to go to the World Series this year," Báez said. "But we weren't us. We were competing. But not the whole time, not as a team."

Báez thought the 2018 Cubs were worrying too much about other teams, a curious statement about a team that had been to three straight NLCS.

"I just feel like our mind was over there and not here," Báez said. "Not on here touching the ground. We were trying to get everybody here together. But at the same time, because we struggled, we were paying attention to how far we were back or how far we were in front of anybody. That's not what we do. In '16, it didn't matter who was out there. We knew we had a lineup and we knew they had to pitch to someone in our lineup. We're not doing that. If we don't do that and we're not playing as a team, we're not going to win. It doesn't matter. We're not going to win."

I think Epstein appreciated that Báez didn't hold back his criticism of the team. Both publicly and privately, Epstein was critical of his players at various points of the season and those feelings came out in myriad ways.

"I'm not pointing fingers at anybody—anybody—because we're all in this together," Epstein said. "But you know when you have it and you know when you don't. And I think we did a good job of keeping an even keel, we did a good job of grinding through, our players were phenomenal in dealing with 42 games in 43 days. It was a really connected clubhouse, there were so many positives and so many things to be proud of, but look, having that sense of urgency and not having any just reliance on the talent and the length of the season, and that everything will just be okay because we're the Cubs. We can't have that. We have to all challenge ourselves to get better and be accountable. And it's all of us. It starts with me."

No, seriously. Epstein hadn't been criticized much since the rebuild started to bear fruit. But Darvish, Chatwood, and Morrow didn't sign themselves. His front office rolled the dice and for one season, at least, they came up snake eyes.

"I think when you fail and you don't reach your goal, yeah, it's great to talk about making something positive about it, but it starts with self-awareness and self-reflection and accountability," he said. "And so, I'll be the first to admit the off-season moves we made last year did not lead to immediate productivity on those contracts this year. And it put us in a little hole early with our starting pitching that we all had to work hard to overcome. We have to own that and I have to own that and find a way to be better with those decisions and how certain things worked out. We started that process and I think a lot of things we did in-season really helped to rectify that and by the end, our starting pitching was our strength and addressed some things with the bullpen and the offense too. There's obviously some things we need to do better and I need to do better and we should look at this season this way: we won 95 games, great. But we didn't accomplish our ultimate goal. How can we get better? How can we be accountable?"

For the first time since 2014, the Cubs didn't have games past October 1. How would they spend the time? Brainstorming ways to improve on a limited budget.

For all the talk about staying under the self-imposed "competitive balance tax," it turned out that wasn't to set up a spending spree in 2018. The Cubs were never in the Bryce Harper and Manny Machado derbies, which would hang over the entire MLB off-season. Soon the public talk concerning the Cubs shifted from big changes to improvements from within.

Epstein had a knack for underpromising and overdelivering in off-seasons. After the 2015 season, he didn't know what kind of budget he would have. But a run to the NLCS fattened his pockets and he got creative on Jason Heyward's contract. After the 2017 season, he benefitted from a slow free-agent market and signed Yu Darvish.

Uh, maybe austerity would be a good thing for the Cubs?

Still, through Christmas 2018, Epstein's big addition was infielder Daniel Descalso, who had remade his swing going into his thirties and looked like he could be a nice utility player for the next couple years. For sure, the Cubs had the talent on the roster to compete and win in 2019.

But the 2018 off-season looked like it would be as unproductive as the previous two, except this time there was no built-up anticipation, no false hope.

In 2016, it felt like the Cubs had multiple World Series parades in their future. But two years later, we were left to think about what would happen if they don't get another one before the band breaks up. Lucrative TV money wasn't ready for this free agent class, though the Cubs finally agreed on a deal with Sinclair Broadcast Group to distribute their TV channel, which would begin after the 2019 season. WGN had been synonymous with the Cubs for 72 years, but 2019 will mark the end of their relationship. In truth, it was overdue, as teams in other markets had left over-the-air TV years and years ago.

Joe Maddon's five-year contract will also end in 2019, making an unlikely lame duck manager and one with a new staff once again. Tommy Hottovy, the former major leaguer turned analytics liaison, was named the pitching coach at 37 years old. Anthony Iapoce, a former Cubs minor league hitting coach, was named the hitting coach. Former big leaguer Mark Loretta took over as the bench coach.

Epstein spent his free time in the offseason communicating exactly what was expected from his returning major leaguers, several of whom needed to show real maturation or development this season.

This would be critical because the Cubs didn't money to spend on high-end free agents before the 2019 season. They picked up Cole Hamels' $20 million option and signed a handful of cheaper relievers to fill out the bullpen. They let pinch-hitter Tommy La Stella go and added Daniel Descalso in his stead. Bryce Harper was never a realistic option unless the Cubs could shed Yu Darvish or Jason Heyward's contracts.

After signing Darvish, Epstein praised his boss' vision.

"It's wonderful to have an owner like that who sees the big picture," Epstein said. "And then once he's gotten a real taste of winning he isn't necessarily content just to be a contender or in the mix each year. [He] really wants to capitalize on this window that we have and deliver championship baseball to our loyal fans who certainly deserve it.

"We've gotten nothing but support from Tom and the business side. We're starting to capitalize on some new revenue streams, and that allows us to fish in these waters."

Tom Ricketts struck a different tone when he met with the media in spring training as the 2019 season began. When asked about fans' discontent on the Cubs' lack of action this winter, he said there were strict budget limitations and he wasn't going to ignore them. So much for that window.

"Yeah, that's a pretty easy question to answer," he said. "We don't have any more. The fact is that we've been in the top five in spending, in baseball spending, for the last five or six years. We're in the top couple in spending last year. We've put our money back on the field. Unfortunately, you just can't have a high-profile free agent every single year. And part of that is obviously how much it costs, whatever the $25, $30 million are going to cost. Plus it's a 10-year commitment, and you've gotta pay those dollars. So we like the team we have. We made the bets we have over the last few years. I think that we're well positioned to win the division again. And as much as I would love to have a great new exciting player every single season, it just can't happen every year."

Even the most delusional fans could agree you can't sign a big-name free agent every year. But Harper, specifically, seemed like a good fit, even if that meant the Cubs would've had to move a position player or two to make room.

Baseball Prospectus' preseason PECOTA projections predicted the Cubs to finish in last place in the NL Central with a sub-.500 record. While these projections are designed to be conservative, there was reason for some skepticism, if not a 79-win prediction.

As Epstein said, the 2019 season would be a "definitional" year. And not just on the field.

Off the field, there was the Russell mess. He spoke as spring training began and impressed almost no one with a rehearsed, robotic press conference. Tom Ricketts had to address his father's racist, Islamophobic emails, which came out as part of a series of email dumps from the Univision website Splinter News.

The Cubs' brand had taken a hit, whether or not Tom Ricketts wanted to admit it, because the brand had gotten so big.

The Cubs were now expected to be something for everyone: big spenders, good citizens, trendsetter, and, most importantly, perennial World Series contenders.

After the heartbreaking NLCS loss in 2003, the Cubs of yesteryear couldn't get back to the mountaintop. These Cubs not only got there, they planted their flag at the top and took selfies. It was an amazing feat worth all the adulation that came their way.

But after you conquer one mountain, what's left to do but go back down to Earth and try to scale another one. Could the Cubs make that trip again? We used to say the Cubs winning the World Series would be the greatest story in sports and it was. But we also learned that the only story left now is: Can the Cubs win another one? And if not, why?